Wischner

THE INTERNATIONAL PSYCHO-ANALYTICAL LIBRARY

No. 8

THE INTERNATIONAL PSYCHO-ANALYTICAL LIBRARY

EDITED BY ERNEST JONES, M D.

No. 8

SIGMUND FREUD, M.D., LL.D.

COLLECTED PAPERS

VOLUME II

*Authorized Translation
under the supervision of*
JOAN RIVIERE

SIXTH IMPRESSION

LONDON

THE HOGARTH PRESS, 42 WILLIAM IV ST., W.C.2.

AND THE INSTITUTE OF PSYCHO-ANALYSIS

1949

PUBLISHED BY
The Hogarth Press Ltd
and
The Institute of Psycho-Analysis
LONDON
★
Clarke, Irwin & Co. Ltd
TORONTO

First Published 1924
Second Impression 1933
Third Impression 1942
Fourth Impression 1946
Fifth Impression 1948
Sixth Impression 1949

COPYRIGHT 1924

PRINTED BY THE REPLIKA PROCESS
IN GREAT BRITAIN BY
LUND HUMPHRIES
LONDON . BRADFORD

COLLECTED PAPERS

VOLUME II

CLINICAL PAPERS

★

PAPERS ON TECHNIQUE

EDITORIAL PREFACE

IN the regrouping of the COLLECTED PAPERS, the present volume has proved to be the most miscellaneous, and can indeed be termed ' Clinical ' only *a potiori*. The word ' clinical', however, as the present writer has expounded at length elsewhere, has greatly widened in its meaning of late years, and has now come mainly to indicate a certain characteristic mode of approach to various problems—psychological, medical, and others.

The third, forthcoming volume will consist of five long case-histories studied psycho-analytically, and is thus the most valuable as regards actual clinical material. The fourth volume will contain a number of papers on ' Metapsychology ', together with most of those dealing with the application of psycho-analysis to non-medical topics.

The present volume contains all the other papers written between 1906 and 1924. Many are purely clinical in the narrower sense, such as Hysterical Phantasies, Types of Nosogenesis, Disposition to Obsessional Neurosis, Case of Homosexuality in a Woman, etc. ; others concern matters of wider interest, such as the ascertainment of truth in legal proceedings, the sexual enlightenment of children, children's lying, etc., while the first application of psycho-analysis to the study of character-development will also be found here.

A word should be said about two groups of papers which are more homogeneous. The last four in the first section were written only this year, 1924, and one of them has not yet even appeared in German ; Professor Freud, however, kindly supplied the manuscript of it to the Institute for the purposes of this translation. These are all written on the basis of his recent important brochure entitled *Das Ich und Das Es*, of which a separate translation will shortly appear, and they are so recondite that the reader is advised to postpone the study of them until he is familiar with the contents of that book.

The second section contains all those papers relating directly to Technique ; six of them were published in a group in the *Zeitschrift*.

It should be pointed out, however, that they were in no sense intended to form a comprehensive or consecutive exposition of the technique, but merely deal with certain points arising in the course of psycho-analytic treatment. In spite of several attempts, no completely satisfying account of psycho-analytic technique has yet been provided. Indeed, it is probable that, as with bacteriology and many other disciplines, no written account of technique can do more than supplement the only satisfactory method of acquiring it, namely, first-hand study with someone who possesses a mastery over it.

We wish to express our gratitude to Fräulein Anna Freud for her invaluable assistance in revising the translation.

REFERENCES

ALL the references in the footnotes contain only the title, and in some cases the date, of the book or paper referred to ; further details will in all cases be found at the end of this volume in the List of Books and Papers referred to in the Text.

The following abbreviations are used in the footnotes and at the end in the List of Books and Papers referred to :

1. *Imago* = *Imago*, Vienna.

2. *Jahrbuch* = *Jahrbuch für psychoanalytische und psychopathologische Forschungen*, Vienna.

3. *Sammlung* = Freud, *Sammlung kleiner Schriften zur Neurosenlehre*, Vienna.

4. *Zeitschrift* = *Internationale Zeitschrift für ärztliche Psychoanalyse*, later called *Internationale Zeitschrift für Psychoanalyse*, Vienna.

5. *Zentralblatt* = *Zentralblatt für Psychoanalyse*, Vienna.

CONTENTS OF VOLUME II

PAPERS ON TECHNIQUE

CLINICAL PAPERS

I

PSYCHO-ANALYSIS AND THE ASCERTAINING OF TRUTH IN COURTS OF LAW [1]

(1906)

THERE is a growing recognition of the untrust-worthiness of statements made by witnesses, at present the basis of so many judgements in Courts of Law ; and this has quickened in all of you, who are to become judges and advocates, an interest in a new method of investigation, the purpose of which is to lead the accused person to establish his own guilt or innocence objectively. This method is of a psychological and experimental character, and is based upon psychological research ; it is closely connected with certain views which have only recently been propounded in medical psychology. I understand that you are already engaged in testing the utility and bearing of this new method by means of what one might call ' mock trials ', and I have gladly accepted the invitation of your President, Professor Löffler, to explain to you more fully the relation of this method to psychology.

You are all acquainted with the game played at parties, where a word is called out at random and some-one has to add a second word forming a compound with the first—for example, ' steam ', ' ship ', giving the compound word ' steam-ship '. It is nothing more than a modification of this children's game which the Wundt school has introduced into psychology under the name of ' association test ', and it omits only one

[1] Lecture delivered to Prof. Löffler's Seminar in June 1906. First published in the *Archiv für Kriminalanthropologie und Kriminalistik*, von H. Gross, Bd. 26, 1906 ; reprinted in *Sammlung*, Zweite Folge. [Translated by E. B. M. Herford.]

rule of the game. The experiment is as follows : a word (termed the ' stimulus-word ') is called out to the subject, and he replies as quickly as possible with some other word that occurs to him (the so-called ' reaction '), his choice of this reaction not being restricted in any way. The points to be specially observed are the *time* required for this reaction, and the very variable *relation* of the stimulus-word to the reaction-word. Now it cannot be claimed that much fresh knowledge was gained as the immediate result of these experiments. This was to be expected, however, since they were carried out without any decided aim in view, and without any guiding principle which could be brought to bear on the results. The experiments only became significant and fruitful when Bleuler in Zurich and his pupils, especially Jung, began to pay attention to ' association tests '. Their experiments acquired practical value when the hypothesis was applied that the connection between the stimulus-word and the reaction-word could not be one of chance, but must be determined by a pre-existing group of ideas in the mind of the person reacting.

It has become customary to call a group of ideas of this kind, having an influence on the reaction to the stimulus-word, a ' complex'. The influence works either by the stimulus-word actually touching a complex directly or by the complex succeeding in getting into touch with the word by intermediate links. This determination of the reaction is a very remarkable fact, as you can see by the undisguised amazement expressed in the literature on the subject. The truth of it admits of no doubt, however ; for as a rule you can lay bare the particular complex at work by asking the subject of the experiment to give the reasons for his reaction, and so explain a reaction which could not otherwise be understood. Examples like those given by Jung, on pp. 6 and 8-9 of his treatise,[1] are well

[1] Jung, *Die psychologische Diagnose des Tatbestandes*, 1906.

suited to make us doubt the existence of chance and
of what appears to be arbitrariness in mental processes.

Let us consider for a moment the early history of
the view put forward by Bleuler and Jung, namely,
that these reactions are determined by complexes in
the mind of the subject. In 1901 I published a work [1]
in which I pointed out that a whole series of actions
previously held to be due to chance were on the
contrary strictly determined, and to that extent I have
therefore contributed towards circumscribing the field
of mental free will. I took as examples slight slips of
memory, tongue or pen, and the mislaying of objects.
I showed that when someone makes a slip of the tongue
it is not chance, nor difficulty in articulation either,
nor similarity in sound that is responsible ; but that
in every case a disturbing group of ideas—a complex
—can be brought to light which alters the meaning of
the intended speech under the guise of an apparent
slip of the tongue. Further, I took for consideration
people's little actions that are apparently purposeless
and due to chance—their petty habits of playing,
fiddling with things and so on—and revealed them as
' symptomatic actions ' connected with a hidden meaning and intended to give this hidden meaning un-
obtrusive expression. I found, moreover, that even a
Christian name cannot occur to the mind by chance,
but must have been determined by a powerful complex ;
and that the numbers that one may think one chooses
arbitrarily can be traced to the influence of such a
hidden complex. A few years later a colleague of
mine, Dr. Alfred Adler, was able to substantiate this
most astonishing statement of mine by some very
striking examples.[2] Once one has accustomed oneself
to such a conception of determinism in mental processes it is a justifiable deduction, drawn from the
study of the psychopathology of everyday life, that the

[1] Freud, *Zur Psychopathologie des Alltagslebens.*
[2] Adler, *Drei Psychoanalysen von Zahleneinfällen und obsedierenden
Zahlen,* 1905.

the method is called psycho-analysis ; it was evolved by me from the ' cathartic ' method of therapeutics first practised by Breuer in Vienna.[1] To allay your surprise I must work out an analogy between the criminal and the hysteric. In both we are concerned with a secret, with something hidden. But in order that I may not appear paradoxical, I must point out the difference at once. In the case of the criminal it is a secret which he knows and hides from you, but in the case of the hysteric it is a secret hidden from him, a secret he himself does not know. How is this possible ? Now, through laborious investigations, we know that all these illnesses are the result of the patient having succeeded in repressing certain ideas charged with strong feeling, together with the wishes that arise from them, in such a way that they play no part in his deliberate thought-processes, cannot enter into his conscious thoughts, and therefore remain unknown to him. But from this repressed psychic material (complexes) are generated the somatic and psychic symptoms, which plague the patient just as a guilty conscience does. In this one point, therefore, the difference between the criminal and the hysterical is fundamental.

The task of the therapeutist is, however, the same as the task of the judge ; he must discover the hidden psychic material. To do this we have invented various methods of detection, some of which lawyers are now going to imitate.

It will interest you, from the point of view of your own profession, to hear how we physicians proceed in psycho-analysis. When the patient has recapitulated his history for the first time, we ask him to be completely passive and to allow all thoughts that occur to him free expression without any selection, criticism or suppression on his part. We start, as you see, with an assumption he does not in any way share, that his thoughts are not arbitrary but are determined by

[1] Breuer und Freud, *Studien über Hysterie*, 1895.

their reaction to his secret complexes, and may be
regarded to a certain extent as derived from these
complexes. You will note it is the same assumption
which helped us to arrive at the significance of the
association test. But although we have impressed
upon the patient the rule to communicate all his
thoughts, he does not seem able to keep to it. He
holds back first this and then the other thought, and
gives various reasons to account for this, either that
it is unimportant or that it is irrelevant, or that it is
quite meaningless. We insist that he should communicate the thought in spite of these objections and
that he should follow it up ; for this criticism is precisely evidence to us that the thought belongs to the
' complex ' which we are seeking. It is precisely in
this attitude of the patient that we recognize a manifestation of his ' resistance ', which will continue
through the whole course of his treatment. I would
only indicate briefly that this conception of resistance
has gained the utmost significance for us in understanding the origin of the illness as well as the
mechanism of the healing process.

Now a similar attitude of criticism of associations
does not occur directly in your tests, whereas we are
able in psycho-analysis to observe all those striking
signs of a ' complex ' which you notice in your tests.
Even when the patient no longer ventures to evade the
rule which has been imposed upon him, we notice that
sometimes, nevertheless, he hesitates and stops, sometimes pauses in his flow of ideas. Every hesitation of
this kind is to us an expression of his resistance and
an indication of its relation to the ' complex '. Indeed,
for us it is the most important sign of such a significance, just as for you the lengthening of reaction-time
is a very important indication. We are accustomed
to interpret the hesitation in this light even when the
content of the idea held back seems to contain nothing
difficult, and when the patient assures us he cannot
imagine why he should hesitate to communicate it.

The pauses which occur in psycho-analysis are as a rule many times longer than the delays which you notice in reaction-tests.

The second of your complex-indicators, the alteration of the reaction-content, also plays its part in the technique of psycho-analysis. We are wont to regard even the smallest digressions from the ordinary form of expression in our patients generally as a sign of some hidden meaning ; and for the time being we lay ourselves open to the ridicule of the patient by such interpretations. We are literally on the alert for remarks that hint at a double meaning, and in which the hidden meaning glimmers through the harmless expression. Not only patients, but colleagues ignorant of the technique of psycho-analysis and its immediate bearings, are incredulous and accuse us of petty jokes and of playing with words, but we are nearly always in the right. After all, it is not difficult to understand that the only way in which a carefully guarded secret betrays itself is by distant, or at best by ambiguous, allusions. At last the patient becomes accustomed to disclosing, by means of so-called ' indirect representation ', all we require in order to discover the complex.

The third of your complex-indicators, that of error in reproduction (such as you observe when something repeated a second time shows a discrepancy with the first), is also made use of in a narrower field in the technique of psycho-analysis. One task which is often set us is the interpretation of dreams, i.e. the translation of the remembered dream-content into its hidden meaning. It sometimes happens that we are uncertain at which point to begin the task, and in this case we make use of a rule discovered empirically, according to which we let the dreamer recount his dream again. In doing so he usually changes the expressions used in some parts whilst faithfully repeating the rest. These points, in regard to which discrepancies arise in the two accounts or which are omitted in the second telling, are the points to which

we pay special attention ; for the inaccuracy indicates
that the complex is being touched, and promises the
best approach to the secret meaning of the dream.[1]

You will not now suppose that the points of similarity are exhausted when I state that a phenomenon
corresponding exactly to perseveration does not appear
in psycho-analysis. This apparent difference only
arises from the particular conditions of your test.
For you do not allow the effect on the complex time
to develop itself. It has scarcely begun to act when
you distract the attention of the subject under examination by a new and probably harmless stimulus-word,
and then you may observe that the subject delays,
being still occupied with the complex in spite of your
interference. On the other hand, in psycho-analysis
we avoid such interruptions, keeping the patient
occupied with his complex, and since in our method
everything is, so to speak, ' perseveration ', we cannot
observe the phenomenon as an isolated occurrence.

We may claim that it is by means of this kind of
technique that we, on the whole, succeed in making
the patient aware of what he has repressed, of his
secret, and thus in removing the psychological cause
of the symptom from which he is suffering. Before
you draw any conclusions as to the possibilities these
successful results offer for your profession, we will
consider some points of difference in the psychological
situation in the two cases.

We have already pointed out the chief difference.
With the neurotic, the secret is hidden from his own
consciousness ; with the criminal it is hidden only from
you. In the first we have a genuine ignorance (though
not altogether complete), whilst in the latter this
ignorance is merely simulated. Connected with this is
another difference more important in practice. In
psycho-analysis the patient consciously helps to overcome his resistance because he expects to gain something from the investigation—cure. The criminal, on

[1] Cf. Freud, *Die Traumdeutung.*

the contrary, does not co-operate with you ; he would be working against his whole ego. As a compensation for this, however, you are only endeavouring to arrive at a conviction objectively ; whereas our therapy demands that the patient himself should also arrive at the same conviction subjectively. It remains to be seen, however, how far your difficulties are increased or altered by the lack of co-operation on the part of the subject ; for this is a situation which you can never bring about in your class experiments, since your colleague playing the part of the accused is, in spite of his conscious determination not to betray himself, your co-worker and assistant.

Looking more deeply into the comparison of the two situations, it will become clear to you that on the whole psycho-analysis is concerned with a simple, special form of the problem of discovery of hidden material in the mind ; whereas in your profession, on the other hand, the problem is a much broader one. The case of the psychoneurotic is regularly concerned with a repressed sexual complex (in the widest sense of the term), but this is a difference which does not concern you. There is another point, however, which does. The aim of psycho-analysis is identical in all cases ; the analysis aims at laying bare the complexes which have been repressed as a result of the painful feelings associated with them, and which produce signs of resistance when there is an attempt to bring them into consciousness. The resistance is localized ; it arises at the boundary between the unconscious and the conscious. In your case we are concerned with a resistance originating entirely within the conscious life. You cannot simply discount this difference. You must first determine experimentally whether the conscious resistance betrays itself by exactly the same signs as the unconscious resistance does. Further, in my opinion you cannot yet be certain whether you may interpret your objective signs of a ‘ complex ’ as resistance in the same way that we psychotherapeutists do. It may happen in the case of your experimental subjects, though not very often in the case of criminals, that the complex you touch on is one tinged with pleasure, and the question then arises whether this complex will give the same reaction as one charged with painful affect.

I would also lay stress on the consideration that your experiments may possibly be subject to a complication which naturally does not arise in psychoanalysis. You may be led astray in your examination by a neurotic who reacts as though he were guilty even though he is innocent—because a lurking sense of guilt already existing in him assimilates the accusation made against him on this particular occasion. You must not regard this possibility as an idle one ; you have only to think of the nursery, where you can often observe it. It sometimes happens that a child who has been accused of a misdeed denies the accusation, but at the same time weeps like a sinner who has been caught. You might think that the child lies, even while it asserts its innocence ; but this need not be so. The child is really not guilty of the specific misdeed of which he is being accused, but he is guilty of a similar misdemeanour of which you know nothing and of which you do not accuse him. He therefore quite truly denies his guilt in the one case, but in doing so betrays his sense of guilt with regard to the other. The adult neurotic behaves in this and in many other ways just as the child does. People of this kind are often to be met, and it is indeed a question whether your technique will succeed in distinguishing such self-accused persons from those who are really guilty. Finally, one more point : you know that, according to law, you may not use any procedure which takes the accused off his guard. He will therefore be aware that his whole effort must be directed to avoid betraying himself in your experiments ; and a further question then arises, whether you can expect the same reactions when attention is directed towards the complex as when it is diverted from it ? How far does the conscious intention to avoid self-betrayal affect reactions in different people ?

Just because the situations on which your investigations are based can be so manifold, psychology takes a very lively interest in its results, and one would like to suggest that you should not too readily doubt their practical value. Although my work lies so far from the sphere of your legal practice, allow me to make one other suggestion. In spite of the fact that experiments in class are essential for your training and for the examination of witnesses, you will never be able to reproduce in your experiments the same psychological situation as in the examination of a guilty person in the criminal court. They remain ' mock trials ', and no practical conclusions can be based on them for use in a criminal case. If we do not wish to give up experimental study, the following alternative suggests itself : it might be arranged for you, even to the extent of becoming a duty, to undertake such examinations for a series of years in all actual cases of accusation *without your conclusions being allowed to influence the decision of the judge.* It would, indeed, be best if the latter never knew the conclusions which you drew from your experiments with regard to the guilt of the accused. After years of collecting and comparing the results thus obtained, all doubt with regard to the value of this psychological method of examination should be solved. I know, however, that the realization of this proposal does not rest only with you or with your eminent teachers.

II

OBSESSIVE ACTS AND RELIGIOUS PRACTICES [1]

(1907)

I AM certainly not the first to be struck by the resemblance between what are called obsessive acts in neurotics and those religious observances by means of which the faithful give expression to their piety. The name ' ceremonial ', which has been given to certain of these obsessive acts, is evidence of this. The resemblance, however, seems to me to be something more than superficial, so that an insight into the origin of neurotic ceremonial may embolden us to draw by analogy inferences about the psychological processes of religious life.

Persons who are addicted to obsessive acts or ceremonials belong to the same class as those who suffer from obsessive thoughts and ideas, obsessive impulses and the like, and form with them a definite clinical group, the customary term for which is obsessional neurosis.[2] But one should not attempt to deduce the character of the disease from its name, for, strictly speaking, there are other morbid psychological phenomena which have an equal claim to the ' obsessional character ', as it is called. In place of a definition we must for the present be content with a detailed description of these conditions, for it has not yet been possible to demonstrate the essential feature which probably lies at the root of the obsessional neurosis,

[1] First published in the *Zeitschrift für Religionspsychologie*, Bd. I., 1907 ; reprinted in *Sammlung*, Zweite Folge. [Translated by R. C. McWatters.]
[2] Cf. Löwenfeld, *Die psychische Zwangserscheinungen*, 1904.

though one seems to find indications of it at every turn in clinical manifestations of the disorder.

The neurotic ceremonial consists of little prescriptions, performances, restrictions, and arrangements in certain activities of every-day life which have to be carried out always in the same or in a methodically varied way. These performances make the impression that they are mere ‘ formalities ’ ; they appear quite meaningless to us. Nor do they appear otherwise to the patient himself ; yet he is quite incapable of renouncing them, for every neglect of the ceremonial is punished with the most intolerable anxiety, which forces him to perform it instantly. Just as trivial as the ceremonial performances themselves are the occasions which give rise to them, and the kind of actions which are thereby caricatured, hindered, and invariably also delayed, *e.g.* dressing and undressing, going to bed, and the satisfaction of bodily needs. The carrying out of a ceremonial may be described as the fulfilment of a series of unwritten rules ; for example, in the bed ceremonial the chair must stand in a particular place by the bed, and the clothes must be folded and laid upon it in a particular order ; the coverlet must be tucked in at the bottom, and the bed-clothes evenly spread ; the pillows must be arranged in such and such a manner, and the body must lie in a particular position—only when all is correct is it permissible to go to sleep. In slight cases the ceremonial appears to be only an exaggeration of an ordinary and justifiable orderliness, but the remarkable conscientiousness with which it is carried out, and the anxiety which follows its neglect, gives the ceremonial the character of a sacred rite. Any disturbance of it is tolerated with difficulty, and the presence of other persons during the performance of it is almost always out of the question.

Any activities whatsoever may become obsessive acts in a wide sense if they become elaborated by petty modifications or develop a rhythmic character by pauses and repetitions. A sharp distinction between 'obsessive acts' and 'ceremonials' is not to be expected; as a rule an obsessive act develops from a ceremonial. Besides these, prohibitions and hindrances (*aboulia*) complete the picture of the disorder; the latter only carry further the work of the obsessive acts, for in the one case a certain activity is interdicted altogether, and in the other it is only possible when the patient follows the prescribed ceremonial.

It is remarkable that both compulsions and prohibitions (that one thing must be done and another may not be done) originally relate only to the solitary activities of the persons concerned; for a long time their social activities remain unaffected, so that for many years such patients can treat their affliction as a private matter and hide it from others. Moreover, far more persons suffer from these forms of the obsessional neurosis than ever come to the knowledge of physicians. For many patients, too, concealment is not a difficult matter, because it is quite possible for them to fulfil their social duties during part of the day, after having devoted several hours to their secret performances in Melusina-like seclusion.

It is easy to see wherein lies the resemblance between neurotic ceremonial and religious rites ; it is in the fear of pangs of conscience after their omission, in the complete isolation of them from all other activities (the feeling that one must not be disturbed), and in the conscientiousness with which the details are carried out. But equally obvious are the differences, some of which are so startling that they make the comparison into a sacrilege : the greater individual variability of neurotic ceremonial in contrast with the stereotyped character of rites (prayer, orientation, etc.) ; its private nature as opposed to the public and communal character of religious observances ; especially, however, the distinction that the little details of religious ceremonies are full of meaning and are understood symbolically, while those of neurotics seem silly and meaningless. In this respect an obsessional neurosis furnishes a tragi-comic travesty of a private religion. But this, the sharpest distinction between neurotic and religious ceremonials, disappears as soon as one penetrates by means of psycho-analytic investigation to insight into obsessive actions. By this process the outward appearance of being foolish and meaningless, which is characteristic of obsessive acts, is completely demolished, and the fact of their having this appearance is explained. It is found that obsessive acts are throughout and in all their details full of meaning, that they serve important interests of the personality, and that they give expression both to persisting impressions of previous experiences and to thoughts about them which are strongly charged with affect. This they do in two ways, either by direct or by symbolic representation, so that they are to be interpreted either historically or symbolically.

I must here give a few examples to illustrate these remarks. Those who are familiar with the results of the psycho-analytic investigation of the psychoneuroses will not be surprised to learn that what is expressed in an obsessive act or ceremonial is derived from the most intimate, and for the most part from the sexual, experiences of the patient.

(a) A girl of my acquaintance was under the compulsion to rinse out the basin many times after washing. The significance of this ceremonial lay in the proverbial saying, ' Don't throw away dirty water until you have clean '. The action had the meaning of a warning to her sister, to whom she was much attached, not to separate from her unsatisfactory husband until she had established a relationship with a better man.

(b) A woman who was living apart from her husband was subject to a compulsion to leave the best of whatever she ate ; for example, she would only take the outside of a piece of roast meat. This renunciation was explained by the date of its origin. It appeared the day after she had refused marital relations with her husband, that is to say, had given up the best.

(c) The same patient could only sit on one particular chair, and could leave it again only with difficulty. In connection with certain details of her married life the chair symbolized to her her husband, to whom she remained faithful. She found the explanation of her compulsion in the sentence, ' It is so hard to part from anything (chair or husband) in which one has once settled oneself.'

(d) For a long time she used to repeat a very curious and senseless obsessive act. She ran out of her room into the next, in the middle of which stood a table with a cloth upon it. This she pulled straight in a particular manner, rang for the housemaid, who had to approach the table, and then sent her off again on some indifferent errand. During her efforts to explain this compulsion it occurred to her that at one place on the tablecloth there was a stain and that she always arranged the cloth so that the housemaid was bound to see it. The whole scene proved to be a reproduction of an incident in her marriage. On the wedding-night her husband had met with a not unusual mishap. He found himself impotent, and ' many times in the course of the night came hurrying from his room to hers ' in order to try again. In the morning he said he would be shamed in the eyes of the hotel chambermaid who made the bed, so he took a bottle of red ink and poured its contents over the sheet ; but he did it so clumsily that the stain came in a place most unsuitable for his purpose. With her obsessive act, therefore, she was reproducing the bridal night. (' Bed and board ' indeed comprise marriage.)

(e) She started a compulsion to note the number of each currency-note before parting with it, and this also was to be interpreted historically. At a time when she had still had an intention to leave her husband if she could find a more trustworthy man, she allowed herself to become the object of the attentions of a man she met at a watering-place, but was in doubt whether he was altogether in earnest. One day, as she was short of small change, she asked him to change a 5-kronen piece for her. He did so, and put the large coin in his pocket, saying with a gallant air that he would never part with it since it had passed through her hands. At their later meetings she was frequently tempted to challenge him to show her the 5-kronen piece, as if to convince herself that she could believe in his attentions. But she refrained, for the good reason that one cannot distinguish coins of the same value. Her doubts therefore remained unsolved ; they left her with a compulsion to note the number of each currency-note by which each one can be distinguished from others of the same value.

These few examples, selected from many I have met with, are intended merely to illustrate the statement that in obsessive acts everything has its meaning and interpretation. The same is true of ceremonials in the strict sense, only that the evidence for this would require a more detailed presentation. I quite realize, however, how far we seem to be getting from any connection between this interpretation of obsessive acts and the line of thought peculiar to religious practices.

It is one of the features of the disease that the person who is affected with a compulsion submits to it without understanding its meaning—or at any rate its chief meaning. It is only under the influence of psycho-analytic treatment that the meaning of the obsessive act, and therewith of the impelling motive underlying it, becomes conscious. We express this important fact by saying that the obsessive act serves to express *unconscious* motives and ideas. Here we seem to find a further departure from religious rites ; but we must remember that as a rule the ordinary religious observer carries out a ceremonial without concerning himself with its significance, although priests and investigators may be familiar with its meaning, which is usually symbolic. In all believers, however, the *motives* impelling them to religious practices are unknown, or are replaced in consciousness by others which are advanced in their stead.

The analysis of obsessive acts has already given us some sort of insight into their causes and into the network of motives which bring them to effect. One may say that a sufferer from compulsions and prohibitions behaves as if he were dominated by a sense of guilt, of which, however, he is ignorant—an unconscious sense of guilt, as one must call it in spite of the apparent contradiction in terms. The sense of guilt has its origin in certain early psychological occurrences, but is constantly revived by temptations which are renewed at every present opportunity ; it gives rise, moreover, to a state of anxious expectation, or anticipation of misfortune, which through the idea of punishment is linked with the inner perception of temptation. When the compulsion is first being formed, the patient is conscious that he must do this or that lest misfortune occur, and as a rule the nature of the expected misfortune is also recognized in consciousness. But the relation between the occasion which gives rise to this anxiety and the danger to which it refers is already hidden from him, though it is always capable of demonstration. Thus a ceremonial begins as an act of defence or security—as a *protective measure*.

The protestations of the pious that they know they are miserable sinners in their hearts correspond to the sense of guilt of the obsessional neurotic ; while the pious observances (prayers, invocations, etc.) with which they begin every act of the day, and especially every unusual undertaking, seem to have the significance of defensive and protective measures.

Deeper insight into the mechanism of the obsessional neurosis is gained when the primary factor underlying it is taken into account : this is always the repression of an impulse (one component of the sexual instinct) which is inherent in the constitution of the person, and which for a while found expression in his childhood but succumbed later to suppression. In course of this repression a special type of conscientiousness directed towards opposing the aim of the impulse is developed ; but this mental reaction is felt to be insecure and constantly threatened by the impulse which lurks in the unconscious. The influence of the repressed impulse is felt as a temptation, and anxiety is produced by the process of repression itself, which is dealt with by directing it towards the future in the form of anxious expectation. The process of repression which leads to the obsessional neurosis must be described as imperfectly carried through and as constantly threatening to break down. It may be compared, consequently, with an insoluble conflict ; fresh mental efforts are continually required to counterbalance the constant forward pressure of the impulse. Thus the ceremonial and obsessive acts arise partly as a defence against temptation and partly as a protection against the misfortune expected. Against the temptation the protective measures seem to become rapidly ineffective ; then the prohibitions come into play, for these are intended to keep at a distance situations which give rise to temptation. We thus see that prohibitions replace obsessive acts just as a phobia serves to hold off an hysterical attack. From another point of view a ceremonial represents the sum of all the conditions under which something not yet absolutely forbidden becomes permissible, just as the marriage ceremony of the Church signifies a sanction of sexual enjoyment, which is otherwise sinful. It is in the nature, moreover, of the obsessional neurosis—as of all similar affections —that its manifestations (symptoms, including also the obsessive acts) fulfil the condition of a compromise between the opposing forces in the mind. Thus they always reproduce something of the identical pleasure they were designed to prevent ; they serve the repressed impulse no less than the repressing element. Indeed, as the disease develops the performances which at first were concerned chiefly with defence approximate ever more and more nearly to those proscribed actions in which the impulse was able to find an outlet in childhood.

This state of things has some counterparts in the sphere of religious life, as follows : the structure of a religion seems also to be founded on the suppression or renunciation of certain instinctual trends ; these trends are not, however, as in the neurosis, exclusively components of the sexual instinct, but are egoistic, antisocial instincts, though even these for the most part are not without a sexual element. The sense of guilt in consequence of continual temptation, and the anxious expectation in the guise of fear of divine punishment, have indeed been familiar to us in religion longer than in neurosis. Possibly on account of the sexual elements which are also involved, possibly on account of some characteristic of instincts in general, the suppression active in religion proves here also to be neither completely effective nor final. Unredeemed backslidings into sin are even more common among the pious than among neurotics, and these give rise to a new form of religious activity, namely, the acts of penance of which one finds counterparts in the obsessional neurosis.

We saw a curious feature of the obsessional neurosis, one that seems to render it unworthy and trivial, in the fact that these ceremonials are concerned with such petty performances of daily life, and are expressed in foolish regulations and restrictions in regard to them. One first understands this remarkable feature of the clinical picture when one finds that the mechanism of the psychical displacement, which I first discovered in the formation of dreams,[1] dominates the mental processes in the obsessional neurosis. It is already clear from the few examples of obsessive acts given above that their symbolism and the details of their execution are effected as if by a displacement from the actual important thing on to an insignificant one which

[1] Cf. Freud, *Die Traumdeutung*.

replaces it, *e.g.* from the husband to the chair. It is this tendency to displacement which progressively changes the clinical picture of the symptoms, and eventually succeeds in turning apparently trivial matters into those of great and urgent importance. It cannot be denied that in the religious sphere also there is a similar tendency to a displacement of psychical values, and indeed in the same direction, so that petty ceremonials gradually become the essence of religious practices, and replace the ideas underlying them. It is for this reason that religions are subject to retroactive reforms which aim at the re-establishment of the original relative values.

The element of compromise in those obsessive acts which we find as neurotic symptoms is the feature least easy to find reproduced in corresponding religious observances. Yet here, too, one is reminded of this trait in the neurosis when one recalls how commonly all those acts which religion forbids—expressions of the instincts it represses—are yet committed precisely in the name of, and ostensibly in the cause of, religion.

In view of these resemblances and analogies one might venture to regard the obsessional neurosis as a pathological counterpart to the formation of a religion, to describe this neurosis as a private religious system, and religion as a universal obsessional neurosis. The essential resemblance would lie in the fundamental renunciation of the satisfaction of inherent instincts, and the chief difference in the nature of these instincts, which in the neurosis are exclusively sexual, but in religion are of egoistic origin.

A progressive renunciation of inherent instincts, the satisfaction of which is capable of giving direct pleasure to the ego, appears to be one of the foundations of human civilization. Some part of this repression is effected by means of the various religions, in that they require individuals to sacrifice the satisfaction of their instincts to the divinity. 'Vengeance is mine, saith the Lord.' In the development of the ancient religions one seems to find that many things which mankind had renounced as wicked were surrendered in favour of the god, and were still permitted in his name ; so that a yielding up of evil and asocial impulses to the divinity was the means by which man freed himself from them. For this reason it is surely no accident that all human characteristics—along with the crimes they prompt—were freely attributed to the ancient gods, and no anomaly that it was nevertheless not permissible to justify one's own misdeeds by reference to divine example.

III

THE SEXUAL ENLIGHTENMENT OF CHILDREN [1]

(1907)

AN OPEN LETTER TO DR. M. FÜRST, EDITOR OF *SOZIALE MEDIZIN UND HYGIENE*

DEAR SIR—When you ask me for an expression of opinion on the matter of sexual enlightenment for children, I assume that what you want is the independent opinion of an individual physician whose professional work offers him special opportunities for studying the subject, and not a regular conventional treatise dealing with all the mass of literature that has grown up around it. I am aware that you have followed my scientific efforts with interest, and that, unlike many other colleagues, you do not dismiss my ideas without a hearing because I regard the psycho-sexual constitution and certain noxiae in the sexual life as the most important causes of the neurotic disorders that are so common. My *Drei Abhandlungen zur Sexualtheorie*, in which I describe the components of which the sexual instinct is made up, and the disturbances which may occur in its development into the function of sexuality, has recently received favourable mention in your Journal.

I am therefore to answer the questions whether children may be given any information at all in regard to the facts of sexual life, and at what age and in what way this should be done. Now let me confess at the outset that discussion with regard to the second and

---

[1] First published in *Soziale Medizin und Hygiene*, Bd. II., 1907 ; reprinted in *Sammlung*, Zweite Folge. [Translated by E. B. M. Herford.]

third points seems to me perfectly reasonable, but that
to my mind it is quite inconceivable how the first of
these questions could ever be the subject of debate.
What can be the aim of withholding from children, or
let us say from young people, this information about the
sexual life of human beings ?   Is it a fear of arousing
interest in such matters prematurely, before it spontaneously stirs in them ?   Is it a hope of retarding by
concealment of this kind the development of the sexual
instinct in general, until such time as it can find its
way into the only channels open to it in the civilized
social order ?   Is it supposed that children would show
no interest or understanding for the facts and riddles
of sexual life if they were not prompted to do so by
outside influence ?   Is it regarded as possible that the
knowledge withheld from them will not reach them in
other ways ?   Or is it genuinely and seriously intended
that later on they should consider everything connected
with sex as something despicable and abhorrent, from
which their parents and teachers wish to keep them
apart as long as possible ?

I am really at a loss to say which of these can be the
motive for the customary concealment from children
of everything connected with sex.   I only know that
these arguments are one and all equally foolish, and
that I find it difficult to pay them the compliment of
serious refutation.   I remember, however, that in the
letters of that great thinker and friend of humanity,
Multatuli, I once found a few lines which are more than
adequate as an answer.[1]

'To my mind it seems that certain things are
' altogether too much wrapped in mystery.   It is well
' to keep the fantasies of children pure, but their purity
' will not be preserved by ignorance.   On the contrary,
' I believe that concealment leads a girl or boy to
' suspect the truth more than ever.   Curiosity leads
' to prying into things which would have roused little
' or no interest if they were talked of openly without

---

[1] Multatuli, *Briefe*, 1906, Bd. I. S. 26.

' any fuss. If this ignorance could be maintained
' I might be more reconciled to it, but that is im-
' possible; the child comes into contact with other
' children, books fall into his hands which lead him
' to reflect, and the mystery with which things he has
' already surmised are treated by his parents actually
' increases his desire to know more. Then this desire
' that is only incompletely and secretly satisfied gives
' rise to excitement and corrupts his imagination, so
' that the child is already a sinner while his parents
' still believe he does not know what sin is.'

I do not know how the case could be better stated,
though perhaps one might amplify it. It is surely
nothing else but habitual prudery and a guilty conscience in themselves about sexual matters which
causes adults to adopt this attitude of mystery towards
children; possibly, however, a piece of theoretical
ignorance on their part, to be counteracted only by
fresh information, is also responsible. It is commonly
believed that the sexual instinct is lacking in children,
and only begins to arise in them when the sexual
organs mature. This is a grave error, equally serious
from the point of view both of theory and of actual
practice. It is so easy to correct it by observation
that one can only wonder how it can ever have arisen.
As a matter of fact, the new-born infant brings
sexuality with it into the world; certain sexual sensations attend its development while at the breast and
during early childhood, and only very few children
would seem to escape some kind of sexual activity and
sexual experiences before puberty. A more complete
exposition of this statement can be found in my
Drei Abhandlungen zur Sexualtheorie, to which reference
has been made above. The reader will learn that the
specific organs of reproduction are not the only portions
of the body which are a source of pleasurable sensation,
and that Nature has stringently ordained that even
stimulation of the genitals cannot be avoided during
infancy. This period of life, during which a certain

degree of directly sexual pleasure is produced by the stimulation of various cutaneous areas (erotogenic zones), by the activity of certain biological impulses and as an accompanying excitation during many affective states, is designated by an expression introduced by Havelock Ellis as the period of auto-erotism. Puberty merely brings about attainment of the stage at which the genitals acquire supremacy among all the zones and sources of pleasure, and in this way presses erotism into the service of reproduction, a process which naturally can undergo certain inhibitions ; in the case of those persons who later on become perverts and neurotics this process is only incompletely accomplished. On the other hand, the child is capable long before puberty of most of the mental manifestations of love, for example, tenderness, devotion, and jealousy. Often enough the connection between these mental manifestations and the physical sensation of sexual excitation is so close that the child cannot be in doubt about the relation between the two. To put it briefly, the child is long before puberty a being capable of mature love, lacking only the ability for reproduction ; and it may be definitely asserted that the mystery which is set up withholds him only from intellectual comprehension of achievements for which he is psychically and physically prepared.

The intellectual interest of a child in the riddle of sexual life, his desire for knowledge, finds expression at an earlier period of life than is usually suspected. If they have not often come across such cases as I am about to mention, parents must either be afflicted with blindness in regard to this interest in their children, or, when they cannot overlook it, must make every effort to stifle it. I know a splendid boy, now four years old, whose intelligent parents abstain from forcibly suppressing one side of the child's development. Little Herbert, who has certainly not been exposed to any seducing influence from servants, has for some time shown the liveliest interest in that part of his body which he calls his weewee-maker. When only three years old he asked his mother, ' Mamma, have you got a weewee-maker, too ? ' His mother answered, ' Of course, what did you think ? ' He also asked his father the same question repeatedly. At about the same age he was taken to a barn and saw a cow milked for the first time. ' Look, milk is coming out of the weewee-maker ! ' he called in surprise. At the age of three and three-quarters he was well on the way to establish correct categories by means of his own independent observation. He saw how water is run off from a locomotive and said, ' See, the engine is making weewee, but where is its weewee-maker ? ' Later on he added thoughtfully, ' Dogs and horses have weewee-makers, but tables and chairs don't have them '. Recently he was watching his little sister of one week old being bathed, and remarked, ' Her weewee-maker is still tiny ; it will get bigger when she grows '. (I have heard of this attitude towards the problem of sex difference in other boys of the same age.) I must expressly assert that Herbert is not a sensual child nor even morbidly disposed ; in my opinion, since he has never been frightened or oppressed with a sense of guilt, he gives expression quite ingenuously to what he thinks.

The second great problem which exercises a child's mind—probably at a rather later date—is that of the origin of children, and is usually aroused by the unwelcome arrival of a baby brother or sister. This is the oldest and most burning question that assails immature humanity ; those who understand how to interpret myths and legends can detect it in the riddle which the Theban Sphinx set to Oedipus. The answers usually given to children in the nursery wound the child's frank and genuine spirit of investigation, and generally deal the first blow at his confidence in his parents ; from this time onwards he commonly begins to mistrust grown-up people and keeps to himself what interests him most. The following letter may show

how torturing this very curiosity may become in older children ; it was written by a motherless girl of eleven and a half who had been puzzling over the problem with her younger sister.

' DEAR AUNT MALI—Please will you be so kind as ' to write and tell me how you got Chris or Paul. You ' must know because you are married. We were ' arguing about it yesterday, and we want to know the ' truth. We have nobody else to ask. When are you ' coming to Salzburg ? You know, Aunt Mali, we ' simply can't imagine how the stork brings babies. ' Trudel thought the stork brings them in a shirt. ' Then we want to know, too, how the stork gets them ' out of the pond, and why one never sees babies in ' ponds. And please will you tell me, too, how you ' know beforehand when you are going to have one. ' Please write and tell me *all* about it. Thousands ' of kisses from all of us.—Your inquiring niece,

' LILY.'

I do not think that this touching request brought the two sisters the information they wanted. Later on the writer developed the neurosis that arises in unanswered unconscious questions—obsessive speculating.

I do not think that there is even one good reason for denying children the information which their thirst for knowledge demands. To be sure, if it is the purpose of educators to stifle the child's power of independent thought as early as possible, in order to produce that ' good behaviour ' which is so highly prized, they cannot do better than deceive children in sexual matters and intimidate them by religious means. The stronger characters will, it is true, withstand these influences ; they will become rebels against the authority of their parents and later against every other form of authority. When children do not receive the explanations for which they turn to their elders, they go on tormenting themselves in secret with the problem,

and produce attempts at solution in which the truth
they have guessed is mixed up in the most extraordinary
way with grotesque inventions ; or else they whisper
confidences to each other which, because of the sense
of guilt in the youthful inquirers, stamp everything
sexual as horrible and disgusting. These infantile
sexual theories are well worth collecting and examining.
After these experiences children usually lose the only
proper attitude to sexual questions, many of them
never to find it again.

It would seem that the overwhelming majority of
writers, both men and women, who have dealt with the
question of explaining sexual matters to children have
expressed themselves in favour of enlightenment. The
clumsiness, however, of most of their proposals how
and when this enlightenment should be carried out
leads one to conclude that they have not found it very
easy to venture this admission. As far as my knowledge of the literature goes, the charming letter of
explanation which a certain Frau Emma Eckstein
gives as written to her ten-year-old boy stands out
conspicuously.[1] The customary method is obviously
not the right one. All sexual knowledge is kept from
children as long as possible, and then on one single
occasion an explanation, which is even then only half
the truth and generally comes too late, is proffered them
in mysterious and solemn language. Most of the
answers to the question ' How can I tell my children ? '
make such a pitiful impression, at least upon me, that
I should prefer parents not to concern themselves with
the explanation at all. It is much more important that
children should never get the idea that one wants to
make more of a secret of the facts of sexual life than of
any other matter not suited to their understanding.
To ensure this it is necessary that from the very beginning everything sexual should be treated like everything else that is worth knowing about. Above all,
schools should not evade the task of mentioning sexual

---

[1] Emma Eckstein, *Die Sexualfrage in der Erziehung des Kindes*, 1904.

matters ; lessons about the animal kingdom should
include the great facts of reproduction, which should
be given their due significance, and emphasis should
be laid at the same time on the fact that man shares
with the higher animals everything essential to his
organization. Then, if the atmosphere of the home
does not make for suppression of all reasoning, something similar to what I once overheard in a nursery
would probably occur oftener. A small boy said to
his little sister, ' How can you think the stork brings
babies ! You know that man is a mammal, do you
suppose that storks bring other mammals their young
too ?' In this way the curiosity of children will never
become very intense, for at each stage in its inquiries
it will find the satisfaction it needs. Explanations
about the specific circumstances of human sexuality
and some indication of its social significance should be
provided before the child is eleven years old.[1]   The age
of confirmation would be a more suitable time than any
other at which to instruct the child, who already has
full knowledge of the physical facts involved, in those
social obligations which are bound up with the actual
gratification of this instinct. A gradual and progressive course of instruction in sexual matters such
as this, at no period interrupted, in which the school
takes the initiative, seems to me to be the only method
of giving the necessary information that takes into
consideration the development of the child and thus
successfully avoids ever-present dangers.

I consider it a most significant advance in the science
of education that in France, in place of the catechism,
the State should have introduced a primer which gives
the child his first instruction in his position as a citizen
and in the ethical obligations which will be his in time
to come. The elementary instruction provided there,
however, is seriously deficient in that it includes no
reference to sexual matters. Here is the omission

---

[1] [The original has also : *am Schlusse des Volksschulunterrichtes und
vor Eintritt in die Mittelschule.*—Trans.]

which stands in such need of attention on the part of educators and reformers. In those countries which leave the education of children either wholly or in part in the hands of the priesthood, the method urged would of course not be practicable. No priest will ever admit the identity in nature of man and beast, since to him the immortality of the soul is a foundation for moral training which he cannot forgo. Here again we clearly see the unwisdom of putting new wine into old bottles, and perceive the impossibility of carrying through a reform in one particular without altering the foundations of the whole system.

IV

CHARACTER AND ANAL EROTISM [1]

(1908)

AMONG those whom one tries to help by means of
psycho-analytic treatment, one very often meets
with a type of character in which certain traits
are strongly marked, while at the same time one's
attention is arrested by the behaviour of these persons
in regard to a certain bodily function and of the organ
connected with it during their childhood. I can no
longer say on what precise occasions I first received the
impression that a systematic relationship exists between
this type of character and the activities of this organ,
but I can assure the reader that no theoretical anticipations of mine played any part in its production.

My belief in such a relationship has been so much
strengthened by accumulated experience that I venture
to make it the subject of a communication.

The persons whom I am about to describe are
remarkable for a regular combination of the three
following peculiarities : they are exceptionally *orderly*,
parsimonious, and *obstinate*. Each of these words really
covers a small group or series of traits which are related
to one another. ' Orderly ' comprises both bodily
cleanliness and reliability and conscientiousness in the
performance of petty duties : the opposite of it would
be ' untidy ' and ' negligent '. ' Parsimony ' may be
exaggerated up to the point of avarice ; and obstinacy
may amount to defiance, with which irascibility and
vindictiveness may easily be associated. The two
latter qualities—parsimony and obstinacy—hang to-

---

[1] First published in the *Psychiatrisch-Neurologische Wochenschrift,*
Bd. IX., 1908 ; reprinted in *Sammlung*, Zweite Folge. [Translated by
R. C. McWatters.]

gether more closely than the third, orderliness ; they are, too, the more constant element in the whole complex. It seems to me, however, incontestable that all three in some way belong together.

From the history of the early childhood of these persons one easily learns that they took a long time to overcome the infantile *incontinentia alvi*, and that even in later childhood they had to complain of isolated accidents relating to this function. As infants they seem to have been among those who refuse to empty the bowel when placed on the chamber, because they derive an incidental pleasure from the act of defæcation [1] ; for they assert that even in somewhat later years they have found a pleasure in holding back their stools, and they remember, though more readily of their brothers and sisters than of themselves, all sorts of unseemly performances with the stools when passed. From these indications we infer that the erotogenic significance of the anal zone is intensified in the innate sexual constitution of these persons ; but since none of these weaknesses and peculiarities are to be found in them once childhood has been passed, we must conclude that the anal zone has lost its erotogenic significance in the course of their development, and that the constant appearance of this triad of peculiarities in their character may be brought into relation with the disappearance of their anal erotism.

I know that no one feels inclined to accept a proposition which appears unintelligible, and for which no explanation can be offered, but we can find the basis of such an explanation in the postulates I have formulated in my *Drei Abhandlungen zur Sexualtheorie*. I there attempt to show that the sexual instinct of man is very complex and is made up of contributions from numerous components and partial impulses. The peripheral stimulation of certain specialized parts (genitals, mouth, anus, urethra), which may be called erotogenic zones, furnishes

[1] Cf. Freud, *Drei Abhandlungen zur Sexualtheorie,* 1905.

important contributions to the production of sexual excitation, but the fate of the stimuli arising in these areas varies according to their source and according to the age of the person concerned. Generally speaking, only a part of them finds a place in the sexual life ; another part is deflected from a sexual aim and is directed to other purposes, a process which may be called sublimation. During the period of life which may be distinguished as the ' sexual latency period ', *i.e.* from the end of the fourth year to the first manifestations of puberty at about eleven, reaction-formations, such as shame, disgust, and morality, are formed in the mental economy at the expense of the excitations proceeding from the erotogenic zones, and these reaction-formations erect themselves as barriers against the later activity of the sexual instinct. Now anal erotism is one of those components of the instinct which in the course of evolution and in accordance with our present civilizing education has become useless for sexual aims : it would therefore be no very surprising result if these traits of orderliness, parsimony, and obstinacy, which are so prominent in persons who were formerly anal erotics, turned out to be the first and most constant results of the sublimation of anal erotism.[1]

[1] Since it is just these remarks about the anal erotism of infants in my three contributions to the sexual theory that have most scandalized uncomprehending readers, I venture to insert here an observation which I owe to a very intelligent patient. ' An acquaintance of mine who has read the *Drei Abhandlungen zur Sexualtheorie* was talking about the book and said he fully accepted it, but one passage—though naturally he also accepts and understands it—appeared to him so grotesque and comic that he sat down and laughed over it for a quarter of an hour. This passage runs : " It is one of the best signs of later eccentricity or nervousness if an infant obstinately refuses to empty its bowel when placed on the chamber, that is, when the nurse wishes, but withholds this function at his own pleasure. Naturally it does not matter to the child if he soils his bed ; his only concern is not to lose the pleasure incidental to the act of defæcation." The picture of this infant sitting on the chamber and deliberating whether he should allow such a limitation of his personal independence, and of his anxiety not to lose the pleasure of defæcation, caused my friend the greatest merriment. Some twenty minutes later, as we were sitting at tea, my acquaintance suddenly remarked without any preliminary, " Do you know, there just occurs to me, as I see the cocoa in front of me, an idea that I always had as

The inherent necessity of this relationship is naturally not clear even to myself, but I can make some suggestions which help towards an understanding of it. The cleanliness, orderliness, and reliability give exactly the impression of a reaction-formation against an interest in things that are unclean and intrusive and ought not to be on the body (' Dirt is matter in the wrong place '). To bring obstinacy into relation with interest in defæcation seems no easy task, but it should be remembered that infants can very early behave with great self-will about parting with their stools (see above), and that painful stimuli to the skin of the buttocks (which is connected with the anal erotogenic zone) are an instrument in the education of the child designed to break his self-will and make him submissive. As an expression of defiance or of defiant mockery, a challenge referring to a caress on this part of the body is used even at the present day, as in former times—that is, it represents a tender feeling which has undergone repression. An exposure of the buttocks corresponds

---

a child. I then always pretended to myself that I was the cocoa manufacturer Van Houten '' (he pronounced it '' Van Hauten ''), '' that I possessed a great secret for the preparation of this cocoa, and that all the world was trying to get this valuable secret from me, but that I carefully kept it to myself. Why it was Van Houten that I hit upon I do not know. Probably it was that his advertisements made the greatest impression on me.'' Laughing, and without thinking much about the meaning of my words, I replied, '' *Wann haut'n* (Van Houten) *die Mutter* ? '' [When do mothers smack ?] It was only later that I realized that my pun really contained the key to the whole of his sudden recollection from childhood, which I now recognized as a striking example of a screen-phantasy, setting at rest the sense of guilt by means of a complete reversal of the value of its memory content, while it retained its reference to actual experience (the nutritional process) and was supported by a phonetic association : '' cocoa '' — '' *Wann haut'n* '' (Van Houten). (Displacement from behind forwards ; excrement becomes aliment ; the shameful substance which has to be concealed turns into a secret which enriches the world.) It was interesting to me how in this case, after a defence-reaction, which to be sure took the comparatively mild form of a merely formal objection, the most striking evidence was supplied from the subject's own unconscious after a quarter of an hour without any effort on his part.'

[Besides the pun on the word Van Houten, there is probably a further association between the German for cocoa (*Kakao*) and for the nursery term for fæces in that language, *Kakis*. Compare also the English *caca* for fæces.—Trans.]

to the reduction of this speech to a gesture ; in Goethe's
Götz von Berlichingen we find both speech and gesture
introduced most appropriately as expression of defiance.

The connections which exist between the two
complexes of interest in money and of defæcation,
which seem so dissimilar, appear to be the most far-
reaching. It is well known to every physician who
has used psycho-analysis that the most refractory and
obdurate cases of so-called chronic constipation in
neurotics can be cured by this means. This is less
surprising if we remember that this function has shown
itself equally amenable to hypnotic suggestion. But
in psycho-analysis one only attains this result when one
deals with the money complex of the persons concerned, and induces them to bring it into consciousness
with all its connections. One might suppose that the
neurosis is here only following a hint from common
speech which calls a person who keeps too careful a hold
on his money ' dirty ' or ' filthy', but this would be
far too superficial an explanation. In reality, wherever
archaic modes of thought predominate or have persisted—in ancient civilizations, in myth, fairy-tale and
superstition, in unconscious thoughts and dreams, and
in the neuroses—money comes into the closest relation
with excrement. We know how the money which
the devil gives his paramours turns to excrement
after his departure, and the devil is most certainly
nothing more than a personification of the unconscious instinctual forces.[1] The superstition, too, which
associates the finding of treasure with defæcation is
well known, and everyone is familiar with the figure
of the ' excretor of ducats ' (*Dukatenscheisser*).[2] Even
in the early Babylon cult gold is ' the excrement of
Hell ', Mammon = ilu manman.[3] Thus in following

---

[1] Compare hysterical possession and demoniac epidemics.

[2] [Unfamiliar to English readers, but compare ' the goose which
lays golden eggs '.—Trans.]

[3] Jeremias, *Das Alte Testament im Lichte des alten Orients*, 1906,
p. 216, and *Babylonisches im Neuen Testament*, 1906, p. 96. ' Mammon
is Babylonian " Manman ", another name of Nergal, the god of the

common speech, the neurosis, here as elsewhere, takes the words in their original most significant sense, and wherever it appears to express a word figuratively it usually only reproduces its original meaning.

It is possible that the contrast between the most precious substance known to man and the most worthless, which he rejects as ' something thrown out ', has contributed to this identification of gold with fæces.

Yet another circumstance facilitates this equivalence in the mental processes involved in neurosis. The original erotic interest in defæcation is, as we know, destined to be extinguished in later years ; it is in these years that the interest in money is making its appearance as something new which was unknown in childhood. This makes it easier for the earlier impulse, which is in process of relinquishing its aim, to be carried over to the new one.

If there is any reality in the relation described here between anal erotism and this triad of character-traits, one may expect to find but little of the ' anal character ' in persons who have retained the erotogenic quality of the anal zone into adult life, as for example certain homosexuals. Unless I am greatly mistaken experience on the whole is fully in accord with this anticipation.

One ought to consider whether other types of character do not also show a connection with the excitability of particular erotogenic zones. As yet I am aware only of the intense, ' burning ' ambition of those who formerly suffered from enuresis. At any rate, one can give a formula for the formation of the ultimate character from the constituent character-traits : the permanent character-traits are either unchanged perpetuations of the original impulses, sublimations of them, or reaction-formations against them.

---

underworld. According to an Oriental myth which has passed over into sagas and folk-tales, gold is the excrement of hell ; see *Monotheistische Strömungen innerhalb der babylonischen Religion*, S. 16, Anmk. i.'

V

HYSTERICAL PHANTASIES AND THEIR RELATION TO BISEXUALITY [1]

(1908)

WE are all familiar with the delusional phantasies of paranoiacs which portray the person's greatness or his sufferings, and occur in stereotyped forms with almost monotonous regularity. We also come across numerous accounts of the strange conditions under which certain perverts carry out their sexual gratification—either in imagination or in reality. Nevertheless, it may be new to some readers to hear that quite analogous mental productions are regularly present in all the psychoneuroses, particularly in hysteria, and that these so-called hysterical phantasies have important connections with the causes of the neurotic symptoms.

The common origin and normal prototype of all these phantastic creations are the so-called day-dreams of adolescence, to which some, though perhaps inadequate, attention has been given in the literature on the subject.[2] They occur with perhaps equal frequency in both sexes ; in girls and women they are invariably of an erotic nature, in men they may be either erotic or ambitious. The importance of the erotic factor in those of men should not, however, be under-estimated ; a more precise investigation of the day-dreams of a

[1] First published in the *Zeitschrift für Sexualwissenschaft*, Bd. I., 1908 ; reprinted in *Sammlung*, Zweite Folge. [Translated by Douglas Bryan.]

[2] Cf. Breuer und Freud, *Studien über Hysterie*, 1895 ; Pierre Janet, *Névroses et idées fixes*, I., 'Les rêveries subconscientes,' 1898 ; Havelock Ellis, *Studies in the Psychology of Sex*, vol. i., 'The Evolution of Modesty', 1904 ; Freud, *Die Traumdeutung*, 1900 ; A. Pick, *Über pathologische Träumerei und ihre Beziehungen zur Hysterie*, 1896.

man generally shows that all his heroic exploits, all his successes, are for the purpose of pleasing a woman, of being preferred by her to other men.[1] These phantasies are wish-fulfilments, products of frustration and desire ; they are justly called day-dreams, for they give us the key to an understanding of night dreams, the nucleus of which is nothing else than these daytime phantasies, but complicated and distorted, and misunderstood by the conscious psychic system.[2]

These day-dreams are invested with great interest, carefully cherished and usually concealed with some shame, as though they belonged to the person's most intimate possessions. It is easy to recognize a day-dreamer in the street, however, by his sudden absent-minded smile, his way of talking to himself, or the hastening of his steps which marks the climax of the fancied situation. All hysterical attacks which I have been able to investigate up to the present have proved to be involuntary day-dreams of this kind breaking in upon ordinary life. Now our observations leave no room for doubt that phantasies of this sort may be unconscious as well as conscious in nature, and that as soon as they become unconscious they may become pathogenic, i.e. may express themselves in symptoms or attacks. Under favourable circumstances consciousness may just be able to capture such an unconscious phantasy. After I had drawn the attention of one of my patients to her phantasies, she told me that on one occasion she had burst into tears in the street, and that, thinking quickly what she had been crying about, she realized the existence of a phantasy in her mind that a pianist well known in the town (but not personally acquainted with her) had entered into an intimate relationship with her, that she had had a child by him (she was childless), and that he had deserted her and her child and left them in misery. It

---

[1] Havelock Ellis is of the same opinion ; op. cit.
[2] Cf. Freud, Die Traumdeutung, Dritte Auflage, p. 331 et seq.

was at this point of her romance that she burst into tears.

Unconscious phantasies have either always been unconscious and formed in the unconscious, or more often they were once conscious phantasies, day-dreams, and have been purposely forgotten and driven into the unconscious by 'repression'. Their content may then either have remained the same or may have been altered, so that the phantasies which are now unconscious are derivatives of phantasies that were once conscious. Now an unconscious phantasy has a very important connection with the sexual life of the person ; it is actually identical with the phantasy which served the person in his sexual gratification during the period of masturbation. The masturbatory (in the widest sense, onanistic) act at that time consisted of two parts, one of which was the creation of the phantasy, and the other a manipulative performance for attaining auto-erotic gratification at the climax of the phantasy. It is known that these two components of the act have first had to be welded together.[1] Originally the active performance was a purely auto-erotic proceeding for the purpose of obtaining pleasure from a particular erotogenic part of the body. Later this performance became bound up with the idea of a wish emanating from the sphere of object-love, and served as a partial realization of the situation in which the phantasy culminated. If the person subsequently renounces this type of masturbatory gratification with phantasy, the action is given up, but the previously conscious phantasy becomes an unconscious one. It may happen that no other form of sexual gratification supervenes, the person remaining abstinent and not succeeding in sublimating his libido, that is, in deflecting his sexual excitation·into higher channels ; these are, then, the conditions under which the unconscious phantasy is re-stimulated, and under which it will grow and spread and, drawing upon the whole might

[1] Cf. Freud, *Drei Abhandlungen zur Sexualtheorie.*

of the person's need for love, will achieve expression of at least a part of its content in the form of a morbid symptom.

In this way such unconscious phantasies are the immediate precursors in the mind of a whole series of hysterical symptoms. The hysterical symptoms are nothing but the unconscious phantasies made manifest by ' conversion ', and in so far as the symptoms are of a somatic kind they are often enough drawn from within the range of the sexual feelings and motor innervations that originally accompanied the phantasy while it was still conscious. In this way the process of discontinuing masturbation is literally reproduced again backwards ; while the final aim of the whole pathological process, restoration of the original primary sexual gratification, is achieved, though never, it is true, completely, yet always by a sort of approximation.

Those who study hysteria find their attention therefore very soon diverted from the symptoms and directed to the phantasies which give rise to the symptoms. The technique of psycho-analysis enables us first of all to infer the unconscious phantasies from the symptoms and then to enable the patient to become conscious of them. Now it has been found by this means that the content of the unconscious phantasies of hysterical patients is in complete accordance with the conscious ways in which perverts actually obtain gratification ; and if any one requires examples of such situations he need only call to mind the world-famed orgies of the Roman Emperors, the madness of which, of course, was the product of the unrestrained power and liberty possessed by their creators. The delusions of paranoiacs are of a similar nature but are phantasies which achieve direct access to consciousness ; they are based on the masochistic-sadistic component of the sexual instinct, and they too have their complete counterpart in certain unconscious phantasies of hysterical persons. Of practical importance, too, is the case of hysterical persons who may not express their phantasies as symptoms, but consciously realize them in action and thus imagine and actually bring about assaults, attacks, or sexual aggressions.

This method of psycho-analytic investigation, which proceeds from the conspicuous symptoms to the hidden unconscious phantasies, reveals everything that can be found out about the sexuality of psychoneurotics, including the fact which is the subject of this short preliminary publication.[1]

The reason why the relationship between the phantasies and the symptoms is no simple one but very complicated, is in all probability due to the obstacles which the unconscious phantasies meet with in seeking to find expression.[1] As a rule, *i.e.* when the neurosis is fully developed and has persisted for some time, a particular symptom corresponds not to a single unconscious phantasy, but to several such; and this correspondence, moreover, is no arbitrary one but obeys definite laws. At the beginning of the illness these complications are not likely to be all fully developed.

For the sake of general interest I will here trespass beyond the continuity of my argument and try to describe the nature of hysterical symptoms in a series of successively exhaustive formulas. They do not contradict one another, but they consist partly in attempts at greater completeness and more precise classification, and partly of applications of different points of view.

1. The hysterical symptom is the memory-symbol of the operation of certain (traumatic) impressions and experiences.

2. The hysterical symptom is a substitute, produced by 'conversion', for the reactivation of these traumatic experiences by association.

3. The hysterical symptom is, like other mental products, the expression of a wish-fulfilment.

---

[1] The same is true of the relation between the 'latent' dream-thoughts and the elements of the 'manifest' dream-content. See the section on dream-work in my *Traumdeutung*.

4. The hysterical symptom is a realization of an unconscious phantasy which serves as a wish-fulfilment.

5. The hysterical symptom serves the purposes of sexual gratification and represents a part of the sexual life of the person (corresponding to one of the components of his sexual instinct).

6. The hysterical symptom corresponds to the recurrence of a form of sexual gratification which was real in infantile life and has since been repressed.

7. The hysterical symptom arises as a compromise between two opposing affects or instinctual trends, of which one is attempting to express a partial impulse or component of the sexual constitution, while the other tries to suppress it.

8. The hysterical symptom may represent various unconscious non-sexual impulses, but can never dispense with a sexual significance.

Among these various definitions the seventh is the one which defines the hysterical symptom most completely as the realization of an unconscious phantasy, and the eighth recognizes the proper significance of the sexual factor. Some of the previous formulas lead up to this and are contained in it.

The connection between the symptoms and the phantasies makes it easy to arrive, by psycho-analysis of the former, at a knowledge of the components of the sexual instinct dominating the person concerned, which I have described in my *Drei Abhandlungen zur Sexualtheorie*. In some cases, however, investigation by this means yields an unsuspected result. It shows that for many symptoms it is not enough to resolve only one unconscious sexual phantasy or even a number of them, of which one, the most important and fundamental, is of a sexual nature ; to resolve the symptom one has, on the contrary, to deal with two sexual phantasies, of which one has a masculine and the other a feminine character, so that one of these phantasies has its source in a homosexual trend. This new statement does not alter our seventh formula ; an hysterical symptom must necessarily be a compromise between a libidinal and a repressing force, but incidentally it may represent a combination of two libidinal phantasies of an opposite sexual character.

I shall refrain from giving examples of this law. I have found from experience that short condensed analyses always fail in the convincing effect for which they are intended, and I must leave an account of fully analysed cases for another time.

I will, therefore, merely state the following formula and explain its import.

9. An hysterical symptom is the expression of both a masculine and a feminine unconscious sexual phantasy.

I must expressly mention that I cannot claim the same general validity for this formula as for the others. As far as I can see, it applies neither to all the symptoms of one case nor to all cases. On the contrary, it is not hard to find cases in which the antithetical sexual impulses have found expression in separate symptoms, so that the symptoms of the heterosexuality and the homosexuality can be as clearly distinguished from each other as the underlying latent phantasies. Nevertheless, the condition stated in this ninth formula is frequent enough, and important enough when it occurs to deserve particular emphasis. It seems to me to mark the highest degree of complexity in the way in which an hysterical symptom can be determined, and one may expect, therefore, to meet with it only when a neurosis has persisted for a long time and undergone considerable organization.[1]

The bisexual nature of hysterical symptoms can nevertheless be demonstrated in numerous cases, and this is in any event an interesting confirmation of my view that the assumption of a bisexual predisposition

---

[1] J. Sadger has recently discovered this independently in his own psycho-analyses, and even vouches for its general validity : *Die Bedeutung der psychoanalytischen Methode nach Freud.*

in man [1] is particularly clearly brought out by psycho-analysis of neurotics. A quite analogous condition occurs when anyone in his conscious masturbatory phantasies pictures himself both as the man and as the woman in an imagined situation ; further counterparts of this are found in certain hysterical attacks in which the patient acts at one and the same time both parts of the underlying sexual phantasy—for instance, in one case I observed, the patient pressed her dress to her body with one hand (as the woman) while trying to tear it off with the other (as the man). These simultaneous contradictory actions largely obscure the situation which is otherwise so plastically portrayed in attacks, and thus serve very well to conceal the unconscious phantasy which is actually at work.

In treatment by psycho-analysis it is very important to be prepared for the bisexual meaning of a symptom. One need not then be surprised or misled if a symptom seems to persist with undiminished force though one of its sexual meanings has already been resolved. It is then still being maintained by the perhaps unsuspected opposite sexual trend. In the treatment of such cases one may also observe how the patient finds an easy way of *evading* analysis of one sexual meaning by diverting his associations constantly to the opposite meaning, as if along a parallel line.

[1] *Drei Abhandlungen zur Sexualtheorie.*

ON THE SEXUAL THEORIES OF CHILDREN [1]

(1908)

THE material on which the following synthesis is built up is derived from many sources. First, from the direct observation of what children say and do; secondly, from what adult neurotics consciously remember of their childhood and retail during psycho-analytic treatment; and thirdly, from the conclusions, reconstructions and unconscious memories translated into consciousness which result from the psycho-analysis of neurotics.

That the first of these three sources has not alone supplied all that is worth knowing on the subject is due to the attitude of adults towards childish sexual life. Children are not credited with any sexual activities, therefore no pains are taken to observe anything of the kind, while on the other hand any expressions of such a thing which would be worthy of attention are suppressed. Consequently the opportunity of gaining information from this most genuine and fertile source is greatly restricted. Whatever we derive from the uninfluenced communications of adults concerning their conscious childhood is at best subject to the objection that it is perhaps falsified in looking back and, further, has to be estimated in the light of the fact that the persons in question have later become neurotic. The material from the third source is subject to all the attacks that are in general directed against the trustworthiness of psycho-analysis and the reliability of the conclusions drawn from it, so that

---

[1] First published in *Sexualprobleme*, new issue of the periodical *Mutterschutz*, Bd. IV., 1908; reprinted in *Sammlung*, Zweite Folge. [Translated by Douglas Bryan.]

no justification of it can be attempted here ; I will only assert that those who know and make use of the psycho-analytic technique acquire extensive confidence in its results.

I cannot guarantee the completeness of my collection, but I can answer for the care taken in gathering the material.

There remains a difficult question to decide. How far ought one to take for granted what is here reported about children in general as being true of all children, i.e. of every individual child ? Pressure of education and the varying intensity of the sexual instinct certainly render possible great individual variations in the sexual behaviour of children, and, above all, these things influence the date at which the childish interest in sexuality appears. Therefore I have not arranged my material according to the successive epochs of childhood, but have included in one recital what applies to various children, in one early, and in another late. It is my conviction that no child—none, at least, who is mentally sound, still less one who is mentally gifted—can avoid being occupied with sexual problems in the years *before* puberty.

I do not think much of the objection that neurotics are a special class of people marked by a degenerative disposition, whose child-life must not be regarded as evidence of the childhood of others. Neurotics are human beings like every one else, and cannot be sharply differentiated from normal people ; in their childhood they are not easily distinguishable from those who later remain healthy. It is one of the most valuable results of our psycho-analytic investigations to have found that their neuroses have no special mental content peculiar to them, but that, as C. G. Jung has expressed it, they fall ill of the same complexes with which we who are healthy also have to contend. The difference is only that the healthy know how to overcome these complexes without great and practically demonstrable harm ; while the suppression of

these complexes in nervous people only succeeds at the
price of costly substitute-formations, thus in practice
proving unsuccessful. In childhood nervous and normal
people naturally approximate much more closely than
in later life, so that I cannot recognize it as an error
in method to make use of the communications of
neurotics concerning their childhood as analogies for
normal child-life. Since those who later become
neurotics very frequently include in their constitution
an especially strong sexual instinct and a disposition
to precocity and to premature expression of this
impulse, they enable us in this way to recognize much
of the infantile sexual activities more plainly and more
correctly than, with our blunted talent for observation
of ordinary children, would otherwise be possible.
The true value of these communications by adult
neurotics can only be estimated, to be sure, when a
collection of the childhood-memories of adult healthy
people, made after the manner of Havelock Ellis, has
also been taken into account.

In consequence of both external and internal
unfavourable circumstances, the following remarks
apply chiefly to the sexual development of one sex
only, namely, the male. The value of a compilation
such as I attempt here, however, need not be merely
descriptive. The knowledge of the infantile sexual
theories in the form in which they appear in childish
thoughts can be of interest in various directions—for
instance, surprisingly so for an understanding of myths
and fairy-tales. They are indispensable for the understanding of the neuroses, where these childish theories
are still in operation and have acquired a determining
influence upon the form taken by the symptoms.

* * *

If, forgetting our mortality and imagining ourselves
to be merely thinking beings, gazing, for instance,
from another planet, we could apprehend the things
of this earth afresh, perhaps nothing would arrest our

attention more forcibly than the existence of two sexes among human beings, who otherwise resemble each other so closely and yet emphasize their difference even in the most superficial indications. Now it does not seem that children also choose this fundamental fact as the starting-point of their investigations concerning sexual problems. Since they have known a father and a mother as far back as they can remember in life, they accept their existence as a reality which needs no further inquiry, and in just the same way does a boy behave towards a little sister from whom he is only separated by a slight difference of age, by one or two years. The child's desire for knowledge does not awaken spontaneously on this point at all, as it would if prompted perhaps by an inborn need to seek for causes, but arises under the goad of a self-seeking impulse which dominates him when he is confronted by the arrival of a new child—perchance at the end of the second year. Those children whose own nursery at home does not become divided up in this way are nevertheless able as a result of their own observations to put themselves in the place of others who are in this situation in other homes. The loss of the parents' care and concern, which they actually experience or with justice fear, the presentiment that they must from now and for ever share all possessions with the newcomer, has the effect of awakening the emotions of the child and sharpening its thinking capacities. The elder child expresses unconcealed hostility against the newcomer, which finds vent in unfriendly criticisms of it, in wishes that ' the stork should take it back again ', and occasionally even in attempts at little outrages upon the helpless creature lying in the cradle. A greater difference of age as a rule modifies the expression of this primary hostility ; just as in somewhat later years, if brothers and sisters fail to appear, the wish for a playmate like those observed elsewhere obtains the upper hand.

Under the stimulus of these feelings and anxieties

the child thus comes to consider the first of the great problems of life, and asks itself the question where children come from, which at first runs, 'Where did this particular tiresome child come from?' The after-echo of this first riddle seems to be observable in the innumerable riddles of myths and sagas. The question itself, like all inquiry, is a product of dire necessity, as if to thought were entrusted the task of preventing the repetition of an event so greatly feared. At the same time, we may assume, the child's thinking becomes independent of the stimulus, and continues its activity as a separate impulse towards investigation. Where a child is not already too much intimidated, it takes sooner or later the shortest way by demanding answers from its parents or attendants, who signify for it the source of all knowledge. This way, however, fails. The child receives either evasive answers or a rebuke for its curiosity, or is dismissed with that mythologically significant information which in German runs : ' The stork brings the children ; it fetches them out of the water '. I have grounds for supposing that far more children than parents suspect are dissatisfied with this solution, and respond to it with pronounced doubt, which, however, is not always outspoken. I know of a three-year-old boy who, to the terror of his nurse, was missed after receiving this enlightenment, and found at the edge of the big lake of the castle, where he had run, in order to see the children in the water! I know of another who could allow his disbelief only hesitating expression by saying he knew better, it was not storks who bring the children, but herons. It appears to me from much of the evidence conclusive that children refuse to believe the stork theory, and that from the time of this first deception and rebuff they nourish a mistrust against adults, have the presentiment of something forbidden which is being withheld from them by the ' grown-ups ', and con-sequently conceal their further investigations by secrecy. With this, however, it comes about that they experience the first occasion of a 'psychical conflict', in that ideas for which they 'by instinct' feel a preference, but which adults consider ' naughty ', come into opposition with others which are maintained by the authority of the adults without being acceptable to them themselves. Out of these mental conflicts there may soon arise a 'mental dissociation'; the one idea which is bound up with 'being good', but also with a cessation of thinking, becomes the prevailing conscious one ; the other, for which meanwhile the inquiries prosecuted have brought new evidence, which is not supposed to count, becomes suppressed and unconscious. The nuclear complex of neurosis is formed in this way.

Lately, by the analysis of a five-year-old boy [1] which his father undertook and permitted me to publish, I have received an irrefutable proof of a piece of knowledge towards which the psycho-analysis of adults had for long led me. I now know that the changes in the mother during pregnancy do not escape the sharp eyes of a child, and that the latter is very well able subsequently to establish the correct connection between the increase in size of the mother's body and the appearance of a baby. In the case mentioned, the boy was three and a half when his sister was born, and four and three-quarters when he showed his better knowledge by the most unmistakable allusions. This precocious knowledge is, however, always kept secret, and later, in connection with the future fate of childish sexual inquiry, is repressed and forgotten.

The stork fable, therefore, is not one of the infantile sexual theories ; indeed, the observation of animals, who hide so little of their sexual life and to whom children feel so closely related, strengthens their disbelief. With the knowledge independently obtained that babies grow in the mother's body, a child would be on the right path to solve the problem on which it

[1] Freud, 'Analysis of a Phobia in a Five-year-old Boy,' COLLECTED PAPERS, vol. iii.

first tries its thinking powers. Its further progress is stopped, however, by a piece of ignorance which cannot be made good, and by false theories which the condition of its own sexuality imposes on it.

These false sexual theories, which I will now describe, all have one very curious characteristic. Although they go astray in a grotesque way, yet they all, each one of them, contain a bit of the real truth, so that they are analogous to those adult attempts at solution, which we call flashes of genius, of the problems of the universe that are too difficult for human comprehension. What is correct and hits the mark in these theories is to be explained by their origin in those components of the sexual instinct which are already active in the childish organism ; for it is not due to an arbitrary mental act or to chance impressions that these notions arise, but to the necessities of the psycho-sexual constitution, and this is why we are able to speak of typical sexual theories in children, this is why we find the same false ideas in all children whose sexual life is accessible to us.

The first of these theories begins with a neglect of sex-differentiation, the neglect to which we called special attention at the commencement as being characteristic of children. It consists in attributing to everybody, including women, a penis just like the one the boy knows of from his own body. It is precisely in that sexual constitution which we must recognize as a normal one that the penis is already in childhood the governing erotogenic zone, the most important auto-erotic sexual object, and the estimate of its value is logically reflected in the impossibility of imagining a person similar to the self without this essential part. If a little boy obtains a sight of the genitals of a little sister, what he says will show that his prejudice is already strong enough to influence the perception ; he does not remark on the lack of the penis but *invariably* says, as if consoling and reconciling : that her ' widdler ' is still small, but when she is bigger it will soon grow. The idea of a woman with a penis returns still later in the dreams of adults ; in a state of nocturnal sexual excitation he throws down a woman, exposes her and prepares for coitus ; then on beholding the well-formed penis at the site of the female genitals, the dream and excitation break off. The numerous hermaphrodites of classic antiquity faithfully reproduce this once general infantile idea ; one may observe that to most normal people they cause no offence, while actual hermaphroditic formations of the genitals in nature nearly always excite the greatest abhorrence.

If this idea of woman with a penis becomes ' fixated ' in a child, it resists all the influences of later life and makes the man incapable of dispensing with a penis in his sexual object, so that such a person, if otherwise he has a normal sexual life, must become homosexual, seeking his sexual object in men who through other physical and mental qualities remind him of women. Real women, as they become known to him later, are excluded from being sexual objects to him because they lack the essential sexual attraction ; indeed, in connection with another impression of childhood-life they may become abhorrent to him. A child who is chiefly dominated by penis-excitation usually produces pleasure by stimulation of it with his hand, is detected doing this by his parents or by the persons in charge of him, and is terrorized by the threat that his penis will be cut off. The effect of this ' castration threat ' is in direct proportion to the value set upon this part of the body, i.e., quite extraordinarily deep-rooted and persistent. Sagas and myths testify to the revolt in the childish feelings, to the horror which is then linked to the castration complex, and this later is remembered with corresponding reluctance by consciousness. The woman's genitalia, seen subsequently and regarded as mutilated, recall this threat, and thus awaken in the homosexual horror instead of pleasure. This reaction is not altered by his learning through science that

the childish assumption is not so far wrong after all,
namely, that a woman also possesses a penis. Anatomy
has recognized the clitoris within the female pudenda
as an organ homologous to the penis, and the physiology
of sexual processes has been able to add that this little
penis which no longer grows behaves in the childhood
of the woman like a genuine and real penis, that it is
the site of excitations which leads to its being touched,
that its excitability gives the sexual activity of little
girls a male character, and that it needs an effort of
repression in the years of puberty to make the woman
develop through discarding this male sexuality. The
fact that the sexual function of many women is crippled
by their obstinately clinging to this clitoris excitability
—so that they remain anæsthetic in coitus, or that
repression succeeds so excessively that its action is
partly nullified by hysterical compensatory formations
—all this shows that the infantile sexual theory that a
woman possesses a penis like a man has some truth in it.

One can easily observe that little girls are quite in
agreement with their brothers' estimate. They develop
a great interest in this part of a boy's body, but this
interest is at once dominated by jealousy. They feel
themselves injured ; they make attempts to urinate
in the position that is possible to the boy by his possession of the big penis, and when they express the wish,
' I should love to be a boy ', we know what lack the
wish is to remedy.

If children could follow the hint given them by the
excitation in the penis, they would get a little nearer
to the solution of their problems. That the baby
grows in the mother's body is obviously not a sufficient
explanation. How does it get there ? What starts it
developing there ? That the father has something to
do with it is probable ; indeed, he declares that the
baby is also *his* child.[1] The penis, too, certainly also
has its share in these mysterious happenings ; it testi-
fies to this by the accompanying excitation in it

[1] Freud, *op. cit.*

during all this thought-work. Along with this excitation obscure impulses are roused, which the child does
not know how to account for—to do something violent,
to press in, to knock to pieces, to burst open a hole
somewhere. But when the child seems thus in a fair
way to arrive at the existence of the vagina, and to
attribute to the father's penis an act of incursion into
the mother which should create the baby in the body
of the mother, the inquiry breaks off helplessly ; for
at this point there stands in the way the theory that
the mother possesses a penis like a man, and the
existence of the cavity which receives the penis remains
undiscovered to the child. One can readily surmise
that the lack of success of this effort of thought
facilitates a rejection and forgetting of it. These
speculations and doubts, however, become the prototype
of all later thought-work on problems, and the first
failure has a crippling effect for ever after.

Their ignorance of the vagina again makes it possible
for children to have a conviction which constitutes the
second of their sexual theories. If the baby grows in
the body of the mother and is then detached from it,
this can only happen by the sole possible way of the
anal aperture. The child must be expelled like
excrement, like a motion. If in later childhood the
same question is the subject of solitary reflection or of
a discussion between two children, then the explanations probably are that the baby comes out of the
navel, which opens, or that the belly is slit and the
child taken out, as happens to the wolf in the tale of
Little Red Riding-Hood. These theories are expressed
aloud and later consciously remembered ; they no
longer contain anything shocking. These same children
have then completely forgotten that in earlier years
they believed another sexual theory, which since then
has undergone the subsequent repression of the anal
sexual components. At that time an evacuation was
something which could be spoken about in the nursery
without shame ; the child was still not so far distant

from his constitutional coprophilic inclinations ; it was no degradation then to come into the world like a mass of fæces, which had not yet been attainted by disgust. The *cloaca* theory, which is valid for so many animals, was the most natural and the only one which could force itself upon the child as probable.

Then, however, it was only logical that the child should refuse to grant women the painful monopoly of giving birth to children. If babies are born through the anus then a man can give birth just as well as a woman. A boy can therefore fancy that he too has children of his own without our needing to accuse him of feminine inclinations. It is only his still active anal erotism at work.

If the cloaca theory of birth is preserved in consciousness in later years of childhood, which occasionally happens, it is then accompanied by another solution of the question concerning the origin of children, one which, it is true, is no longer the original one. It is like that in fairy-tales. One eats some particular thing and from this one gets a child. The insane re-animate this infantile birth theory. A maniac, for instance, will lead the visiting physician to a heap of fæces which she has deposited in a corner of her cell, and say to him, laughing, ' That is the child I bore to-day '.

The third of the typical sexual theories appears in children when through some unforeseen domestic occurrence they witness parental sexual intercourse, concerning which they are then able to obtain only a very incomplete idea. Whatever detail it may be that comes under their observation, whether it is the position of the two people, or the sounds, or certain accessory circumstances, in all cases they arrive at the same conclusion, that is, at what we may call the *sadistic conception of coitus*, seeing in it something that the stronger person inflicts on the weaker by force, and comparing it, especially the boy, to a fight as they know it from their childish play, in which, by the way, an admixture of sexual excitation is also not wanting.

I have not been able to establish whether children recognize this procedure which they observe between the parents as the necessary missing link in the problem of the birth of children ; more often it appears that this connection is overlooked by children for the very reason that they had interpreted the love-act as an act of violence. But this sadistic conception itself gives the impression of a re-appearance of that obscure impulse towards cruel activity which was linked up with penis-excitation when the child first reflected upon the puzzle of where children come from. The possibility cannot be excluded that that precocious sadistic impulse, which might have led to discovery of the mystery of coitus, itself appeared first under the influence of very dim memories of parental intercourse for which the child had obtained material, without at the time making use of it, when it shared the bedroom of its parents in the first years of its life.[1]

The sadistic theory of coitus, which by itself becomes a false guide where it might have led to enlightenment, is again the expression of one of the inborn components of the sexual instinct, any one of which may be more or less strongly marked in any particular child, and thus the sadistic conception is to a certain extent true ; in part it divines the essence of the sexual act and the ' antagonism of the sexes ' which precedes it. Often, too, the child is in a position to support this conception by accidental observations which it understands in part correctly, in part falsely. In many marriages the wife, in fact, regularly opposes the matrimonial embrace, which to her brings no pleasure and the risk of a fresh pregnancy, and thus to the child who is supposed to be asleep (or pretending to be asleep) the mother might give an impression that could only be explained as meaning warding off an act of violence. At other times the whole marriage presents to the observant child

---

[1] In his autobiographical book entitled *Monsieur Nicolas*, published in 1794, this sadistic misconception of coitus is confirmed by Restif de la Bretonne, who there relates an experience from his fourth year.

the spectacle of an unceasing quarrel, expressed by loud words and unfriendly gestures, so that the child need not wonder that this quarrel goes on in the night, too, and is finally decided by the very same means which the child himself is accustomed to make use of in its intercourse with its brothers, sisters and companions, that is, by a fight.

The child also regards it as a confirmation of his idea if he discovers spots of blood in the bed or on his mother's linen. These are to him a proof that in the night an attack of this kind by the father on the mother has again taken place, while we should rather take the fresh spots of blood to mean that sexual intercourse for the time being had ceased. Much of the inexplicable ' horror of blood ' in the nervous finds its explanation in this connection. The child's mistake again covers a small part of the truth, for in certain well-known circumstances a trace of blood is indeed regarded as a sign of initiated sexual intercourse.

In less direct connection with the insoluble problem of where children come from, the child occupies itself with the question of what the nature and the content is of the state called ' being married ' ; and it answers the question differently according to its accidental observations of its parents combined with its own impulses which are still invested with pleasurable feeling. All that these answers appear to have in common is that marriage promises pleasurable gratification, and presupposes a disregard for modesty. The idea I have most frequently met with is that ' one urinates before the other ' ; a variation of this which sounds as if it signified better knowledge symbolically is that ' the man urinates into the woman's chamber '. On other occasions the meaning of marriage is supposed to be that the two persons show their buttocks to each other (without shame). In one case in which training had succeeded in postponing sexual knowledge especially late, a fourteen-year-old girl who had already begun to menstruate arrived at the idea from reading that being married signified 'mixing blood', and since her own sister had not yet had a period the lustful girl attempted to outrage a visitor who confessed that she was just menstruating, so as to compel her to take part in this 'mixing blood'.

The infantile ideas about the nature of marriage, which are not seldom retained by the conscious memory, have great significance for the symptoms of later neurotic illness. They come into evidence first of all in childish games, in which one does with the other whatever it is that constitutes being married, and then later on the wish to be married can choose the infantile form of expression when it appears in a phobia or some similar symptom which at first sight seemed incomprehensible.[1]

These are the most important of the typical sexual theories that children produce spontaneously in early childhood-years under the influence of the components of the sexual instinct. I know that the material is far from complete and that I have not established a full connection between it and the rest of child-life. I can here add a few supplementary remarks which otherwise every experienced person would have missed in my account. Thus, for instance, the significant theory that one gets a child by a kiss, which obviously betrays a pre-eminence of the erotogenic mouth zone. In my experience this theory is exclusively feminine and is sometimes met with as pathogenic in girls whose sexual curiosity had undergone very strong inhibition in childhood. One of my female patients through an accidental observation happened upon the theory of the 'couvade', which is well known among many races as a general practice, and probably has the purpose of contradicting that doubt about paternity that is never quite to be overcome. After the birth of his child, a rather strange uncle of hers remained for days at home and received visitors in his night-

[1] The games that are significant in later neuroses are the 'doctor' game and the game of 'father and mother'.

shirt, so she concluded that both parents had a share in the birth and must go to bed.

About the tenth or eleventh year information about sexual matters comes to children. A child who has grown up unchecked in its social relations, or who in some other way has found a good opportunity for observation, communicates to other children what he knows, because by doing so he can feel himself to be grown-up and superior. What children learn in this way is mostly correct, that is, the existence of the vagina and its use is revealed to them, but otherwise the enlightenment which they get from one another is frequently mixed with false ideas, and burdened with the remains of older infantile sexual theories. It is scarcely ever complete and sufficient to solve the original problems. Just as formerly with the ignorance of the vagina, so now ignorance of the semen prevents understanding of the whole process. The child cannot guess that out of the male sexual organ another substance can be expelled besides urine, and occasionally an ' innocent ' girl on her wedding night is still indignant because the man has ' urinated into her '. This information acquired before puberty links up with a fresh impetus in childish inquiries ; the theories which the child now produces, however, have no longer the typical and original stamp, which was characteristic of the early primary ones as long as the infantile sexual components were uninhibited and untransformed and could come to expression in these theories. The later intellectual efforts to solve the sexual puzzle seemed to me not worth the trouble of collecting, nor have they much claim to a pathogenic significance. Their multiplicity is naturally mainly dependent upon the nature of the first information received, their significance consists rather in that they re-awaken the unconscious vestiges of that first period of sexual interest, so that not seldom masturbatory sexual activities and a part of the detachment of feeling from the parents is linked up with them. Hence the condemning judgement of teachers that such information at this age ' corrupts ' children.

A few examples may show what elements often enter into these later speculations by children about sexual life. A girl had heard from her school companions that the man gives the woman an egg, which she hatches in her body. A boy who had also heard of the egg, identified it with the testicle, which is vulgarly called by the same name, and thereupon puzzled his head how the content of the scrotum could always become renewed. The information given seldom reaches as far as to prevent important doubts on the matter of sexual processes. Thus girls may come to expect that coitus happens only on one single occasion but lasts very long, for twenty-four hours, and that from this one occasion come all the successive children. One would suppose that this child had knowledge of the process of propagation in certain insects : however, this conjecture was nót confirmed and the theory appeared to be an independent creation. Other girls ignore the time of gestation, the life in the womb, and suppose that the child appears immediately after the night of the first connection. Marcel Prévost has turned this mistake of young girls into an amusing story in one of his *Lettres de femmes*. Hardly to be exhausted and perhaps in general not uninteresting is this theme of the later sexual inquiries of children, or of adolescents who have been delayed at a childish stage ; but it lies further from my purpose, and I must only call special attention to the fact that many errors are invented by children in order to contradict older, better but now unconscious and repressed knowledge.

The way in which the child behaves when he receives information also has its significance. In many children sexual repression has gone so far that they will not hear anything, and these may also succeed in remaining ignorant until even later (apparently, at least) till the knowledge dating from early childhood comes to light in the psycho-analysis of neurotics. I know also of two boys between ten and thirteen years old, who certainly listened to sexual information but gave their informant the averting answer : ' It is possible that your father and other people do such things, but I know for certain that my father would never do it '. However this later attitude in children towards satisfying their sexual curiosity may vary, we can postulate a thoroughly uniform behaviour in them in early years and believe that at that period they were all eager to find out what it is the parents do with each other to make the babies.

VII

'CIVILIZED' SEXUAL MORALITY AND MODERN NERVOUSNESS [1]

(1908)

IN his recently published book on sexual ethics, von Ehrenfels dwells on the difference between 'natural' and 'civilized' (cultural) sexual morality. By 'natural' sexual morality he understands that system of control which enables a race to preserve its health and efficiency; by 'civilized', that system which when followed spurs man to more intensive and productive cultural activity. According to him this contrast is best elucidated by comparing the innate character of a people with its cultural attainments. While referring to von Ehrenfels' paper [2] for the better appreciation of this significant line of thought, I shall take from it only so much as I need to establish the connection with my own contribution to the subject.

It is natural to suppose that under the domination of a 'civilized' morality the health and efficiency in life of the individuals may be impaired, and that ultimately this injury to the individual, caused by the sacrifices imposed upon him, may reach such a pitch that the 'civilized' aim and end will itself be indirectly endangered. Indeed, von Ehrenfels points to a series of injurious effects, responsibility for which he attributes to the code of sexual morality at present prevailing in our Western society; and although he fully acknowledges its high value for the furtherance of civilization, he concludes by judging it to be in need of reform.

[1] First published in *Sexual Probleme*, new issue of the periodical *Mutterschutz*, Bd. IV., 1908; reprinted in *Sammlung*, Zweite Folge. [Translated by E. B. Herford and E. Colburn Mayne.]
[2] *Sexualethik*, Grenzfragen des Nerven- und Seelenlebens.

Characteristic of· present-day sexual morality is the extension of the demands made upon women on to the sexual life of the male, and the taboo on all sexual intercourse except in monogamous marriage. Even so, consideration of the natural difference in the sexes necessitates less condemnation of lapses in the male, and so in effect admission of a double code of morality for him. But a society which accepts this double code cannot attain to 'love of truth, honesty and humanity'[1] except to a certain narrowly limited degree, and must incline its members to concealment of the truth, to euphemism, to self-deception, and to the deception of others. Civilized sexual morality does worse, indeed, than this, for by glorifying monogamy it cripples virile selection—the sole influence by which an improvement of the race can be attained, for among civilized peoples vital selection is reduced to a minimum by humane and hygienic considerations.[2]

Among the injurious effects attributed to sexual morality the physician misses precisely the one whose significance we are now to consider. I refer to the way in which it promotes modern nervousness, which under our present social conditions is rapidly spreading. Occasionally a nervous patient will himself draw the physician's attention to the part played in the causation of his sufferings by the opposition between his constitution and the demands of civilization, and will remark : 'We in our family have all become nervous because we wanted to be something better than what with our origin we were capable of being.' The physician is also frequently given matter for thought by observing that neurosis attacks precisely those whose forefathers, after living in simple, healthy, country conditions, offshoots of rude but vigorous stocks, came to the great cities where they were successful and were able

---

[1] *Loc. cit.*, p. 32 *et seq*.
[2] *Loc. cit.*, p. 35. [The preceding paragraph is clearly an abstract of v. Ehrenfels' views, and does not necessarily represent Freud's own.—ED.]

in a short space of time to raise their children to a high level of cultural attainment. But, most cogent of all, neurologists themselves have loudly proclaimed the connection between the ' increasing nervousness ' of the present day and modern civilized life. A few extracts from the opinions of eminent observers will show clearly upon what they base this connection.

W. Erb : [1] ' The original question may now be summarized thus : Are those causes of nervousness which have been put before you so markedly on the increase under modern conditions of life as to declare those conditions responsible ? This question can be answered without hesitation in the affirmative, as a cursory glance at our modern life and its character will show.

' This is already clearly evidenced by an array of general facts : the extraordinary achievements of modern times, the discoveries and inventions in every field, the maintenance of progress in the face of increasing competition, have been gained and can be held only by great mental effort. The demands on the ability of the individual in the struggle for existence have enormously increased, and he can meet them only by putting forth all his mental powers ; at the same time the needs of the individual, and the demand for enjoyment, have increased in all circles ; unprecedented luxury is displayed by classes hitherto wholly unaccustomed to any such thing ; irreligion, discontent, and covetousness are spreading widely through every degree of society. The illimitable expansion of communication brought about by means of the network of telegraphs and telephones encircling the world has completely altered the conditions of business and travel. All is hurry and agitation : night is used for travel, day for business ; even " holiday trips " keep the nervous system on the rack ; important political, industrial, financial crises carry excitement into far wider circles than formerly ; participation in political life has become quite general ; political, religious, and

[1] *Über die wachsende Nervosität unserer Zeit*, 1893.

social struggles, party-interests, electioneering, endless associations of every kind heat the imagination and force the mind to ever greater effort, encroaching on the hours for recreation, sleep and rest ; life in large cities is constantly becoming more elaborate and more restless. The exhausted nerves seek recuperation in increased stimulation, in highly-seasoned pleasures, only thereby to become more exhausted than before ; modern literature is concerned predominantly with the most questionable problems, those which stir all the passions—sensuality and the craving for pleasure, contempt of every fundamental ethical principle and every ideal demand ; it brings pathological types, together with sexual psychopathic, revolutionary and other problems, before the mind of the reader. Our ears are excited and overstimulated by large doses of insistent and noisy music. The theatres captivate all the senses with their exciting modes of presentation ; the creative arts turn also by preference to the repellent, ugly and suggestive, and do not hesitate to set before us in revolting realism the ugliest aspect offered by actuality.

' This merely general picture suffices to show a series of dangers in our modern cultural evolution, the details of which may be filled in by a few strokes! '

Binswanger : [1] ' Neurasthenia especially has been described as essentially a modern disorder, and Beard, to whom we are first indebted for a general description of it, believed that he had discovered a new nervous disease which had developed specifically in America. This assumption was of course erroneous ; nevertheless the fact that an *American* physician was the first to perceive and maintain—as the fruit of great experience —the particular symptoms of this disorder cannot fail to point to a close connection between them and the modern·way of life—the unbridled lust and haste for gold and possessions, those immense advances in technical spheres which have reduced to insignificance

[1] *Die Pathologie und Therapie der Neurasthenie,* 1896.

all limitations of time and space where communication is concerned.'

Von Krafft-Ebing : [1] ' The mode of life of innumerable civilized peoples shows at the present time an abundance of anti-hygienic factors which make it easy to understand the deplorable increase of nervousness, for these harmful factors take effect first and foremost on the brain. Changes have taken place in the political and social, and particularly in the mercantile, industrial and agricultural conditions of civilized peoples, in the course of no more than the last decade, which have abruptly transformed professional life, citizenship and property at the direct cost of the nervous system ; this is then called upon to meet the increased social and domestic demands by a greater expenditure of energy, unredressed by any satisfactory forms of recuperation.'

Of these and many other similarly-worded opinions I have to observe, not that they are erroneous, but that they show themselves insufficient to explain in detail the manifestations of nervous disturbance, and that they leave out of account the most important ætiological factor. If one passes over the less definite forms of ' nervousness ' and considers the actual forms of nervous disease, the injurious influence of culture reduces itself in all essentials to the undue suppression of the sexual life in civilized peoples (or classes) as a result of the ' civilized ' sexual morality which prevails among them.

The proof of this statement I have attempted to establish in a series of technical papers.[2] It cannot be repeated here ; still I will at this point put forward the most important arguments arising from my researches.

Close clinical observation empowers us to distinguish two groups of nervous disorder, the true neuroses, and the psychoneuroses. In the former, the disturbances (symptoms), whether bodily or mental, appear to

---

[1] *Nervosität und neurasthenische Zustände*, 1895, p. 11.
[2] COLLECTED PAPERS, vol. i.

be of a toxic character.   The phenomena are essentially
the same as those due to excess or deficiency of certain
nerve-poisons.   These neuroses, usually designated col-
lectively as ' neurasthenia ', can be induced by certain
injurious influences in the sexual life, without any
hereditary taint being necessarily present ; indeed, the
form taken by the disease corresponds with the nature
of these noxiæ, so that not seldom the clinical picture
can be directly employed as a key to the particular
sexual ætiology.   Any such regular correspondence
between the form of nervous disorder present and the
other injurious influences of civilization to which the
writers quoted above attribute so much is, however,
entirely absent.   It may, therefore, be maintained that
the sexual factor is the essential one in the causation
of the true neuroses.

With the psychoneuroses, hereditary influence is
more marked, and the causation less transparent.   A
peculiar method of investigation known as psycho-
analysis has, however, enabled us to recognize that the
symptoms of these disorders (hysteria, obsessional
neurosis, etc.) are psychogenic, and depend upon the
operation of unconscious (repressed) ideational complexes.   This same method has taught us what these
unconscious complexes are, and has shown us that,
speaking quite generally, they have a sexual content.
They originate in the sexual needs of unsatisfied people,
and represent a kind of substitute for gratification
of them.   So that we must regard all factors which
operate injuriously upon the sexual life and suppress
its activity or distort its aims as likewise pathological
factors in the psychoneuroses.

The value of the theoretical distinction between the
toxic and the psychogenic neuroses is, of course, in no
way lessened by the fact that disturbances arising in
both sources are to be observed in most nervous people.

Anyone who is prepared to look with me for the
ætiology of nervousness pre-eminently in influences
which cripple .the sexual life, will willingly give his

attention to some further considerations, to be appended here, which are intended to review the question of increasing nervousness in a broader application.

Our civilization is, generally speaking, founded on the suppression of instincts. Each individual has contributed some renunciation—of his sense of dominating power, of the aggressive and vindictive tendencies of his personality. From these sources the common stock of the material and ideal wealth of civilization has been accumulated. Over and above the struggle for existence, it is chiefly family feeling, with its erotic roots, which has induced the individuals to make this renunciation. This renunciation has been a progressive one in the evolution of civilization ; the single steps in it were sanctioned by religion. The modicum of instinctual satisfaction from which each one had abstained was offered to the divinity as a sacrifice; and the communal benefit thus won was declared ' holy '. The man who in consequence of his unyielding nature cannot comply with the required suppression of his instincts, becomes a criminal, an outlaw, unless his social position or striking abilities enable him to hold his own as a great man, a ' hero '.

The sexual instinct—or, more correctly, the sexual instincts, since analytic investigation teaches us that the sexual instinct consists of many single component impulses—is probably more strongly developed in man than in most of the higher animals ; it is certainly more constant, since it has almost entirely overcome the periodicity belonging to it in animals. It places an extraordinary amount of energy at the disposal of ' cultural ' activities ; and this because of a particularly marked characteristic that it possesses, namely, the ability to displace its aim without materially losing in intensity. This ability to exchange the originally sexual aim for another which is no longer sexual but is psychically related, is called the capacity for sublimation. In contrast with this ability for displacement in which lies its value for civilization, the sexual

instinct may also show a particularly obstinate tendency
to fixation, which prevents it from being turned to
account in this way, and occasionally leads to its
degenerating into the so-called abnormalities. The
original strength of the sexual instinct probably differs
in each individual ; certainly the capacity for sublimation is variable. We imagine that the original
constitution pre-eminently decides how large a part
of the sexual impulse of each individual can be
sublimated and made use of. In addition to this, the
forces of environment and of intellectual influence on
the mental apparatus succeed in disposing of a further
portion of it by sublimation. To extend this process of
displacement illimitably is, however, certainly no more
possible than with the transmutation of heat into
mechanical power in the case of machines. A certain
degree of direct sexual satisfaction appears to be
absolutely necessary for by far the greater number of
natures, and frustration of this variable individual
need is avenged by manifestations which, on account
of their injurious effect on functional activity and of
their subjectively painful character, we must regard
as illness.

Further aspects are opened up when we take into
consideration the fact that the sexual instinct in man
does not originally serve the purposes of procreation,
but has as its aim the gain of particular kinds of
pleasure.[1] It manifests itself thus in infancy, when it
attains its aim of pleasurable gratification not only in
connection with the genitalia, but also in other parts
of the body (erotogenic zones), and hence is in a position
to disregard any other than these easily accessible
objects. We call this stage that of auto-erotism, and
assign to the child's training the task of circumscribing
it, because its protracted continuance would render the
sexual instinct later uncontrollable and unserviceable.
In its development the sexual instinct passes on from
auto-erotism to object-love, and from the autonomy

[1] Cf. my *Drei Abhandlungen zur Sexualtheorie*.

of the erotogenic zones to the subordination of these under the primacy of the genitals, which come into the service of procreation. During this development a part of the self-obtained sexual excitation is checked, as being useless for the reproductive functions, and in favourable cases is diverted to sublimation. The energies available for ' cultural ' development are thus in great part won through suppression of the so-called perverse elements of sexual excitation.

It would be possible to distinguish three stages in cultural development corresponding with this development in the sexual instinct : first, the stage in which the sexual impulse may be freely exercised in regard to aims which do not lead to procreation ; a second stage, in which the whole of the sexual impulse is suppressed except that portion which subserves procreation ; and a third stage, in which only *legitimate* procreation is allowed as a sexual aim. This third stage represents our current ' civilized ' sexual morality.

If we regard the second of these stages as our standard, we must acknowledge that a number of people, on account of their constitution, are not equal to its demands. With whole classes of individuals, the development of the sexual impulse referred to above, from auto-erotism to object-love, with its aim of union of the genitalia, has not been correctly and sufficiently completed. As a result of this disturbance of development there arise two kinds of harmful deviation from normal or ' civilized ' sexuality ; and these are related to one another almost as positive to negative. They are, first (disregarding altogether those persons with an over-powerful and uncontrollable sexual instinct in general), the different varieties of perverts, in whom an infantile fixation on a preliminary sexual aim has impeded the establishing of the primacy of the reproductive function ; secondly, the homosexuals or inverts, in whom, in a way not yet quite understood, the sexual aim has been deflected from the opposite sex. If the injurious results of these two

forms of disturbance in development are less than
might have been expected, this can be directly ascribed
to the complicated co-ordination within the sexual
instinct, which makes it possible for the sexual life to
express itself finally in some form or other, even if
one or more components of the instinct have been
excluded from development.   The constitution of those
suffering from inversion—the homosexuals—is indeed
often distinguished by the sexual impulse lending itself
to ' cultural ' sublimation in a special degree.

Stronger developments of the perversions and of
homosexuality, especially if exclusive, do indeed make
those who harbour them socially unadaptable and
unhappy, so that even the cultural demands of the
second stage must be recognized as a source of suffering
for a certain proportion of human beings.   The fate
of those persons who differ constitutionally in this way
from their fellows depends on whether they are
endowed with comparatively stronger or weaker sexual
impulses in an absolute sense.   In the latter case, that
of an impulse which is on the whole weaker, perverts
succeed in completely suppressing those tendencies
which bring them into conflict with the moral demands
of their level of civilization.   But this, from the ideal
point of view, remains also their only achievement,
because for this repression of their sexual instinct
they make use of all those energies which otherwise
they would employ in cultural activity.   They are at
once inwardly stunted, and outwardly crippled.   What
we shall presently say about the state of abstinence
(of men and women) demanded by the third state of
culture applies to these also.

Where the sexual instinct is very strong but yet
perverted, there are two possible outcomes.   In the
first, which it is not necessary to consider further, the
afflicted person remains perverted, and has to bear the
consequences of his deviation from the prevailing level
of culture.   The second way is much more interesting.
Here, under the pressure of education and social

demands, a suppression of the perverse impulse is indeed attained, but it is of such a kind as not to be a true one, and can be better described as a miscarriage of suppression. The inhibited sexual impulses are not expressed as such—and to that extent the inhibition is successful—but they are expressed in other ways which are quite as injurious to the person concerned, and make him quite as useless to society as satisfaction of these suppressed impulses in their original form would have done ; and in this lies the failure of the process, which in the long run far outweighs the success of the suppression. The substitute-manifestations which thus present themselves in consequence of suppression of the impulses constitute what we describe as neurosis, in particular the psychoneuroses.[1] Neurotics are that class of people, naturally rebellious, with whom the pressure of cultural demands succeeds only in an apparent suppression of their instincts, one which becomes ever less and less effective. Consequently their co-operation in civilized life is maintained only by means of a great expenditure of energy, combined with inner impoverishment, and at times it has to be suspended altogether during periods of illness. I have, however, described the neuroses as the ' negative ' of the perversions, because in the neuroses the perverse tendencies come to expression from the unconscious part of the mind, after the repression, and because they contain the same tendencies in a state of repression that manifest perverts exhibit.

Experience teaches that for most people there is a limit beyond which their constitution cannot comply with the demands of civilization. All who wish to reach a higher standard than their constitution will allow, fall victims to neurosis. It would have been better for them if they could have remained less ' perfect '. The realization that perversion and neurosis stand to one another as positive and negative is often unambiguously confirmed by observations made on

[1] Cf. introductory remarks above.

members of the same family. Quite often in one family the brother will be sexually perverted, while the sister, who as a woman is endowed with a weaker sexual instinct, becomes a neurotic — one whose symptoms, however, express the same tendencies as the perversion of the brother who has a more active sexual impulse. Accordingly in many families the men are healthy, but from the social point of view undesirably immoral ; while the women are high-principled and over-refined, but highly neurotic. It is one of the obvious injustices of social life that the standard of culture should demand the same behaviour in sexual life from everyone — a course of conduct which, thanks to his nature, one person can attain without effort, whereas it imposes on another the severest mental sacrifices ; though, indeed, the injustice is ordinarily nullified by disregard of the commands of morality.

These considerations have been confined so far to what applies to the second stage of cultural development, postulated as interdicting every ' perverse ' sexual activity, so-called, but allowing the free practice of ' normal ' sexual intercourse. We have found that even when the line between sexual freedom and restriction is drawn at this point, a number of persons have to be ruled out as perverse, while others who endeavour not to be perverse, and yet constitutionally should be so, are forced into neurosis. It is now easy to predict the result which will ensue if sexual freedom is still further circumscribed, and the standard demanded by civilization is raised to the level of the third stage, which taboos every sexual activity other than that in legitimate matrimony. Under these conditions the number of strong natures who openly rebel will be immensely increased : and likewise the number of weaker natures who take refuge in neurosis owing to their conflict between the double pressure from the influences of civilization and from their own rebellious constitutions.

We propose to answer three questions which now arise :

1. What is the task that is laid upon the individual as a result of the demands of the third cultural stage ?

2. Whether the legitimate sexual satisfaction allowed may be said to offer reasonable compensation for the abstention in other directions ?

3. In what relation the possible injurious effects of this abstention stand to the benefit accruing to culture ?

The answer to the first question touches a problem which has often been discussed and cannot here be treated exhaustively, *i.e.* that of sexual abstinence. The third stage of our civilization demands from both sexes abstinence until marriage, and lifelong abstinence for all who do not enter into legal matrimony. The position sanctioned by every authority, that sexual abstinence is not harmful and not difficult to maintain, has also obtained a good deal of support from physicians. It may be said that the task of mastering such a mighty impulse as the sexual instinct is one which may well absorb all the energies of a human being. Mastery through sublimation, diverting the sexual energy away from its sexual goal to higher cultural aims, succeeds with a minority, and with them only intermittently ; while the period of passionate youth is precisely that in which it is most difficult to achieve. Of the others, most become neurotic or otherwise come to grief. Experience shows that the majority of those who compose our society are constitutionally unfit for the task of abstinence. Those who would have fallen ill even under moderate sexual restrictions succumb to illness all the earlier and more severely under the demands of our present civilized sexual morality ; for we know no better security against the menace to normal sexual life caused by defective predisposition and disturbances in development than sexual satisfaction itself. The greater the disposition to neurosis, the less can abstinence be tolerated. For in proportion as the component-impulses have been excluded from development (as described above) they become precisely thereby less controllable. But even those who would have retained their health while complying with the demands of the second stage of civilization will in many cases succumb to neurosis in the third stage ; for the psychical value of sexual satisfaction increases under privation. The frustrated libido is now put in the position of spying out one or other of the weaker spots which are seldom wanting in the structure of the sexual life, so that it may break through at that point as a neurotic substitute-gratification in the form of a morbid symptom. Anyone who understands how to penetrate to the factors conditioning nervous illness will soon be convinced that its increase in our society originates in the greater stringency of sexual restraint.

We thus come closer to the question whether sexual intercourse in legitimate marriage can offer full compensation for the restraint before marriage. The abundance of the material supporting a reply in the negative is so overwhelming that we are obliged to make only the briefest summary of it. We must above all keep in mind that our civilized sexual morality also restricts sexual intercourse even in marriage itself, for it compels the married couple to be satisfied, as a rule, with a very small number of acts leading to conception. As a consequence of this, satisfying sexual intercourse occurs in marriage only over a period of a few years, allowing also, of course, for intervals of abstention on hygienic grounds required by the woman's state of health. After these three, four or five years, marriage ceases to furnish the satisfaction of the sexual needs that it promised, since all the contraceptives available hitherto impair sexual enjoyment, disturb the finer susceptibilities of both partners, or even act as a direct cause of illness. Anxiety for the consequences of sexual intercourse first dissipates the physical tenderness of the married couple for each other, and usually, as a more remote result, also the mental affection between them which was destined to succeed the originally tempestuous passion. Under the spiritual disappointment and physical deprivation which thus become the fate of most marriages, both partners find themselves reduced again to their pre-conjugal condition, but poorer by the loss of an illusion, and are once more driven back to their determination to restrain and 'side-track' their sexual instinct. We will not inquire how far a man in mature years succeeds in this task ; experience seems to show that he very frequently makes use of that amount of freedom which is allowed him even by the strictest sexual code, though but reluctantly and furtively. The 'double' code of morality conceded to the male in our society is the plainest possible admission that society itself does not believe in the possibility of adherence to those precepts which it has enjoined on its members. But experience also shows that women, as the true guardians of the sexual interests of the race, are endowed with the power of sublimation only in a limited degree ; as a substitute for the sexual object the suckling child may suffice, but not the growing child, and under the disappointments of matrimony women succumb to severe, lifelong neurosis affecting the whole course of their lives. Marriage under the present cultural standard has long ceased to be a panacea for the nervous sufferings of women ; even if we physicians in such cases still advise matrimony, we are nevertheless aware that a girl must be very healthy to 'stand' marriage, and we earnestly counsel our male inquirers not to marry a girl who has been neurotic. Marital unfaithfulness would, on the other hand, be a much more probable cure for the neurosis resulting from marriage ; the more strictly a wife has been brought up, the more earnestly she has submitted to the demands of civilization, the more does she fear this way of escape, and in conflict between her desires and her sense of duty she again will seek refuge in a neurosis. Nothing protects her virtue so securely as illness. The conjugal state, which is held out to the youthful among civilized

people as a refuge for the sexual instinct, thus proves
inadequate even to the demands of the later period
which it covers ; beyond all question, it fails to compensate for the earlier abstention.

To our third question, even he who admits the
injurious results thus attributable to civilized sexual
morality may reply that the cultural gain derived from
the sexual restraint so generally practised probably
more than balances these evils, which after all, in their
more striking manifestations, affect only a minority.   I
own myself unable to balance gain and loss precisely :
nevertheless I could advance a good many considerations as regards the loss.   Returning to the theme of
abstinence, already touched on, I must insist that yet
other injurious effects besides the neuroses result
therefrom, and that the neuroses themselves are not
usually appraised at their full significance.

The retardation of sexual development and sexual
activity at which our education and culture aim is
certainly not injurious to begin with ; it is seen to be
a necessity, when one reflects at what a late age young
people of the educated classes attain independence and
begin to earn a living.   Incidentally, one is reminded
here of the intimate relation existing between all our
civilized institutions, and of the difficulty of altering
any part of them irrespective of the whole.   But the
benefit, for a young man, of abstinence continued
much beyond his twentieth year, cannot any longer
be taken for granted; it may lead to other injuries even
when it does not lead to neurosis.   It is indeed said
that the struggle with such powerful instincts and the
consequent strengthening of all ethical and æsthetic
tendencies ' steels ' the character ; and this, for some
specially constituted natures, is true.   The view may
also be accepted that the differentiation of individual
character, now so much in evidence, only becomes possible with sexual restraint.   But in the great majority
of cases the fight against sexuality absorbs the available
energy of the character, and this at the very time when

the young man is in need of all his powers to gain his share of worldly goods and his position in the community. The relation between possible sublimation and indispensable sexual activity naturally varies very much in different persons, and indeed with the various kinds of occupation. An abstinent artist is scarcely conceivable : an abstinent young intellectual is by no means a rarity. The young intellectual can by abstinence enhance his powers of concentration, whereas the production of the artist is probably powerfully stimulated by his sexual experience. On the whole I have not gained the impression that sexual abstinence helps to shape energetic, self-reliant men of action, nor original thinkers, bold pioneers and reformers ; far more often it produces ' good ' weaklings who later become lost in the crowd that tends to follow painfully the initiative of strong characters.

In the results produced by efforts towards abstinence the stubbornness and insubordination characteristic of the sexual instinct also come to expression. Civilized education attempts, in a sense, only a temporary suppression of it up to the period of matrimony, intending then to give it free rein in order to make use of it. Extreme measures, however, are more successful in effecting repression of the instinct than are moderate ones ; but then suppression very often goes too far, with the unwished-for result that when the sexual instinct is set free it shows itself permanently impaired. For this reason complete abstinence during youth is often not the best preparation for marriage in a young man. Women dimly recognize this, and among their suitors prefer those who have already proved themselves men with other women. The injurious results which the strict demand for abstinence before marriage produces are quite particularly apparent where women are concerned. Clearly, education does not look lightly on the task of suppressing the sensuality of the girl until marriage, for it employs the most drastic measures. It not only forbids sexual intercourse and sets a high

premium upon the preservation of sexual chastity, but
it also protects the developing young woman from
temptation by keeping her in ignorance of all the facts
concerning the part she is ordained to play, and
tolerates in her no love-impulse which cannot lead to
marriage. The result is that when the girl is suddenly
allowed by parental authority to fall in love, she cannot
accomplish this mental operation and enters the state
of marriage uncertain of her own feelings. As a result,
the artificial retardation in the development of the
love-function provides nothing but disappointments
for the husband, who has treasured up all his desires
for her. Psychically she is still attached to her parents,
whose authority has brought about the suppression of
the sexual feeling ; and physically she shows herself
frigid, which prevents her husband finding any great
enjoyment in relations with her. I do not know
whether the anæsthetic type of woman is also found
outside the range of civilized education, but I consider
it probable. In any case this type is directly cultivated
by education, and these women who conceive without
pleasure show later little willingness to endure frequent
childbirths, accompanied as they are by pain : so that
the training that precedes marriage directly frustrates
the very aim of marriage. When later the retarded
development of the wife becomes rectified, and during
the climax of her womanly life the full power to love
awakens in her, her relation to her husband has been
long undermined. As a reward for her previous submission, there remains for her only the choice between
unappeased desire, infidelity, or neurosis.

The behaviour of a human being in sexual matters
is often a prototype for the whole of his other modes
of reaction to life. A man who has shown determination in possessing himself of his love-object has our
confidence in his success in regard to other aims as
well. On the other hand, a man who abstains, for
whatever reasons, from satisfying his strong sexual
instinct, will also assume a conciliatory and resigned

attitude in other paths of life, rather than a powerfully active one. A particular application of the general statement that the course of the sexual life is typical for the way in which other functions are exercised is easily demonstrable in the entire female sex. Their training excludes them from occupying themselves intellectually with sexual problems, in regard to which naturally they have the greatest thirst for knowledge, and terrifies them with the pronouncement that such curiosity is unwomanly and a sign of immoral tendencies. And thus they are thoroughly intimidated from all mental effort, and knowledge in general is depreciated in their eyes. The prohibition of thought extends beyond the sexual sphere, partly through unavoidable associations, partly automatically, acting precisely in the same way as the prohibition of religious speculation among men, and the taboo of any thought out of harmony with loyalty in faithful subjects. I do not support Moebius in the view he has put forward, which has met with so much opposition, that the biological contrast between intellectual work and sexual activity explains the ' physiological mental weakness ' of women. On the contrary, I think that the undoubted fact of the intellectual inferiority of so many women can be traced to that inhibition of thought necessitated by sexual suppression.

In considering the question of abstinence, far too little distinction is made between two forms of it, namely, abstention from any kind of sexual activity at all, and abstention from heterosexual intercourse. Many who are proud of maintaining abstinence successfully have only been able to achieve it with the help of masturbation and other similar means of satisfaction, which are connected with the auto-erotic sexual activities of early childhood. But this very connection makes these substitutive measures of sexual satisfaction by no means harmless ; they predispose to the numerous forms of neurosis and psychosis, which are conditional on a regression of the sexual life to its infantile form.

Nor does masturbation at all correspond to the ideal demands of civilized sexual morality, and it therefore drives young people into the same conflicts with the ideals of education which they design to escape by abstinence. Further, the character is undermined in more ways than one by this indulgence ; first, because it shows the way to attain important aims in an otiose manner, instead of by energetic effort, in line with the view that the attitude to sex is the prototype of the attitude to life ; and secondly, because in the phantasies accompanying this gratification the sexual object is exalted to a degree which is seldom to be reproduced in reality. A witty writer, K. Kraus in the Vienna *Fackel*, has, as it were, expressed this truth paradoxically in the cynical saying : ' Coitus is merely an unsatisfactory substitute for onanism ! '

The severe standard demanded by civilization and the arduous task of abstinence have combined to make avoidance of the genital union of the sexes the main point of abstinence, whilst favouring other forms of sexual activity—two results which may be said to betoken obedience by halves. The so-called perverse forms of intercourse between the sexes, in which other parts of the body assume the rôle of the genitalia, have undoubtedly become of greater social significance since normal intercourse has been so remorselessly tabooed in the name of morality—and also on grounds of hygiene because of the possibility of infection. These activities, however, cannot be regarded as so harmless as irregularities of a similar kind interwoven with a normal love-intercourse : ethically they are reprehensible, for they degrade the love-relationship of two human beings from being a serious matter to an otiose diversion, attended neither by risk nor by spiritual participation. The spread of the homosexual means of gratification must be regarded as a further consequence of the difficulties placed in the way of normal sexual life ; and in addition to those who are constitutionally homosexual, or who become so in childhood, must be reckoned the great number of those in whom, by reason of the check on the main stream of the libido, the lateral channel of homosexuality is forced open in maturer life.

All these unavoidable and unintended consequences of the insistence upon abstinence unite in one general result : they strike at the roots of the condition of preparation for marriage, which according to the intentions of civilized sexual morality should after all be the sole heir of all sexual tendencies. All those men whose libido, as the result of masturbatory or perverse sexual practices, has become habituated to situations and conditions of satisfaction other than the normal develop in marriage a diminished potency. And all those women who could preserve their virginity only by similar means show themselves anæsthetic to normal intercourse in marriage. A marriage begun with impaired capacity to love on both sides succumbs to the process of dissolution even more quickly than otherwise. As a result of the diminished potency of the man, the woman will not be satisfied and will remain anæsthetic, whereas a powerful sexual experience might have been the means of overcoming the disposition to frigidity that results from her education. The prevention of conception is also more difficult to such a couple than to a healthy pair, because the weakened potency of the man tolerates the use of contraceptives badly. In such perplexity, sexual intercourse comes to be regarded as the source of all difficulties and is soon abandoned, and with it the fundamental condition of married life.

I call upon all who have studied these matters to aver that I am not exaggerating, but am describing conditions glaringly evident to any observant eye. The uninitiated can hardly believe how rarely normal potency is to be found in the men, and how often frigidity in the women, among those married couples living under the sway of our civilized sexual morality ; what a degree of renunciation, often for both partners, is associated with marriage, and of how little the marriage comes to consist, instead of bringing the happiness that was so ardently desired. I have already shown that neurosis is the most obvious way of escape from these conditions. I would, however, further point out how such a marriage will increasingly affect the only child—or the limited number of children—which spring from it. On appearance it looks as if we then had an inherited condition to deal with, but closer inspection shows the effect of powerful infantile impressions. As a mother, the neurotic woman who is unsatisfied by her husband is over-tender and over-anxious in regard to the child, to whom she transfers her need for love, thus awakening in it sexual precocity. The bad relations between the parents then stimulate the emotional life of the child, and cause it to experience intensities of love, hate and jealousy while yet in its infancy. The strict training which tolerates no sort of expression of this precocious sexual state lends support to the forces of suppression, and the conflict at this age contains all the elements needed to cause lifelong neurosis.

I return now to my earlier assertion that, in appraising the neuroses, their full significance is seldom reckoned with. I do not mean by this the insufficient appreciation of these states exhibited in the frivolous dismissal of them on the part of relatives, or in the magniloquent assurances on the part of physicians that a few weeks of cold-water cure or a few months of rest and convalescence will cure the condition—these are merely the opinions of ignorant physicians and laymen, and mostly nothing but forms of speech designed to afford the sufferer a short-lived consolation. Rather, it is established that a chronic neurosis, even if it does not completely paralyse existence, represents for the person concerned a heavy handicap in life, much the same as tuberculosis or a cardiac affection. We might in a measure compound with this if neurotic illness merely excluded from communal activity a number of individuals in any case infirm, and permitted the remainder to take their share at the cost of merely subjective disabilities ; but I would rather draw attention to the point of view that the neuroses, as far as they extend and in whomever they occur, always succeed in frustrating the social purpose, and thereby actually do the work of the socially inimical mental forces which have been suppressed. So that in paying for compliance with its own exorbitant prescriptions by increased neurosis, society cannot claim an advantage purchased by sacrifice—cannot indeed claim any advantage whatever. Let us examine, for example, the frequent case of a woman who does not love her husband, because, owing to the conditions of the consummation of her marriage and the experience of her married life, she has no cause to love him ; but who ardently wishes to do so, because this alone corresponds to the ideal of marriage in which she has been brought up. She will then suppress in herself all impulses which seek to bring her true feelings to expression and contradict her ideal endeavours, and will take particular pains to play the part of a loving, tender and obedient wife. The result of this self-suppression will be a neurotic illness, and this neurosis will in a short time have taken revenge upon the unloved husband and have caused him precisely as much dissatisfaction and trouble as would have arisen merely from an acknowledgement of the true state of affairs. This example is literally typical of what neurosis can do. A similar miscarriage of compensation can be observed after suppression of other socially inimical impulses not directly sexual. A man, for example, who has become excessively ' kind-hearted ' as the result of powerful suppression of a constitutional tendency to harshness and cruelty, often loses by so doing so much energy that he does not achieve the full measure of his compensatory impulses, and on the whole does rather less good than he would have done without suppression.

Let us add that together with the restrictions on sexual activity in any nation there always goes an increase of anxiety concerning life and of fear of death, which interfere with each individual's capacity for enjoyment, and do away with his willingness to incur risk of death in whatever cause—showing itself in a diminished inclination to beget offspring, thus excluding any people or group of such a type from participation in the future. We may thus well raise the question whether our ' civilized ' sexual morality is worth the sacrifice which it imposes upon us, the more so if we are still so insufficiently purged of hedonism as to include a certain degree of individual happiness among the aims of our cultural development. It is certainly not the physician's business to come forward with proposals for reform, but it seemed to me that, by pointing out what significance the injurious results of our sexual morality, enumerated by von Ehrenfels, have in connection with the increase in modern nervousness, I could supplement the account he gives of them, and could thus support the urgency of such reform.

VIII

GENERAL REMARKS ON HYSTERICAL ATTACKS [1]

(1909)

A. WHEN one psycho-analyses a patient subject to hysterical attacks one soon gains the conviction that these attacks are nothing but phantasies projected and translated into motor activity and represented in pantomime. It is true that these phantasies are unconscious but otherwise they are of the same nature as those that may be observed directly in day-dreams or revealed by an interpretation of nocturnal dreams. A dream frequently takes the place of an attack and still more frequently helps to explain one, since the same phantasy finds different forms of expression both in dreams and in attacks. One might expect by observing an attack to be able to discover the phantasy it represents, but this is rarely possible. As a rule the pantomimic representation of the phantasy undergoes distortions, due to the influence of the censorship, analogous to the hallucinatory ones of dreams, so that to begin with both these manifestations are rendered unintelligible either to the patient's conscious mind or to the observer's comprehension. An hysterical attack, therefore, must be subjected to the same analytic procedure as we use in dream-interpretation. Not only are the forces producing the distortion and the purpose of this distortion the same as those we are familiar with from the interpretation of dreams, but the technique of the distortion is the same also.

[1] First published in the *Zeitschrift für Psychotherapie und medizinische Psychologie*, Bd. I., 1909 ; reprinted in *Sammlung*, Zweite Folge. [Translated by Douglas Bryan.]

1. The attack becomes unintelligible through its representing several phantasies simultaneously by means of the same material, that is, through *condensation*. Features common to two (or more) phantasies form the nucleus of the representation, as in dreams. The phantasies thus made to coincide are often of quite different kinds, for instance, a recent wish and the re-activation of an infantile impression ; the same innervations are then made to serve both purposes, often most cleverly. Hysterical patients who make use of condensation to a considerable extent may find a single type of attack sufficient ; others express a multiplicity of pathogenic phantasies by several types of attack.

2. The attack becomes obscured by the patient's undertaking the parts played by both the persons appearing in the phantasy, that is, through *multiple identification*. For instance, I have mentioned a case [1] in which a patient tore off her dress with one hand (as the man) while she pressed it to her body with the other (as the woman).

3. A particularly effective form of distortion is *antagonistic inversion of the innervation*, which is analogous to the very usual changing of an element into its opposite by dream-work. For instance, in an hysterical attack an embrace may be represented by the arms being drawn back convulsively until the hands meet above the spinal column. Possibly the well-known *arc de cercle* of major hysterical attacks is nothing but an energetic disavowal of this kind, by antagonistic innervation of the position suitable for sexual intercourse.

4. Scarcely less confusing and misleading is the *reversal of the sequence of events* in the phantasy, which again has its complete counterpart in some dreams which begin with the end of an action and finish with its beginning. For instance, an hysterical patient may

[1] 'Hysterical Phantasies and their Relation to Bisexuality.', No. V. of this volume, p. 51.

have a phantasy of seduction, the content of which is that she is reading in a park, her dress being slightly raised so that one foot is visible ; a gentleman approaches and speaks to her ; they then go to some other place where a love-scene takes place. This phantasy may be acted in the attack in such a way as to begin with a convulsive stage corresponding to the act of intercourse ; she may then get up, go to another room, sit down to read and reply to the imaginary remark made in accosting her.

The two last-mentioned forms of distortion give some indication of the intensity of the resistance with which the repressed material has to deal, even when it breaks through in an hysterical attack.

B. The outbreak of hysterical attacks follows laws that are readily understood. Since the repressed complex consists of libidinal cathexis and ideational content (phantasy), the attack may be aroused (1) *associatively*, if the content of the complex (sufficiently charged) is stirred by a conscious occurrence ; (2) *organically*, if from some internal somatic reasons or external influences on the mind the libidinal cathexis exceeds a certain amount ; (3) in the service of the *primary tendency* (paranosic gain) as an expression of ' flight into illness ' if reality becomes painful or frightening, therefore as a *consolation* ; (4) in the service of the *secondary tendencies* (epinosic gain) with which the state of illness becomes connected as soon as the patient can gain a useful purpose by the production of an attack. In the last case the attack is aimed at particular people ; it may be put off until they are within reach, and gives an impression of conscious simulation.

C. Investigation of the childhood history of hysterical patients shows that the hysterical attack is a substitute for an *auto-erotic* gratification previously practised and since given up. In a great number of cases this gratification (masturbation by manipulation or pressure of the thighs, movement of the tongue, etc.)

recurs during the attack itself during the deflection of consciousness. The outbreak of attacks due to an increase of libido and in the service of the primary tendency, as a consolation, then exactly repeats the conditions under which the patient at one time consciously employed this auto-gratification. The anamnesis of the patient then gives the following phases : (a) auto-erotic gratification without ideational content, (b) the same in connection with a phantasy which culminates in the act of gratification, (c) renunciation of the act with retention of the phantasy, (d) repression of this phantasy, which then breaks through in the hysterical attack either unchanged or else modified and adapted to new experiences, and (e) which may even restore the action producing gratification which belongs to the phantasy and has apparently been given up. This is a typical cycle of infantile sexual activity : repression, failure of the repression, and return of the repressed.

The involuntary passing of urine can certainly not be considered irreconcilable with the diagnosis of hysterical attacks ; it merely repeats the infantile form of a violent pollution. Moreover, biting the tongue may be met with in undoubted cases of hysteria ; it is no more inconsistent with hysteria than with love-making. It occurs in attacks more readily when the physician's questions have drawn the patient's attention to the difficulties of a differential diagnosis. Self-injury may occur in hysterical attacks (more frequently in the case of men) and then repeats an accident that happened during childhood (for instance, during a fight).

The loss of consciousness, the ' absence ' of the hysterical attack, is derived from the fleeting but unmistakable loss of consciousness which can be observed at the climax of every intensive (also auto-erotic) sexual gratification. Where hysterical ' absences ' arise from pollutions in young female persons this development can be most clearly followed. The so-called hypnoidal states, ' *absences* ' during day-dreaming so frequent in hysterical cases, reveal the same origin. The mechanism of these ' *absences* ' is comparatively simple. In the first place all the attention is concentrated on the course of the process of gratification and this whole cathexis of attention is suddenly removed at the moment when gratification occurs, so that a momentary void in consciousness takes place. This gap in consciousness, which may be called a physiological one, is then extended in the service of repression until it takes up everything which the repressing faculty rejects.

D. It is that reflex mechanism of the coitus-action which we see becoming manifest during unrestrained surrender to a sexual activity and which is available to everybody, including women, that points the way to the motor discharge of the repressed libido in attacks. Even the ancients called coitus a ' minor epilepsy '. We may alter this statement : the hysterical fit is an equivalent of coitus. The analogy with the epileptic attack helps us little, since its genesis is even less intelligible to us than that of hysterical attacks.

In general, the hysterical attack, like every form of hysteria, in women recalls to action a form of sexual activity which existed during childhood, and had at that time a pronounced masculine character. One may often observe that it is just those girls who in the years before puberty showed a boyish character and inclinations who tend to become hysterical at puberty. In a whole series of cases the hysterical neurosis is nothing but an excessive over-accentuation of the typical wave of repression through which the masculine type of sexuality is removed and the woman emerges.[1]

[1] Cf. Freud, *Drei Abhandlungen zur Sexualtheorie.*

PSYCHOGENIC VISUAL DISTURBANCE ACCORDING TO PSYCHO-ANALYTICAL CONCEPTIONS [1]

(1910)

BY taking psychogenic visual disturbances as an example, I propose to show you what alterations in our idea of the genesis of such ailments have resulted from the psycho-analytic method of investigation. You are aware that hysterical blindness is taken as the type of a psychogenic visual disturbance. It is thought that the researches of the French school of Charcot, Janet, Binet have enabled us to apprehend the genesis of such a disturbance. Indeed, we are now in a position to induce such blindness experimentally if we happen to have at our disposal a somnambulistic subject. If such a person is put into a deep hypnotic trance, and it is suggested to him or her that nothing can be seen with one of the eyes, he or she will behave as if blind of that eye, just as an hysterical subject does under spontaneously developed visual disturbance. We may thus construct the mechanism of the spontaneous hysterical visual disturbance after the pattern of the suggested hypnotic variety. In hysteria the idea of blindness does not arise from the suggestion of the hypnotist, but spontaneously, so to speak, through auto-suggestion ; and this idea is in both cases so powerful that it transmutes itself into actuality, precisely like a suggested hallucination, paralysis, and the like.

This sounds quite reasonable, and will doubtless

---

[1] First published in *Ärztliche Standeszeitung*, Vienna, 1910 ; reprinted in *Sammlung*, Dritte Folge. [Translated by E. Colburn Mayne.]

satisfy all who are able to ignore the enigmas latent in those phenomena we term hypnosis, suggestion, and auto-suggestion. Auto-suggestion, in particular, gives rise to further conjectures. When, and under what conditions, can an idea become so powerful as to reproduce the phenomena of a suggestion and be directly transmuted into actuality? On this point closer investigations have shown that the question is unanswerable without recourse to the concept of ' the unconscious '. Many philosophers refuse to accept the concept of an unconscious part of the mind, because they have not concerned themselves with the pheno- mena which necessitate its postulation. Psycho- pathologists can no longer operate without the concept of unconscious mental processes, unconscious ideas and the like.

Well-directed experiments have shown that the hysterical blind do in a certain sense see, though not in the complete sense. Excitations of the blind eye may thus have definite results of a mental kind—for instance, may evoke affects—although these fail to be consciously apprehended. The hysterical blind are therefore blind in consciousness only, while in the unconscious they are sighted. It is precisely experi- ences of this sort that compel us to make a distinction between conscious and unconscious mental processes. How comes it that these people develop an unconscious auto-suggestion to be blind, while in the unconscious they can see ?

French research replies to this further question by the assertion that patients of hysterical disposition display an inherent proneness to dissociation—to a dissolution of the nexus in the psychic field—as a consequence of which many unconscious processes never reach consciousness. Let us for the present leave entirely unconsidered the value of this attempt at explanation for comprehension of the phenomena we are studying, and let us turn to another point of view. You will surely note that the identity of hysterical

blindness with that produced by auto-suggestion, which
I emphasized in my opening words, is here abandoned.
Hysterical patients are not blind as a result of the
auto-suggestive idea that they cannot see, but as a
result of a dissociation between unconscious and
conscious processes in the visual act ; their idea that
they cannot see is the logical expression of a mental
condition, and not the causation of it.

If you demur to the foregoing delineation on the
ground of obscurity, I shall not find it easy to defend
myself. I have attempted to give you a synthesis of
the views of different investigators, and in doing so
have probably drawn the links too closely together.
My desire was to condense into a homogeneous whole
the prevailing contributions towards an understanding
of psychogenic disturbances—their origin in over-
mastering ideas, the distinction between conscious and
unconscious mental processes, and the hypothesis of
psychic dissociation—and in this I was able to succeed
no better than the French writers, with Pierre Janet
at their head. Pardon me therefore not only the
obscurity but also the inaccuracy of my delineation, and
let me tell you how psycho-analysis has led us to a
more firmly based and probably a more authentic view
of psychogenic visual disturbances.

Psycho-analysis, too, accepts the hypothesis of
dissociation and of the unconscious, but sets them in
a different relation to each other. Psycho-analysis is
a dynamic conception, which reduces mental life to
the interplay of reciprocally urging and checking
forces. When it happens that a group of ideas remains
in the unconscious, psycho-analysis sees in this no
proof of a constitutional incapacity for synthesis,
exhibiting itself through this particular dissociation,
but maintains that an active antagonism of certain
groups of ideas has caused the isolation of another
group in the unconscious. The process which imposes
such a fate upon a given group is termed by psycho-
analysis ' repression ', and it recognizes in it some-

thing analogous to reasoned rejection in the sphere of logic. Psycho-analysis can show that such repressions play an extraordinary part in our mental life, that they may frequently miscarry in individual cases, and that such miscarriages of repression are the primary cause of symptom-formation.

If, then, psychogenic visual disturbance, as we have learnt, is based on the segregation from consciousness of certain ideas connected with seeing, the psycho-analytical mode of thought constrains us to assume that these ideas have come into opposition with other more powerful ideas (which we should ascribe to our conception of the ego, which has had a varying significance) and have therefore become repressed. But where can any such opposition, calling for such repression, arise between the ego and single groups of ideas? You will observe that this question could not have been posed before the advent of psycho-analysis, for before that nothing was known about mental conflict and repression. Our researches have now put us in a position to give the required answer. Our attention has been drawn to the significance of the instincts in the conceptual life; we have learnt that every instinct seeks to come to expression by activating those ideas which are in accordance with its aims. These instincts do not always agree with one another, and this frequently results in a conflict of interests; the contradictions in the ideas are merely the expression of the battle between the various instincts. Of quite peculiar significance for our efforts towards elucidation is the undeniable opposition between the instincts which serve the purposes of sexuality, of gaining sexual pleasure, and those others which aim at the self-preservation of the individual, the ego-instincts. Schiller said that we can classify under ' hunger ' or under ' love ' every active organic instinct of our souls. We have tracked the ' sexual instinct ' from its earliest manifestations in the child to its attainment of what is called the ' normal ' final form of it, and

have found that it is made up of numerous component-
instincts which are rooted in the excitations of certain
regions of the body ; we have clearly seen that these
single instincts must go through a complex process of
development before they can co-operate, in any effective
sense, with the aims of propagation. The light thrown
by psychology on our cultural development has shown
us that culture is acquired essentially at the cost of
the sexual component-instincts, and that these must
be suppressed, restrained, transmuted, directed towards
loftier goals, for civilized psychical achievements to
take place. As a valuable result of these researches we
have been able to recognize, what our colleagues are
not yet prepared to grant us, that those sufferings we
call the neuroses derive from the manifold ways in
which these processes of transformation fail in regard
to the sexual component-instincts. The ego feels itself
menaced by the claims of the sexual instinct and defends
itself from them by repressions, which, however, do
not always produce the desired effect, but result in
dangerous substitute-formations of the repressed instinct and burdensome reaction-formations in the ego.
From these two classes of phenomena are formed what
we term the symptoms of neurosis.

We have apparently wandered far from our theme,
but in doing so have touched on the connection of
neurotic conditions with the whole mental life of man.
Let us now return to our more immediate problem.
Speaking generally, the various organs and systems of
organs are at the disposal of both sexual and ego-
instincts. Sexual pleasure is not connected only with
the function of the genitals ; the mouth serves for
kissing as well as for eating and speaking, the eyes
perceive not only those modifications in the external
world which are of import for the preservation of life,
but also the attributes of objects by means of which
these may be exalted as objects of erotic selection, their
' charms '. We now perceive the truth of the saying
that it is never easy to serve two masters at the same

time. The more intimate the relation of an organ possessing such a duality of function with one of the great instincts, the more will it refuse itself to the other. This principle necessarily leads to pathological consequences when the two fundamental instincts are at variance, when a repression is set up on the part of the ego against the sexual component-instinct in question. It is easy to apply this to the eye and the faculty of vision. If the sexual component-instinct which makes use of sight—the sexual 'lust of the eye' —has drawn down upon itself, through its exorbitant demands, some retaliatory measure from the side of the ego-instincts, so that the ideas which represent the content of its strivings are subjected to repression and withheld from consciousness, the general relation of the eye and the faculty of vision to the ego and to consciousness is radically disturbed. The ego has lost control of the organ, which now becomes solely the instrument of the repressed sexual impulse. It would appear as though repression on the part of the ego had gone too far and poured away the baby with the bath-water, for the ego now flatly refuses to see anything at all, since the sexual interests in looking have so deeply involved the faculty of vision. The other presentation of the situation, however, is probably closer to the facts, the aspect in which we see the *active* part in the process played by the repressed scoptophilia. It is the revenge, the indemnification of the repressed impulse, thus withheld from further psychical development, that it can succeed in so boldly asserting its mastery over the organ which serves it. The loss of conscious control over the organ is a detrimental substitute-formation for the miscarried repression, which was only possible at this cost.

This relation of the dually functioning organs to the conscious ego and the repressed sexuality is even clearer in the case of the motor organs than in that of the eye ; as, for example, when the hand which had been desirous of making a sexual aggression becomes hysterically crippled, and after the inhibition of this desire can do nothing else, exactly as if it insisted stubbornly on accomplishing that repressed innervation, and that only ; or again, when the fingers of persons who have renounced masturbation refuse to acquire the delicate mobility which the piano or violin exacts. In the case of the eye we customarily translate the obscure psychical processes implicit in the repression of scopto-philia and in the outbreak of psychogenic visual dis-turbance as if an accusing voice had uplifted itself within the person concerned, saying : ' Because you have chosen to use your organ of sight for evil indul-gence of the senses, it serves you quite right if you can see nothing at all now ', thus giving its sanction to the outcome of the process. There is here, we perceive, the idea of the talion, and our explanation of psycho-genic visual disturbance is at one with those laws prevailing in saga, myth, and legend. In the beautiful saga of Lady Godiva all the inhabitants of the little town retire behind their shuttered windows in order to make less painful to the lady her ordeal of riding naked through the streets in broad daylight. The one man who peeps through the shutters at her nude beauty is punished by becoming blind. Nor is this the only instance which leads us to suspect that concealed in the study of neurosis lies the key to mythology.

Psycho-analysis is wrongly reproached with tending to purely psychological theories of the processes of disease. Yet its accentuation of the pathogenic part played by sexuality, which is assuredly no exclusively psychical factor, ought to have protected it from this reproach. Psycho-analysis never forgets that the mental is based on the physical, although it can only carry its work back to this foundation and no farther. Hence psycho-analysis is fully prepared to grant, indeed to postulate, that not every functional visual disturbance is necessarily psychogenic, like those resulting from repression of the scoptophilia. When an organ which serves two purposes overplays its

erotogenic part, it is in general to be expected that
this will not occur without alterations in its response
to stimulation and in innervation, which will be manifested as disturbances of the organ in its function as
servant of the ego. And indeed, when we observe an
organ which ordinarily serves the purpose of sensorial
perception presenting as a result of the exaggeration of
its erotogenic rôle precisely the behaviour of a genital,
we shall even suspect that there are toxic modifications
as well in that organ. For both kinds of functional
disturbances resultant from the exaggeration of the
erotogenic office, for those of physiological no less than
for those of toxic causation, we are obliged to retain,
for want of a better, the time-honoured, inapposite
name of ' neurotic ' disturbances. Neurotic disturbances of vision are related to psychogenic as, in general,
are the actual neuroses to the psychoneuroses ; psychogenic visual disturbances can hardly occur without
neurotic disturbances, though the latter surely can
without the former. Unfortunately, these ' neurotic '
symptoms are as yet little appreciated and understood,
for they are not directly accessible to psycho-analysis,
and other modes of investigation have neglected the
sexual aspect.

From psycho-analysis there branches out another
line of thought conducting to organic research. We
may ask ourselves whether the suppression of the
sexual component-instincts induced by environmental
influences suffices in itself to set up functional disturbances of the organs, or whether there must not be
some particular constitutional conditions which predispose the organs to overdo their erotogenic part,
and thus provoke repression of the impulse. These
conditions we should necessarily regard as the part
played by the constitution in the tendency to disease
when considering psychogenic and neurotic disturbances. This would represent that factor which, in
hysteria, I have already designated as the ' somatic
compliance ' of the organs.

X

TYPES OF NEUROTIC NOSOGENESIS [1]

(1912)

IN the ensuing remarks, which are based on impressions obtained empirically, it is proposed to describe those changes of conditions which operate to bring about the onset of neurotic illness in a person predisposed to it. We are concerned, that is, with the exciting cause of illness ; scarcely at all with the form of it. The following view is distinguishable from other formulations concerning the exciting causes of illness in that it connects the changes to be described entirely with the libido of the person concerned. Psychoanalysis has shown us that the course taken by the libido is decisive for nervous health or ill-health. The concept of predisposition needs no discussion in this connection ; for psycho-analytic research has made it possible for us to trace back the predisposition to neurosis to its source in the developmental history of the libido, and to reveal the factors operative in this predisposition as inborn varieties of the sexual constitution and the effects of external experiences in early childhood.

(a) The most immediate, most easily discerned, and most comprehensible exciting cause of the onset of neurotic illness lies in that external factor which may generally be described as *frustration*. The person was healthy as long as his erotic need was satisfied by an actual object in the outer world ; he becomes neurotic as soon as he is deprived of this object and no substitute is forthcoming. Happiness here coincides with health, unhappiness with neurosis. By providing a

[1] First published in *Zentralblatt*, Bd. II., 1912 ; reprinted in *Sammlung*, Dritte Folge. [Translated by E. Colburn Mayne.]

substitute for the lost source of gratification, fate can effect a cure more easily than the physician.

For this type, which may be said to include the majority of mankind, the possibility of an outbreak of illness begins only with abstinence—which may give us some indication of the significance for the causation of neuroses of cultural restrictions in facilities for satisfaction. Frustration operates pathogenically in that it dams up the libido, and thus puts to the test both the person's power of tolerating the increase of mental tension, and his manner of taking steps to release himself from it. There are only two possible methods of retaining health in a continuous state of actual frustration of satisfaction : first, that of transposing the mental tension into active energy which remains directed towards the outer world and finally wrests from that world an actual satisfaction for the libido ; and secondly, that of renouncing the libidinal satisfaction, sublimating the stored-up libido and making use of it to ends which are no longer erotic and thus elude the frustration. Both possibilities can be realized in the destinies of mankind, which shows that unhappiness does not necessarily coincide with neurosis, and frustration is not alone decisive for the health or ill-health of the person concerned. The effect of frustration lies principally in its bringing into action dispositional factors which have hitherto remained inoperative.

When these are present in sufficient strength there arises the danger of the libido becoming *introverted*.[1] It turns away from reality, which on account of the unrelenting frustration experienced has lost all its value for the person concerned, and takes refuge in the life of phantasy where it creates new wish-formations and re-animates the vestiges of earlier, forgotten ones. In consequence of the intimate connection between phantasy-activity and the infantile, repressed, and now unconscious material existing in every indi-

---

[1] A term introduced by C. G. Jung.

vidual, and thanks to that attribute of the life of phantasy which exempts it from the ' testing of reality ',[1] the libido may now begin to flow backward, may seek out infantile paths in the course of its regression, and may strive after corresponding aims. When such strivings, which are incompatible with the person's state of mind in real life, have become sufficiently intensified, there must ensue a conflict between them and the other part of the personality which has remained in relation with reality. This conflict issues in symptom-formations and ends in manifest illness. That the whole process originates in the actual frustration may be clearly perceived from the circumstance that the symptoms by means of which the sphere of reality is regained represent substitutive gratifications.

(b) The second type of occasion for the outbreak of illness is by no means so obvious as the first, and could not indeed be discerned before the searching analytic studies stimulated by the complex-theory of the Zürich School.[2] In these cases the person falls ill not as a result of some alteration in the outer world which has replaced gratification by frustration, but as a result of an inner effort to seize a gratification which reality offers to him. He falls ill of the attempt to adapt himself to reality and to fulfil the *requisitions of reality*, for in doing so he is confronted with insurmountable inward obstacles.

It will be convenient to set these two types of falling ill in sharp antithesis to one another—sharper, indeed, than observation for the most part warrants. In the first type an alteration in the external world is prominent ; in the second, the accent falls upon an internal change. In the first type, the person falls ill from an event ; in the second, from a developmental process. In the first case the task is one of renouncing

---

[1] Cf. Freud, ' Formulations regarding the two Principles in Mental Functioning', COLLECTED PAPERS, vol. iv.

[2] Cf. Jung, *Die Bedeutung des Vaters für das Schicksal des Einzelnen*, 1909.

a gratification, and the person falls ill because of his lack of resistance ; in the second case the task is that of exchanging one kind of gratification for another, and the person is wrecked by his rigidity. In the second case the conflict between the endeavour to keep as he is and the other endeavour to alter himself in accordance with new aims and new demands in reality already exists in him ; in the first case, the conflict does not begin until the dammed-up libido has chosen other and incompatible possibilities of gratification. The part played by the conflict and the previous fixation of the libido is in the second type incomparably more striking than in the first, for in the first it may well be that undesirable fixations of this kind only re-establish themselves in consequence of the external frustration.

The young man who has hitherto gratified his libido by phantasies issuing in masturbation and now desires to exchange this state of affairs, so closely related to auto-erotism, for actual object-choice ; the girl who has given all her affection to her father or brother and now would fain exchange the hitherto unconscious incestuous libido-wishes for the conscious wish towards the man who is wooing her ; the wife who would be glad to abandon her polygamous inclinations and phantasies of prostitution so as to be a faithful companion to her husband and a blameless mother to her child—all these fall ill in consequence of most laudable endeavours if the earlier fixations of their libido are powerful enough to oppose themselves to the displacement ; for this again the factors of pre-disposition, constitutional basis and infantile experiences prove to be of decisive significance. They all, as it were, undergo the fate of the little tree in Grimm's fairy-tale which wanted to have different foliage. From the hygienic standpoint, which is certainly not the only one to be considered, one could but desire for them that they might have remained to the end as un-developed, as inferior, and as good-for-nothing as they were before they fell ill. The change for which such patients strive, but which they achieve only imperfectly or not at all, is regularly equivalent to a step forward for them in real life. It is otherwise if we reckon by ethical standards ; we as often see people fall ill when they divest themselves of an ideal as when they strive to attain it.

Despite the very evident distinctions between the two types of falling ill here described, they have essential points in common, and it is not hard to find a formula which will apply to both. Falling ill of a deprivation (frustration) likewise comes under the head of incapacity for adaptation to reality, only that the incapacity is confined to occasions when reality denies gratification to the libido. Falling ill under the conditions belonging to the second type points merely to a necessary peculiarity in the frustration. What is denied is not every form of gratification in reality, but merely just the one which the person declares to be the one and only form for him ; further, the frustration does not derive directly from the outer world but primarily from certain trends within the ego. Yet the factor of frustration remains common to both, and the most significant one for both. As a result of the conflict which forthwith ensues in the second type, both kinds of gratification, the customary as well as the desired, become equally inhibited ; damming-up of the libido and its attendant results follow as they did in the first case. The mental processes involved in the course of symptom-formation are in the second type more easily discoverable than in the first, since the pathogenic fixations of the libido had not first to be re-established but had been potentially active during the healthy period. A certain degree of introversion of the libido was mostly already existent ; some degree of the regression to the infantile is spared because the development had never traversed its entire course.

(c) The next type seems an exaggeration of the second type, that of succumbing before the requisitions of reality ; I shall describe it as outbreak of illness through *inhibition of development*. There would be no theoretical reason for distinguishing this from the rest, but there is a practical need to do so ; since here we have to deal with those persons who fall ill as soon as they pass beyond the irresponsible age of childhood, and thus never attain a phase of health—that of unrestricted capacity in general for production and enjoyment. The essential part played by the dispositional processes is in these cases quite apparent. The libido has never forsaken its infantile fixations ; the demands of reality do not suddenly confront an individuality which is wholly or partially matured, but arise out of the bare fact of its having grown older, and are of course continually changing with the age of the person concerned. The conflict is subordinate in importance to the incapacity ; but if we take into account the other results of our researches, we must postulate a striving to overcome the infantile fixations, for otherwise the outcome of the process would never be neurosis but only stationary infantilism.

(*d*) Just as the third type shows us the dispositional condition in an almost isolated form, so the now following fourth one directs our attention to another factor, the operation of which has to be reckoned with in all cases, and for that very reason might easily be overlooked in a theoretical discussion. That is to say, we see people fall ill who have hitherto been healthy, to whom no new experience has presented itself, whose relation to the outer world has undergone no change, so that their falling ill makes an inevitable impression of spontaneity. Closer scrutiny of such cases shows us, nevertheless, that a change *has* taken place in them which we cannot but regard as highly significant in the causation of the illness. As a result of reaching a certain period of life, and in accordance with regular biological processes, the *quantity* of libido in their mental economy has increased to an extent which by itself suffices to upset the balance of health and establish the conditions for neurosis. As is well known, such rather sudden intensifications in libido are regularly connected with puberty and the menopause, with the reaching of a certain age in women ; in many people they may in addition manifest themselves in periodicities as yet unrecognized. The damming-up of the libido is here the primary factor ; it becomes pathogenic as a result of the *relative* frustration coming from the outer world, which would have afforded sufficient gratification to a lesser need in the libido. The dissatisfied and dammed-up libido may now open up the path to regression and excite the same conflicts as those found in cases of absolute external frustration. This warns us never to leave the quantitative factor out of consideration when we are dealing with the outbreak of illness. All the other factors—frustration, fixation, inhibition in development—remain inoperative as long as they do not involve a certain amount of libido and produce a definite degree of damming-up. We cannot, it is true, measure the amount of libido essential to produce pathological effects ; we can only postulate it after the effects of the illness have evinced themselves. In only one direction can we define it more closely ; we may assume that it is not a question of an absolute quantity, but of the relation of this effective amount of libido to that quantity of libido which the particular ego in question can control, that is, can hold in suspension, sublimate, or make direct use of. Therefore a relative increase in the quantity of libido may have the same effects as one that is absolute. An enfeeblement of the ego through organic illness or an unusual demand upon its energy will be capable of producing neuroses which would otherwise have remained latent in spite of all dispositional tendencies.

The significance which we must attribute to the quantity of libido in the causation of illness is in satisfactory accord with two axioms of the new theory of neurosis which have emerged from psycho-analysis :

first, with the axiom that the neuroses have their source in a conflict between the ego and the libido ; secondly, with the view that no qualitative distinction exists between the conditions of health and those of neurosis, but rather that the healthy have to contend with the same difficulties in controlling the libido— only they succeed better in doing so.

There still remain a few words to be said about the relation of these ' types ' to clinical experience. When I review the number of patients with whose analysis I am at this moment occupied, I must admit that none of them represents any of the four types in its pure form. Instead, I find in each an element of frustration operating along with a certain degree of incapacity for adaptation to reality ; the standpoint of inhibition in development, which of course coincides with a tenacity of fixations, is to be reckoned with in all of them ; and the significance of the quantity of libido we can never, as was set forth above, afford to overlook. Indeed, it is my experience that in several of these patients the illness has been manifested in accesses, between which there were intervals of health, and that every one of these accesses was to be traced to a different type of exciting cause. The formulation of these four types has therefore no great theoretical value ; they are merely different paths by which a definite pathogenic constellation in the mental economy may be achieved— I refer to a damming-up of the libido which the ego is not able to master with the means at its disposal without some damage. The situation itself, however, becomes pathogenic only as a result of a quantitative factor ; it is in no way a novelty in the mental economy, nor is it created by the advent of a so-called ' cause of illness '.

A certain practical importance may readily be granted to these types of falling ill. Indeed, in individual cases they may be observed in a pure form ; we should not have been made aware of the third and fourth types if they did not comprise the sole exciting causes of onset in some persons. The first type reveals to us the extraordinarily powerful influence of the outer world; the second that, no less significant, of the peculiarities of the individual who opposes himself to that influence. Pathology could never master the problem of the outbreak of illness in the neurotic so long as it was occupied merely with deciding whether these affections were of an endogenous or an exogenous nature. To all the experience which points to the significance of abstinence (in the broadest sense) as an exciting cause, pathology then necessarily objected that other persons suffered a similar fate without falling ill. But if it elected to lay emphasis upon individual peculiarities as essential in sickness or health, it was obliged to bow to the objection that persons with such peculiarities could permanently retain their health provided only that they could preserve their peculiarity. Psycho-analysis warns us to abandon the unfruitful antithesis of external and internal factors, of fate and constitution, and has taught us regularly to discover the cause of an outbreak of neurosis in a definite mental situation, which can be brought into being in different ways.

THE PREDISPOSITION TO OBSESSIONAL NEUROSIS [1]

A Contribution to the Problem of the Option of Neurosis

(1913)

THE problem of why and how a person may fall ill of a neurosis assuredly belongs to those which psycho-analysis is called upon to solve. It is, however, probable that the solution will be found by way of the answer to another and more specific problem —that of why any particular person is bound to succumb to one particular neurosis, and no other. This is the problem of the option of neurosis.

What do we know so far about this problem? Strictly speaking, only one general principle has been established. We divide the causes of neurotic disease into those which the individual himself brings with him into life, and those which life brings to him—that is to say, into constitutional and accidental. It is the interaction of these that as a rule first gives rise to illness. Now the general principle just referred to implies that the basic factors which determine the option of neurosis are entirely of the former kind, that is, are of the nature of dispositions, and are independent of experiences that operate pathogenically.

Where are we to look for the origin of these dispositions? We have come to realize that the mental functions concerned—above all, the sexual function,

---

[1] Paper read before the International Psycho-Analytical Congress at Munich in 1913; reprinted in *Sammlung*, Vierte Folge. [Translated by Edward Glover and E. Colburn Mayne.]

but also various important ego-functions—have to go through a long and complicated process of development before they reach the state characteristic of a normal adult. We must further assume that these developments are not always carried out without a hitch, so that the function as a whole is not always subjected to progressive modification. Should any component of it remain arrested at an earlier phase there results what is known as a ' fixation-point ', to which the function can regress if external hardships give rise to illness.

Our predispositions to various neuroses are thus seen to be inhibitions in development. The analogy with the facts of the general pathology of other diseases strengthens this view. The question of what factors can induce such disturbances in development does not lie within the boundaries of psycho-analytic investigations ; we must leave it to biological research.[1]

With the help of such hypotheses, we were emboldened some years ago to attack the problem of the option of neurosis. The line taken by our method of investigation, which consists in tracing out normal conditions from a study of their disturbances, led us to choose a very singular and unexpected point of attack. The order in which the principal forms of neurosis are customarily ranked—namely, hysteria, obsessional neurosis, paranoia, dementia præcox—corresponds (if not quite exactly) to the order of incidence of these diseases from childhood onward. Hysterical manifestations may be observed already in early childhood ; the first symptoms of obsessional neurosis usually declare themselves in the second period of childhood (from six to eight years of age) ; whilst the two other psychoneuroses, which I have coupled under the joint designation paraphrenia, first appear after puberty and during adult life. Although last in order of incidence,

---

[1] Since the work of W. Fliess has revealed the biological importance of periodicity, it has become conceivable that developmental disturbances may be ascribed to modifications in the duration of the various stages.

these two conditions were the first to yield results from investigations regarding the predispositions determining the option of neurosis. The peculiar characteristics of them both, *i.e.* megalomania, turning from objective reality and difficulty in effecting transference, have forced us to the conclusion that the predisposing fixation is to be sought in a stage of libido-development prior to the establishment of object-choice, that is to say, in the stage of auto-erotism and narcissism.[1] Paranoia and dementia præcox then, although manifesting themselves so late in life, derive from very early inhibitions and fixations.

As a result of this, it seemed reasonable to suppose that the disposition to hysteria and obsessional neurosis, the two transference-neuroses proper, both of which show early symptom-formation, would be found at still earlier stages of libido-development. But where could an arrest in development be found before this, and above all, where could lie that difference between two phases of development which would give rise in one case to an obsessional disposition and in another to that of hysteria ? For a long time no light could be obtained on these points, and earlier surmises of my own about the nature of these dispositions—*e.g.* the idea that hysteria and the obsessional neurosis were conditioned respectively by passivity and activity in infantile experiences—had soon to be discarded as erroneous.

I will now return to individual clinical study, and will consider the case of a woman patient who was under observation for a considerable period, and whose neurosis underwent an unusual transformation. The case was at first one of pure anxiety-hysteria, following on a traumatic experience, and it preserved that character for some years. One day, however, it suddenly changed into an exceedingly severe obsessional neurosis. A case of this kind must be significant from more than one point of view. On the one hand, it

[1] Cf. 'Account of a Case of Paranoia,' COLLECTED PAPERS, vol. iii.

might turn out to have the value of a bilingual document, and show how the two neuroses would express an identical content in different languages. On the other hand, it threatened wholly to overthrow our theory of disposition as a result of arrest in development ; unless we were prepared to assume that an individual could have more than one weak spot in his libido-development. I told myself that one had no right to reject the latter possibility, but I was nevertheless very eager to arrive at an understanding of the case.

As this came to me in the course of the analysis, it became evident that the state of affairs was quite otherwise than I had imagined it. The obsessional neurosis was not a further reaction to the same trauma which had originally called forth the anxiety-hysteria ; it was a reaction to a second experience which had entirely eclipsed the first—it was therefore an exception, although, to be sure, a still debateable one, to our proposition that the option of neurosis does not depend upon experience.

Unfortunately I cannot—for the usual reasons—go into the case-history as fully as I could wish, but must confine myself to the following details. Before she fell ill the patient had been a happy and almost entirely contented married woman. She wished to have children, a wish itself determined by infantile fixation, and fell ill when she realized that her husband, to whom she was entirely devoted, could not satisfy this longing. The anxiety-hysteria with which she reacted to this frustration corresponded to a rejection of seduction-phantasies in which she achieved her enduring wish for a child. She was not long in coming to realize this herself, and did her utmost to prevent her husband guessing that her illness was due to a privation for which he was responsible. It is not without good reason, however, that I have maintained that every man possesses in his unconscious an instrument by which he can interpret the expressions of the unconscious of another ; the husband understood,

without any confession or explanation, what his wife's
anxiety signified, was deeply hurt by the discovery,
though he made no sign, and then began to react
neurotically himself by becoming for the first time
impotent during sexual intercourse.   Immediately after
he went on a journey, and his wife, believing him to be
permanently impotent, produced her first obsessional
symptom on the day before his expected return.

The content of her obsessional neurosis consisted
in a tormenting obsession about washing and cleanliness
and in exceedingly vigorous protective measures against
wicked injuries which others might have to fear from
her ; that is to say, it consisted of reaction-formations
against anal-erotic and sadistic impulses.   In such
forms her sexual need was driven to find expression, as
a result of the entire bankruptcy of her genital life
brought about by the impotence of her husband, who
was the only man to whom she could look for satisfaction.

At this point I was able to fit in a fragment of
a new theory which had recently been shaping in
my mind.   Although seemingly based on the present
isolated observation, it is, as a matter of fact, the result
of numerous earlier impressions, the significance of
which first became clear at this stage of the case under
discussion.   I told myself that my original sketch of
the development of the libidinal function required
another amplification.   Formerly I had simply distinguished a phase of auto-erotism, in which the various
component-impulses, each for itself, seek independent
gratification on the body itself, from a phase when in
the interests of reproduction they unite under the
primacy of the genital system to effect object-choice.
As is already known, the analysis of paraphrenics had
obliged us to interpolate a stage of narcissism during
which object-choice is already effected but in which
the object is still the ego itself.   Now we are faced with
the necessity of reckoning with yet another stage before
the ultimate condition, one in which, although the

component-impulses have been co-ordinated for purposes of object-choice, and although the object does present itself as one outside the self, nevertheless *the primacy of the genital zone has not yet been established*. The component-impulses which govern this *pregenital* organization of the sexual life are, moreover, the anal-erotic and sadistic impulses.

I know that general statements of this kind appear very startling at first hearing. We become reconciled to them only after correlation with our previous knowledge, and it often happens that in the long run they come to be accepted as an insignificant innovation which had already been long suspected. We may proceed therefore to consider this ' pregenital sexual organization ' with somewhat similar anticipations.

(a) The all-important part played by hate impulses and anal erotism in the symptomatology of the obsessional neurosis has impressed many observers, and recently Ernest Jones has called attention to it in a particularly penetrating study.[1] This observation would be established as an immediate corollary to our own views should it prove that the component-impulses referred to, which precede the genital impulses in the process of development, can act for the latter in this neurosis.

At this point we may appropriately refer to a detail in the patient's history which has not so far been mentioned. The patient's sexual life began with sadistic beating-phantasies in her earliest childhood. Following on their suppression an unusually long latency period set in, in the course of which the girl achieved a far-reaching moral development without awakening to the womanly sexual sensations. With her early marriage began a period of normal sexual activity as a happy wife, which lasted for a number of years, until the first great privation brought on the hysterical neurosis. With the ensuing destitution of

[1] Ernest Jones, *Hate and Anal Erotism in the Obsessional Neurosis,* 913.

her genital life, her sexual activity, as has been said, relapsed to the infantile stage of sadism.

It is not difficult to define the characteristic distinguishing this case of obsessional neurosis from those many others which begin in early years and follow a chronic course with more or less notable exacerbations. In these latter, when once the stage of sexual organization which contains the predisposition to obsessional neurosis is established, it is never really overcome ; in our case this organization is, to begin with, superseded by a higher stage of development, then subsequently reactivated by regression from that higher stage.

(b) When we attempt to correlate our views with biological considerations, we must bear in mind that the antithesis of masculine and feminine which is set up by the reproductive function cannot be present at the stage of pregenital object-choice. Instead we find an antithesis of trends with active and passive aims which ultimately resolves into the antithesis of sex (male and female). The active trend is supplied by that general instinct of mastery which when we find it serving the sexual function we call sadism ; in the fully developed normal sexual life it has also important accessory services to render. The passive trend is fed from anal erotism, the erotogenic zone of which corresponds with the old, undifferentiated cloaca. Accentuation of anal erotism at the stage of pregenital organization gives rise in a man to a marked predisposition to homosexuality, when the next stage of the sexual function, that of genital primacy, is reached. The building up of this last phase on the foundation of the previous phases, and the subsequent transformation of the libidinal cathexes, provides us with some of the most interesting openings for psycho-analytic research.

It may be thought that all such difficulties and complications could be avoided by denying the pregenital organization of sexual life and adopting the view that sexual life coincides with the genital and reproductive function, making its appearance at the same time as this. If this course were followed and use were made of such psycho-analytic findings as are beyond dispute, the theory might be advanced that as a result of sexual repression the neuroses are compelled to express sexual strivings by means of other non-sexual instincts, *i.e.* by compensatory sexualization of the latter. Anyone so doing, however, would find himself in complete retreat from the position taken up by psycho-analysis. He would stand where he was before the advent of psycho-analysis and must abandon all the comprehension it affords of the inter-connection between health, perversion and neurosis. Psycho-analysis stands or falls by the recognition of the sexual component-impulses, of the erotogenic zones, and by the consequent expansion of the idea of the ' sexual function ' as opposed to the narrower one of a ' genital function '. Moreover, observation of the normal development of the child is in itself sufficient to obviate any such temptation.

(c) In the sphere of character-development we again meet with the same instinctual forces whose workings we have already discovered in the neuroses. A sharp theoretical distinction between the two becomes, however, necessary from the single circumstance that in character-formation one feature is absent which is peculiar to the mechanism of neurosis— namely, miscarriage of repression and the return of the repressed. In the formation of character either repression is not at work at all or it easily attains its aim, which is to replace the repressed impulses by reaction-formations and sublimations. The processes of character-formation are therefore less transparent and less accessible to analysis than those of neurosis.

In this very sphere of character-formation, however, we do come upon a good analogy to the case of illness described, one which confirms the existence of the pregenital sadistic-anal-erotic sexual organization. It is well known, and has been a matter for much complaint, that women often alter strangely in character after they have abandoned their genital functions. They become quarrelsome, peevish and argumentative, petty and miserly; in fact, they display sadistic and anal-erotic traits which were not theirs in the era of womanliness. Writers of comedy and satirists have in all ages launched their invectives against the ' old termagant ' into which the sweet maiden, the loving woman, the tender mother, has deteriorated. This metamorphosis corresponds, as can be seen, with a regression of sexual life to the pregenital anal-sadistic level, the one in which we have found the predisposition to obsessional neurosis. It would thus be not only the precursor of the genital phase, but often enough its successor and resolvent as well, after the genital function has been fulfilled.

The comparison of this alteration of character with the obsessional neurosis is very impressive. Both are the result of regression, but in the first the regression is complete and follows a process of repression (or suppression) which has been accomplished smoothly; in neurosis we find conflict, followed by efforts to prevent regression, reaction-formations against it and symptom-constructions representing compromises between the opposing tendencies, also a cleavage of the mental processes into those which are capable of reaching consciousness and those which are unconscious.

(*d*) Our formulation of the pregenital sexual organization is incomplete in two directions. First it takes no account of the behaviour of other component-impulses and is content to single out the very definite primacy of sadism and anal erotism. There are many points concerning the other component-impulses which would repay careful investigation and collation; the desire for knowledge, in particular, often gives one the impression that it can actually take the place of sadism in the mechanism of the obsessional neurosis. After all, it is at bottom an off-shoot, sublimated and raised to the intellectual sphere, of the possessive instinct and its rejection in the form of doubt bulks largely in the picture of obsessional neurosis.

The other defect in our formulation is much more important. We know that a full understanding of any neurotic predisposition from the developmental point of view is never complete without taking into account not merely the stage of libido-development at which fixation occurs but also the stage of ego-development. Our concern has been confined to libido-development, however, and consequently does not afford all the information we are entitled to expect. At the present time little is known of the developmental stages of the ego-instincts ; I know only of one highly promising attempt by Ferenczi [1] to approach this problem. I do not know if it will seem too daring if I assume from the clues at our disposal that a premature advance of the ego-development ahead of the libido-development contributes to the obsessional disposition. Precocious development of this kind on the part of the ego-instincts would necessitate the formation of object-choice before the sexual function had reached its final configuration and would thus leave a legacy of fixation at the pregenital stage of sexual organization. When we take into consideration that, in order to protect object-love from the hostility which lurks behind it, the obsessional neurotic is compelled to build up an overconscientious system of ultra-morality, one feels inclined to go a step further and regard a certain degree of precocious ego-development as characteristic of human nature in general and to trace the capacity for morality to the circumstance that, developmentally, hate is the forerunner of love. Perhaps this is the meaning of a statement made by W. Stekel, which seemed incomprehensible to me at the time, that hate, not love, is the primary state of feeling between human beings.[2]

[1] Ferenczi, *Stages in the Development of the Sense of Reality.*
[2] W. Stekel, *Die Sprache des Traumes*, 1911, S. 536.

(*e*) The above considerations have some bearing on the subject of hysteria ; they bring out the intimate relation between this condition and the last phase of libido-development characterized by genital primacy and the introduction of the reproductive function. These newly acquired activities undergo repression in hysteria, but no regression to the pregenital phase takes place. The inadequacy of this description of an hysterical disposition, due to our incomplete understanding of ego-development, makes itself felt more than in the case of the obsessional neurosis.

Nevertheless it is not difficult to see that a different regression to an earlier level occurs in hysteria too. As we know, the sexuality of a female child is governed by an organ that is essentially male (the clitoris) and the manifestations of this sexuality are in many ways similar to those occurring in boys. A final thrust of development at the period of puberty must eliminate this masculine sexuality and promote the vagina, a derivative of the cloaca, to the position of leading erotogenic zone. Hence it is very usual in women suffering from hysteria for a reactivation of this repressed masculine sexuality to take place, against which defensive measures are directed by the ego-syntonic instincts. It seems to me, however, a little premature to discuss the problems of hysterical predisposition at this point.

XII

A DREAM WHICH BORE TESTIMONY [1]

(1913)

A LADY suffering from doubting mania and obsessive ceremonials made a rule that her nurses should never let her out of sight for a single moment : otherwise she would begin to brood about forbidden actions that she might conceivably have committed during this relaxation of vigilance. One evening whilst resting on the sofa she thought she saw that the nurse on duty had fallen asleep. On calling out, 'Have you seen me?', the latter started up and replied, 'Of course I have'. This aroused a fresh doubt in the patient's mind, and after a time she repeated her question, which the nurse met with renewed protestations ; just at that moment a maid-servant came in bringing the patient's supper.

This incident occurred one Friday evening. Next morning the nurse recounted a dream which had the effect of dispelling the patient's doubt.

Dream : *Some one entrusted a child to her whilst the mother was absent on a journey and she had lost it. Going along the street, she inquired from various people whether they had seen the child. Then she came to a large expanse of water and crossed a narrow bridge.* (Supplementing this later : *Suddenly there appeared before her on this bridge, like a* fata Morgana, *the figure of another nurse.*) *Then she found herself in some familiar place where she met a woman she had known as a girl : the latter had in those days been saleswoman in a provision-shop and later had got married. She was standing in*

---

[1] First published in the *Zeitschrift*, Bd. I., 1913 ; reprinted in *Sammlung*, Vierte Folge. [Translated by Edward Glover.]

front of her door and the dreamer asked her, ' Have you seen the child ? ' The woman paid no attention to the question but informed her that she had been divorced, adding that even marriage is not always happy. She woke up feeling reassured and thought : the child will turn up in a neighbour's house.

Analysis : The patient concluded that this dream was connected with the incident of falling asleep which the nurse had denied ; from additional information volunteered by the latter she was able to interpret the dream in a fashion which, although incomplete in many respects, was sufficient for all practical purposes. For myself, not having interviewed the nurse, I have only the lady's report to go on ; first of all I shall quote the patient's interpretation, supplementing this afterwards as far as possible from our general understanding of the laws governing dream-formation.

' Nurse told me that the child in the dream reminded her of a case the treatment of which had given her the most lively satisfaction. It was that of a child who was unable to see on account of inflammation of the eyes (blennorrhœa). The mother, however, was not away : she helped to look after the child. On the other hand, I know that my husband thinks highly of this nurse ; when he went away he left me in her care and she promised him to look after me—as she would a child ! '

On the other hand, we know from the patient's analysis that by insisting on being kept in sight she had put herself once again in the position of a child.

' That she had lost the child ', continued our patient, ' signified that she had not watched me ; she had lost sight of me. It was an admission that she had actually gone to sleep for the time and had not told me the truth later '.

She was quite in the dark about the meaning of that fragment of **dream** where the nurse inquired from people in the street whether they had seen the child : on the other hand she was able to elucidate subsequent details of the manifest dream.

'The expanse of water made nurse think of the Rhine ; she added, however, that it was much larger. Then she remembered that on the previous evening I had read her the story of Jonah and the whale, and had told her that I once saw a whale in the English Channel. I fancy that the water represents the sea and is an allusion to the story of Jonah.

'I think, too, that the narrow bridge comes from the same story, which is told wittily in dialect. A religious instructor describes to his pupils the wonderful adventure of Jonah, whereupon a boy points out that it cannot be true, since the teacher himself had told them before that whales could swallow only the smallest creatures owing to the narrowness of their throats. The teacher got out of the difficulty by saying that Jonah was a Jew, and that Jews would squeeze themselves in anywhere. My nurse is very religious but inclined to scepticism, and I reproached myself that my story-telling might perhaps have stirred her religious doubts.

'Now on this narrow bridge she saw the figure of another nurse whom she knew. From what she said it appears that this nurse drowned herself in the Rhine after being discharged from a case owing to some neglect or other.[1] She herself had feared, therefore, that she would be discharged for having fallen asleep. Moreover, on the day following the incident and after relating the dream, nurse cried bitterly, and when I asked why,

---

[1] I was here guilty of a condensation of the material, which I was able to put right when I read my account to the patient. The nurse who appeared on the bridge had not been discharged on account of neglect. She was discharged because the child's mother, who had to leave home at the time, wanted to leave her child in charge of an older —*i.e.* after all, a more trustworthy !—attendant. This was followed by a reference to yet another nurse who had actually been discharged on account of neglect, but who had not drowned herself. The material necessary for interpretation of the dream element comes, as is often the way, from two sources. My memory completed the synthesis leading to interpretation. For the rest, this story of the drowned nurse contains the element of a mother's departure, which the patient connected with the departure of her husband. We thus have here an overdetermination which detracts somewhat from the elegance of the interpretation.

replied quite rudely : " You know why as well as I do : you won't trust me any more " ! '

Since the appearance of the drowned nurse was an after-thought and an especially distinct item, we should have advised the patient to begin her dream-interpretation at this point. According to the dreamer's report, too, the first half of her dream was accompanied by acute anxiety ; the second part paved the way for that feeling of reassurance with which she awoke.

' I regard the next part of the dream ', said the lady, continuing her analysis, ' as certain corroboration of my view that the dream had to do with what happened on Friday evening, for the person who had formerly been a saleswoman in a provision-shop can only have referred to the servant who brought in the supper on that occasion. I noticed, too, that nurse complained of nausea all day long. The question she puts to this woman, " Have you seen the child ? " is obviously traceable to my question, " Have you seen me ? " I put this question to her for the second time, just as the servant came in with the dishes.'

In the dream, too, inquiry after the child is made on two occasions. The fact that the woman does not reply and shows no sign of interest we shall regard as an aspersion on this other servant made in the dreamer's own interest : she represents herself in the dream as being superior to the other, just because she herself has to face reproach on account of her own lack of attention.

' The woman who appears in the dream is not in actual fact divorced from her husband. The situation is taken from an incident in the life of the other servant, who has been separated from her lover—" separated ", divorced—by her parent's veto. The remark that even marriage is not always happy was in all probability a consoling remark made in the course of conversation between the two servants. On it is modelled the concluding sentence of the dream : the child will turn up.

' I concluded from this dream, however, that on the

evening in question nurse really did fall asleep and that she was afraid of being dismissed for this reason. I had no more doubt about the accuracy of my powers of perception. Moreover, after relating the dream, nurse added that she was very sorry she had no dream-book at hand. To my comment that such books were full of the most ignorant superstitions, she replied that, although she was not at all superstitious, still all the unpleasant happenings of her life had taken place on a Friday. I must add that at the present moment her treatment of me is not at all satisfactory; she is touchy and irritable and makes scenes about nothing.'

I think we must credit the lady with having accurately interpreted and appreciated her nurse's dream. As so often happens with dream-interpretation during analysis, the translation of the dream does not depend solely on associative material, but in addition on the circumstances of its narration, the behaviour of the patient before and after analysis, together with every remark or disclosure made by the patient at the time— during the same analytic session. If we take into account this nurse's touchiness, her attitude to unlucky Fridays, etc., we should confirm the conclusion that the dream contained a confession; in spite of her denial, she had actually fallen asleep and was afraid she would be sent away from her ' foster-child '. [1]

This dream, however, which had a practical bearing for the lady, stimulates our theoretical interest in two directions. It took the form of a consolation, but essentially it represented a significant *avowal* in regard to the nurse's relation to her patient. How does it come about that a dream, which should surely serve the purpose of a wish-fulfilment, can represent a con-fession which is not even in any way advantageous to the dreamer? Must we concede the existence of confession-dreams as distinct from wish- (and anxiety-)

---

[1] As a matter of fact, a few days later the nurse confessed to a third person that she had fallen asleep, thus confirming the lady's inter-pretation.

dreams, or again of warning-dreams, reflection-dreams, adaptation-dreams, and so on ?

I must confess I still do not quite understand why the objections I gave to any such course in my *Traumdeutung* have given rise to misgivings in the minds of so many psycho-analysts, among them some of repute. It seems to me that the differentiation of wish-, avowal-, warning- and adaptation-dreams, and so on, has not much greater value than the differentiation, accepted perforce, of medical specialists into gynecologists, children's specialists, dentists. Let me recapitulate here as briefly as possible the discussion of this question as set forth in my *Traumdeutung*.[1]

The so-called ' residues from the previous day ' can act as disturbers of sleep and dream-producers ; they are thought-processes from the previous day which have retained affective cathexis and to some extent withstood the general lowering of energy through sleep. These residues are discovered by tracing back the manifest dream to the latent dream-thoughts ; they constitute portions of the latter, belong, that is to say, to the activities of waking life—whether they are conscious or unconscious—which are able to persist during sleep. In accordance with the multiformity of thought-processes in the conscious and preconscious systems, these day-residues are present in numerous forms with the most varying significance : they may be wishes or fears that have not been disposed of, or resolutions, reflections, warnings, attempts to adapt oneself to current situations, and so on. To this extent the question of this particular characteristic of dreams would seem to be confirmed by the content discovered on interpretation of them. These residues from the previous day, however, are not the dream itself : they even lack the most essential constituent of a dream. They could not of themselves form a dream. They are, strictly speaking, only the psychical material which the dream-work employs, just as sensory and somatic

---

[1] Dritte Auflage, p. 367 *et seq.*

stimuli, either incidental or produced under experimental conditions, constitute the somatic material for the dream-work. To attribute to them the main part in dream-formation is simply to repeat in a new guise the pre-analytical error by which dreams were explained on the hypothesis of stomach trouble or skin-pressure. Scientific errors indeed have many lives, and even when refuted are ready to creep in again under new guises.

In so far as we comprehend the state of affairs, the conclusion has been forced on us that the essential factor in dream-formation is an unconscious wish— as a rule, an infantile wish—now in a state of repression ; this can come to expression through the somatic or psychic material (therefore also through the day-residues), and thus it can provide these with the energy by which they can force themselves through to consciousness even during the nocturnal suspension of thought. Whatever else it may contain, warning, reflection, or avowal, whatever part of the rich content of preconscious waking life remains unsatisfied and arises during the night, the dream is in every case the fulfilment of *this* unconscious wish. It is *this* unconscious wish that gives the dream-work its peculiar characteristic of an unconscious elaboration of preconscious material. For a psycho-analyst dreams can only be characterized as productions of the dream-work; in spite of the fact that the latent dream-thoughts may only be found after dream-interpretation, he cannot reckon them as part of the dream ; they are a part of preconscious thinking. (Secondary elaboration by the conscious system is reckoned as part of the dream-work. Even if one were to regard it separately, this would not involve any alteration in our conception. The definition would then run : Dreams considered in the analytical sense include the actual dream-work together with the secondary elaboration of the product of this work.) The conclusion to be drawn from these considerations is that one cannot put the dream-characteristic of wish-fulfilment in the same category with dream-characteristics such as warnings, avowals, attempts at solution, etc., without denying the concept of psychic dimensions of depth, that is to say, without rejecting the psycho-analytical standpoint.

At this point we may revert to the dream related by the nurse, in order to demonstrate the dimensional character of the wish-fulfilment contained therein. We already know that the lady's interpretation of this dream was by no means complete ; there were portions of the day-content which she was unable to appraise accurately. Moreover she suffered from an obsessional neurosis, a condition which seems to me to make it harder for the patient to understand dream-symbols, in contrast with dementia præcox in which the reverse is true.

Nevertheless our knowledge of dream-symbolism enables us to understand uninterpreted portions of this dream and to perceive a deeper significance behind the interpretations already given. We cannot but observe how some of the material employed by the nurse comes from the complex of giving birth, of having children. The expanse of water (the Rhine, the Channel where the whale was seen) is certainly the water out of which children come. She too comes to the water ' in search of a child '. The Jonah legend behind this determination of the water, the question how Jonah (the child) could get through such a narrow passage, belong to the same association. The nurse, too, who out of mortification threw herself into the Rhine, found some comfort in her despair of life by the sexual-symbolic mode of her death—by going into water. The narrow bridge on which the nurse makes her appearance is in all probability also a genital symbol, although I must admit that here we lack more precise knowledge.

The wish to have a child seems therefore to be the unconscious creator of the dream in this instance ; no other would be better calculated to comfort the nurse for the painful state of affairs in real life. ' I

shall be discharged : I shall lose my foster-child.
What matter ? I shall get a real child of my own
instead '. That uninterpreted portion of the dream
where she questions everyone in the street about the
child perhaps belongs here ; the interpretation would
then run, ' and even if I have to offer myself on the
streets I know how to get a child for myself '. A
strain of defiance in the dreamer hitherto disguised
suddenly declares itself here : her avowal fits in here
for the first time. ' What if I have shut my eyes and
compromised my professional reputation for conscientiousness and lost my post ? Shall I be such a
fool as to drown myself like Nurse X ? Not I : I'll
give up nursing altogether and get married : I'll be
a woman and have a real child ; nothing shall prevent
me.' This interpretation is justified by the consideration that ' having children ' is really the infantile
expression of a desire for sexual intercourse : indeed it
can be consciously chosen as an euphemistic expression
of this shocking wish.

In her waking life itself the dreamer showed some
tendency to confess ; in the dream a confession which
would be detrimental to her interests is made possible ;
one of the nurse's latent character-traits makes use of
the confession to bring about an infantile wish-fulfilment. We may surmise that this character has a close
connection—in regard both to time and to content—
with the wish for a child and for sexual enjoyment.

Subsequent inquiry of the lady to whom I owe the
first part of this interpretation afforded some unexpected information about the previous career of the
nurse. Before she took up nursing she had wished
to marry a man who had courted her assiduously ;
she had then abandoned this projected marriage on
account of the opposition of an aunt towards whom
her relations were a curious mixture of dependence and
defiance. This aunt who prevented the marriage was
the superintendent of a nursing association, and was
regarded by the nurse as the pattern on which she

modelled her life. The latter expected to be her
aunt's heir, and was dependent on her in this way ;
nevertheless she thwarted the aunt by not entering
the particular branch of nursing the latter had destined
her for. The defiance shown in the dream was therefore directed against the aunt. We have ascribed an
anal-erotic origin to this character-trait, and may
take into consideration that the interests binding her
to the aunt are of a financial nature ; we are also
reminded that children favour the anal theory of
birth.

This factor of infantile defiance may perhaps allow
us to assume a closer relation between the first and last
scenes in the dream. The former saleswoman in a
provision-shop represents in the dream the servant who
brought the lady's supper into the room just when she
was asking the question, ' Have you seen me ? ' It
appears, however, that she is intended in every way to
play the part of hostile rival. Depreciation of her
nursing capacity is indicated by the fact that she takes
not the slightest interest in the lost child, her answer
dealing with her own private affairs. The dreamer
had thus displaced on to this figure the indifference
about her patient which applied to herself. The
unhappy marriage and divorce which the former
dreaded in connection with her most secret wishes are
attributed to the same person. We know, however,
that it was the aunt who had separated the nurse
and her fiancé. Hence the ' provision-seller ' (a figure
not lacking in infantile symbolic significance) may
represent the aunt-superintendent, who was in fact not
much older than the nurse and who had played the
necessary part of mother-rival in the nurse's life. A
satisfactory confirmation of this interpretation is to
be found in the fact that the ' familiar ' district where
she comes upon this person standing in front of her
door was the place where her aunt carried out her
official duties.

Owing to the lack of contact between the analyst

and the object of the analysis, it is scarcely advisable to penetrate deeper into the structure of the dream. It may perhaps be stated that even in the slight degree to which interpretation was possible the dream showed itself rich in corroborative material and in new problems.

XIII

INFANTILE MENTAL LIFE

Two Lies told by Children [1]

(1913)

IT is comprehensible that children should tell lies
when in doing so they mimic the lies of grown-up
people. But a number of the lies of well-brought-up
children have a peculiar significance, and should cause
their instructors to reflect rather than to be angry.
These lies proceed from the influence of an excessive
love motive, and become momentous if they lead to a
misunderstanding between the child and the person
whom it loves.

I

A girl of seven (in her second year at school) had
asked her father for money to buy colours for painting
Easter eggs. The father had refused, saying he had
no money. Shortly afterwards the girl again asked
for some money for a contribution towards a wreath
for the funeral of the late reigning princess. Each of
the school-children was to bring fifty pfennigs. The
father gave her ten marks ; she paid her contribution,
put nine marks on her father's writing-table, and with
the remaining fifty pfennigs bought paints, which she
hid in her toy-cupboard.

At dinner the father asked suspiciously what she
had done with the missing pfennigs, and whether she
had not bought the colours with them. She denied it ;
but her brother, who was two years older, and together

---

[1] First published in *Zeitschrift*, Bd. I., 1913 ; reprinted in *Sammlung*,
Vierte Folge. [Translated by E. Colburn Mayne.]

with whom she had planned to paint the eggs, betrayed
her ; the colours were found in the cupboard. The
father, very angry, handed the culprit over to her
mother for punishment, which was severely administered. Afterwards the mother herself was overwhelmed
when she saw the child's extreme despair. She
caressed the little girl after punishing her, and took her
for a walk to console her. But the effects of this
experience, described by the patient herself as the
' turning-point ' of her life, proved to be immitigable.
She had hitherto been a wild, self-confident child ;
thenceforth she became timid and vacillating. During
her engagement she flew into a rage that was incomprehensible even to herself, when her mother was
buying furniture and trousseau-garments for her. She
had the feeling that after all it was *her* money, and no
one else ought to buy anything with it. As a young
wife she was shy of asking her husband for any expenditure for her personal needs, and made an unnecessary
distinction between ' her ' money and his. During
the course of her treatment it happened now and again
that her husband's remittances to her were delayed,
so that she was resourceless in the foreign city. After
she had once told me this, I made her promise that if it
happened again she would borrow the small necessary
sum from me. She gave the promise, but on the next
occasion of embarrassment she did not keep it and
preferred to pawn her jewellery. She explained that
she could not take money from me.

The appropriation of the fifty pfennigs in her childhood had a significance which the father could not
divine. Some time before she began going to school,
she had played a singular little prank with money.
A neighbour with whom she was friendly had sent the
girl with a small sum of money, as companion for her
own still younger little boy, to make some purchase
in a shop. As the elder of the two, she was bringing the
change from the purchase back to the house. But
when she met the neighbour's servant-maid in the

street, she flung the money down on the pavement.
In the analysis of this action, even to herself inexplicable, the thought of Judas occurred to her, when he
flung away the silver pieces gained by him through the
betrayal of his Master. She declared that she was
certainly acquainted with the story of the Passion
before she went to school. But in what manner could
she have identified herself with Judas ?

At the age of three and a half she had a nursemaid
of whom she was extremely fond. This girl had a
love-affair with a doctor, and visited his surgery with
the child. It appears that the child was the witness
of various sexual proceedings. Whether she saw the
doctor give money to the nursemaid is not certainly
established ; there is, however, no doubt that the girl
gave the child little presents of money to ensure her
silence, and that purchases (probably sweets) were
made with these on the way home. It is possible, too,
that the doctor himself occasionally gave money to
the child. Nevertheless, the child betrayed the girl
to her mother out of jealousy. She played so osten-
tatiously with the pfennigs she had brought home that
the mother could not but ask : ' Where did you get
that money ? ' The maid was dismissed.

To take money from anyone had thus early come
to mean for her the yielding of the body, the erotic
relation. To take money from her father was equivalent to a declaration of love. The phantasy that her
father was her lover was so seductive that the childish
desire for colours for the Easter eggs was easily, by
its aid, indulged in spite of the prohibition. But she
could not confess to the appropriation of the money ;
she was obliged to disavow it, because the motive of
the deed, unknown to herself, could not be confessed.
The father's chastisement was thus a refusal of the
tenderness offered him, a humiliation, and so it broke
her spirit. During the treatment a period of severe
depression ensued, the explanation of which led to her
remembering the events described, when I was once

obliged to copy that humiliation by asking her not to
bring me any more flowers.

It will scarcely be necessary, for the psycho-analyst,
to insist upon the fact that in this child's little experience we are confronted with one of those extremely
common cases of persistence of early anal erotism in
the later erotic life. Even the desire to paint the eggs
with colours derives from the same source.

II

A woman, now very ill as the consequence of a disappointment in life, was in earlier years a particularly
healthy, truth-loving, earnest and admirable girl, and
became a tender-natured woman. But still earlier, in
the first years of her life, she had been a wilful and dis-
contented child, and though she developed fairly early
into an excessively good and conscientious one, there
were occurrences in her schooldays which, when she
fell ill, caused her deep remorse and were regarded by
her as proofs of fundamental depravity. Memory told
her that she had frequently in those days bragged and
lied. Once, on the way home, a schoolfellow boasted :
' Yesterday we had ice at dinner.' She answered :
' Oh, we have ice every day.' In reality she did not
know what ice at dinner could mean ; she knew ice
only in the long blocks in which it is carted about,
but she perceived that there was something grand in
having it for dinner, and so she would not be excelled
by her schoolfellow.

When she was ten years old they were given in
their drawing-lesson the task of drawing a circle in
free-hand. But she made use of the compasses, thus
easily producing a perfect circle, and showed her
achievement triumphantly to her neighbour in class.
The teacher came up, heard her boasting, discovered
the marks of the compasses in the delineation of the
circle, and took the girl to task. But she stubbornly
denied it, would not be abashed by any proofs, and took

refuge in sullen silence. The teacher conferred with her father ; both were influenced by the girl's usual good behaviour to decide against any further notice of the occurrence.

This child's two lies were instigated by the same complex. As the eldest of five children, the little girl early manifested an unusually strong attachment to her father, which was destined in later years to wreck her happiness in life. But she could not long escape the discovery that her beloved father was not so great a personage as she was inclined to think him. He had to struggle against money-difficulties ; he was not so powerful nor so distinguished as she had imagined. This departure from her ideal she could not put up with. Since, as women do, she based all her ambition upon the beloved man, it became a dominating idea with her that she must support her father against the world. So she boasted to her schoolfellows, in order not to have to belittle her father. When, later on, she learnt to translate ice for dinner by ' glace ', the path lay open for her remorse about this reminiscence to take its course as a dread of pieces or splinters of glass.

The father was an excellent draughtsman, and had often enough called forth the delight and wonderment of the children by exhibitions of his skill. In her identification of herself with her father, she had in school drawn that circle which she could produce successfully only by underhand means. It was as though she wanted to boast : ' Look here—see what my father can do ' ! The consciousness of guilt that hung round her excessive fondness for her father found its outlet in the attempted deception ; a confession was impossible for the same reason that was given in the earlier observation—it could not but have been the confession of the hidden incestuous love.

We should not think lightly of such episodes in child-life. It would be a grave misconception to read into such childish errors the prognosis of a developing

immoral character. Nevertheless, they are intimately
connected with the most powerful motivations of the
childish soul, and are prophetic of tendencies which
will take shape either in the later destiny or in a future
neurosis.

XIV

A CASE OF PARANOIA RUNNING COUNTER TO THE PSYCHO-ANALYTICAL THEORY OF THE DISEASE [1]

(1915)

SOME years ago a well-known lawyer consulted me about a case which had raised some doubts in his mind. A young woman had asked him to protect her from the molestations of a man who had drawn her into a love-affair. She declared that this man had abused her confidence by getting invisible witnesses to photograph them in the act of love-making, and that by exhibiting these pictures he could bring shame upon her and force her to resign her position. Her legal adviser was experienced enough to recognize the pathological stamp of this accusation ; he remarked, however, that, as what appears to be incredible often actually happens, he would appreciate the opinion of a psychiatrist in this matter. He promised to call on me again, accompanied by the plaintiff.

Before I continue the account, I will say that I have altered the *milieu* of this case in order to preserve the incognito of those concerned, but that I have altered nothing else. I consider it an undesirable practice, however excellent the motive may be, to alter any detail in the presentation of a case. One can never tell which aspect of a case may be picked out by a reader of independent judgement, and one runs the risk of giving the latter a false impression.

Shortly afterwards I met the patient in person. She was thirty years old, a singularly attractive and

---

[1] First published in *Zeitschrift*, Bd. III., 1915 ; reprinted in *Sammlung*, Vierte Folge. [Translated by Edward Glover.]

handsome girl, who looked much younger than her
age and was of a distinctly feminine type. She
obviously resented the interference of a doctor and
took no trouble to hide her distrust. It was clear that
only the influence of her legal adviser, who was present,
induced her to tell the following story, one which set
me a problem to be referred to later. Neither in her
manner nor by any kind of expression of emotion did
she betray the slightest shame or shyness, although
some such state of mind would naturally arise on such
an occasion in the presence of a stranger. She was
completely under the spell of the apprehension that
her experience had induced in her.

For many years she had been on the staff of a big
institution, where she held a responsible post. Her
work had given her satisfaction and had been appreciated by her employers. She had never sought any
love-affairs with men, but had lived quietly with her
old mother whose only support she was. She had no
brothers or sisters ; her father had died many years
before. Recently an official in the same institution, a
cultured and attractive man, had paid her attentions
and she had inevitably been drawn towards him. For
external reasons, marriage was out of the question,
but the man would not hear of giving up their relationship on that account. He had pleaded that it was
senseless to sacrifice to social convention all that they
longed for, that they had an indisputable right to
enjoy and that could enrich their life as nothing else
could. As he had promised not to expose her to any
risk, she had at last consented to go to his bachelor
rooms in the daytime. There they kissed and embraced
as they lay side by side, and he began to admire the
charms which were now partly revealed. In the midst
of their love-making she was suddenly frightened by
a noise, a kind of knock or tick. It came from the
direction of the writing-desk, which was standing
sideways in front of the window ; the space between
desk and window was partly filled up by a heavy

curtain. She had at once asked her friend what this noise meant, and was told, so she said, that it probably came from the small clock on the writing-desk. I shall take the liberty, however, of commenting below on this part of her narrative.

As she left the house she had met two men on the staircase who whispered to each other as she passed. One of the strangers was carrying something which was wrapped up and looked rather like a box. She was much exercised over this meeting, and even on the way home her thoughts had already taken the following shape : the box could easily have been a camera, and the man a photographer who had been hidden behind the curtain while she was in the room ; the tick had been the noise of the shutter ; the photograph had been taken as soon as he saw her in a particularly compromising position of which he had wished to obtain pictorial evidence. From that moment nothing could abate her suspicion. She pursued her lover with reproaches and pestered him for explanations and reassurances, not only when they met but also by letter. In vain did he try to convince her that his feelings were sincere and that her suspicions were entirely without foundation. At last she called on the lawyer, told him of her experience and handed over the letters which the accused had written to her about the incident. Later I had an opportunity of seeing some of these letters. They made a very favourable impression on me, and contained mainly expressions of regret that such an unspoilt and tender understanding should have been destroyed by this ' unfortunate morbid idea '.

I need hardly justify my agreement with this view. But the case had a special interest for me other than a merely diagnostic one. The view had already been put forward in psycho-analytical literature that patients suffering from paranoia are struggling against an intensification of their homosexual trends, this pointing back to a narcissistic object-choice. And a further interpretation had been made : that the persecutor is in reality the loved person, past or present. A synthesis of the two propositions would lead us to expect that the persecutor must be of the same sex as the persecuted. We had not, it is true, asserted that paranoia is always without exception conditioned by homosexuality ; but only because our observations were not sufficiently numerous. It was one of those conceptions which in view of certain connections become important only when universal application can be claimed for them. In psychiatric literature there is certainly no lack of cases in which the patient imagines himself persecuted by a person of the opposite sex. It is one thing, however, to read of such cases, and quite a different thing to come into personal contact with one. The relation between paranoia and homosexuality had so far been easily confirmed by my own observations and analyses and by those of my friends. But the present case emphatically contradicted it. The girl seemed to defend herself against love for a man by transforming the lover straightaway into a persecutor : there was no sign of the influence of a woman, no trace of a struggle against a homosexual attachment.

In these circumstances the simplest thing to do would have been to abandon the theory that the delusion of persecution invariably depends on homosexuality, and with it everything based on this view. Either that theory must be given up or else, in view of this lack of conformation to rule, one must side with the lawyer and assume that this was no paranoiac combination but an actual experience which had been accurately interpreted. But I saw another way out, by which a final verdict could for the moment be postponed. I recollected how often wrong views were taken about psychotic patients simply because they had not been studied carefully enough and had not told enough about themselves. I therefore said that I could not form an immediate opinion, and asked the lady to call on me a second time, when she could relate her story again and add any details that had

perhaps been omitted. Thanks to the lawyer's influence I secured this promise from the reluctant
patient ; while the former aided me in another way by
saying that at our second meeting his presence would
be superfluous.

The story told on this second occasion did not conflict with the previous narrative, but the additional
details supplied resolved all doubts and difficulties.
To begin with, she had visited the young man not once
but twice. It was on the second occasion that she
had been disturbed by the suspicious noise : she had
suppressed, or omitted to mention, the first visit
because it had no longer seemed of importance to her.
On the first day nothing had happened, but something
did happen on the day following. Her department in
the business concern was under the direction of an
elderly lady whom she described as follows : ' She has
white hair like my mother '. This elderly superintendent had a great liking for her and treated her with
affection, though sometimes she teased her ; the girl
regarded herself as her particular favourite. On the
day after her first visit to the young man's rooms he
appeared in the office to discuss some business matter
with this elderly woman. During their whispered
conversation the patient suddenly felt convinced that
he was telling her about their adventure of the previous
day, and even concluded that there had been for some
time a love-relationship between the two which she
had overlooked. The white-haired motherly old lady
now knew everything, and her speech and conduct
throughout the rest of the day seemed to confirm the
patient's suspicion. At the first opportunity she took
her lover to task about his treachery. He naturally
raised a vigorous protest against what he called a
senseless accusation. This time he succeeded in freeing
her from her delusion and she regained enough confidence to repeat her visit to his room a short time, I
believe a few weeks, afterwards. The rest we know
from her first narrative.

These new details remove first of all any doubts as to the pathological nature of her suspicion. It is easy to see that the white-haired elderly manageress is a mother-substitute, that in spite of his youth the lover has been put in the place of the father, and that the strength of the mother-complex has driven the patient to suspect a love-relationship between these ill-matched partners, however unlikely such a relation might be. Moreover, this fresh information resolves the apparent contradiction with the view maintained by psycho-analysis, that the development of a delusion of perse-cution is conditioned by an over-powerful homosexual bond. The *original* persecutor—the agency whose influence the patient wishes to escape—is here again not a man but a woman. The manageress knows about the girl's love-affairs, disapproves of them, and shows her disapproval by mysterious allusions. The woman's attachment to her own sex hinders her attempts to adopt a person of the other sex as a love-object. Love for the mother becomes the protagonist of all those tendencies which, acting as her ' conscience ', would arrest the girl's first step along the new road to normal sexual satisfaction, in many respects a dangerous one ; and indeed it succeeds in destroying her relation with the man.

When the mother hinders or arrests a daughter's sexual activity she fulfils a normal function. This function is outlined in the early relationship between mother and infant ; it is based on powerful, unconscious motivations, and has the sanction of society. It is the daughter's business to emancipate herself from this influence and to decide for herself on broad and rational grounds what her share of enjoyment or denial of sexual pleasure shall be. If in the attempt to emanci-pate herself she falls a victim to a neurosis there is present a mother-complex, which is as a rule over-powerful, and is certainly unmastered. This conflicts with the new direction taken by the libido, and the conflict is disposed of in the form of this or that neurosis, according to the disposition present. The manifestations of the neurotic reaction will always be determined, however, not by the actual relation to the actual mother, but by the infantile relation to the original mother-imago.

We know that our patient had been fatherless for many years : we may also assume that she would not have kept away from men up to the age of thirty if she had not been sustained by a powerful emotional attachment to her mother. This supporting tie becomes a burdensome obstacle when her libido begins to respond to the call of a man's insistent wooing. She tries to free herself, to throw off her homosexual bond ; and her disposition, which need not be discussed here, enables her to achieve this by the formation of a paranoiac delusion. The mother thus becomes the hostile and jealous watcher and persecutor. As such she could be overcome, were it not that the mother-complex retained power enough to carry out its purpose of keeping her at a distance from men. At the end of the first phase of the conflict the patient has thus become estranged from the mother without having definitely gone over to the man. Indeed, both of them are plotting against her. Then with a vigorous effort the man draws her to himself. She conquers the mother's opposition in her mind and is willing to grant her lover a second meeting. In the later developments the mother does not reappear, but we may rightly assume that in this earlier phase the lover was not a persecutor directly ; his character as such was acquired, as it were, through the mother and in virtue of his relationship to the mother, a factor which played the chief part in the formation of the first delusion.

One would think that the resistance was now definitely overcome, that the girl who had until now been bound to her mother had succeeded in coming to love a man. But after the second visit a new delusion appears, which by making ingenious use of accidental circumstances, destroys this love and thus successfully carries through the purpose of the mother-complex. It still seems strange that a woman should protect herself against the love of a man by means of a paranoiac delusion ; but before examining this state of things more closely, let us glance at the accidental circumstances that form the basis of this second delusion, the one aimed exclusively against the man.

Lying partly undressed on the sofa alongside her lover, she hears some noise, a tick, knock, or tap. She does not know its cause but she arrives at an interpretation of it after meeting on the staircase two men, one of whom carries something that looks like a covered box. She is convinced that someone acting on instructions from her lover has watched and photographed her during their intimate tête-à-tête. We, of course, are far from thinking that had the fatal noise not occurred the delusion would not have been formed ; on the contrary, we see behind this accidental circumstance something compulsive, asserting itself again as inevitably as when the patient divined a love-relationship between her lover and the elderly manageress, her mother-substitute. Among the wealth of unconscious phantasies of neurotics, and probably of all human beings, there is one which is seldom absent and can be disclosed by analysis, concerning the watching of sexual intercourse between the parents. I call these phantasies, together with those of seduction, castration, and others, *primal phantasies* ; and I shall discuss more fully elsewhere their origin and the relation of them to individual experience. The accidental noise is merely a stimulus which activates the typical phantasy of eavesdropping, itself a component of the parental complex. Indeed, it is doubtful whether we can rightly call it ' accidental '. As O. Rank has remarked to me, it is an essential part of the phantasy of listening, and it reproduces either the sounds which betray parental intercourse or those by which the listening child fears to betray itself. But now we know at once where we stand. The lover is still the father, but the patient herself has taken the mother's place. The part of the listener must then be allotted to a third person. We can see by what means the girl has freed herself from her homosexual dependence on the mother. A partial regression has taken place ; instead of choosing her mother as a love-object, she has identified herself with her, she herself has become the mother. The possibility of this regression points to the narcissistic origin of her homosexual object-choice and with that to the paranoiac disposition in her. One might sketch a train of thought which would bring about a similar result : ' If mother does it, I can do it too ; I've just as good a right as she '.

One can go a step further in disproving the acci-dental nature of the noise. We do not, however, ask our readers to follow us, since the absence of thorough analytic investigation makes it impossible in this case to go beyond a certain probability. The patient mentioned in her first interview with me that she had immediately demanded an explanation of the noise, and had been told that it was probably the ticking of the little clock on the table. I take the liberty of assuming that this piece of information was a mistaken memory. It seems to me much more likely that at first she did not react to the noise at all, and that it became significant only after she met the two men on the staircase. Her friend, who had probably not even heard the noise, ventured the explanation, perhaps or some later occasion when she assailed him with her suspicions, ' I don't know what noise you can have heard. Perhaps it was the little clock ; it sometimes ticks like that.' A subsequent use of impressions and displacement of recollections such as this occurs fre-quently in paranoia and is characteristic of it. But as I never met the man and did not continue the analysis of the woman, my hypothesis cannot be proved.

I might go still further in the analysis of this apparently real ' accident '. I do not believe that the clock ever ticked or that any noise was to be heard at all. The woman's situation justified a sensation of throbbing in the clitoris. This was what she subsequently projected as a perception of an external object. Similar things occur in dreams. An hysterical patient of mine once related to me a short 'awakening' dream to which she could bring no spontaneous associations. She dreamt simply that someone knocked and then she awoke. Nobody had knocked, but during the previous nights she had been awakened by unpleasant sensations of pollutions : she had thus a motive for awakening as soon as she felt the first sign of genital excitation. There had been a ' knocking ' of the clitoris. In the case of our paranoiac patient, I should substitute for the accidental noise a similar process of projection. I certainly cannot guarantee that during our short acquaintance the patient, who was reluctantly yielding to necessity, gave me a truthful account of all that had taken place during the two meetings. But an isolated clitoris-contraction would be in keeping with her statement that no contact of the genitals had taken place. In her subsequent rejection of the man, lack of satisfaction undoubtedly played a part as well as ' conscience '.

Let us consider again the outstanding fact that the patient protects herself against her love for a man by means of a paranoiac delusion. The key to the understanding of this is to be found in the evolution of the delusion. As we might have expected, the latter was at first aimed against the woman ; *the subsequent progression from a female to a male object* was, however, made on a *paranoiac basis*. Such a progression is unusual in paranoia ; as a rule we find that the victim of persecution remains fixated to the same persons and therefore to the same sex as before the paranoiac transformation set in. But neurotic disorder does not preclude a progression of this kind, and our observation may be the prototype of many others. There are many similar processes beside that in paranoia which have never yet been classified under this heading, amongst them some which are very familiar. The so-called neurasthenic, for example, is prevented by his unconscious incestuous fixation from choosing a strange woman as a love-object ; his sexual activity must remain within the limits of phantasy. But within the limits of this phantasy he achieves the progress denied him in reality and he succeeds in replacing mother and sister by new objects. Since the veto of the censorship does not then come into action, he can become conscious of his choice of these substitute-figures.

Alongside the phenomena of attempted progression from a position recently achieved, as a rule by regression, we may group the efforts made in some neuroses to regain a libido-position once held and subsequently lost. Indeed we can hardly draw any abstract distinction between these two categories. We are too apt to think that the conflict underlying a neurosis is removed when the symptom has been formed. In reality the struggle often goes on after this. Fresh instinctual components arise on both sides, and these continue it. The symptom itself becomes an object of this struggle ; certain trends anxious to preserve it conflict with others which strive to remove it and to re-establish the *status quo*. In the attempt to render the symptom nugatory the expedient is often adopted of trying to regain through new channels what has been lost and is now frustrated by the symptom. These facts throw much light on a statement made by C. G. Jung to the effect that a peculiar psychic inertia, hostile to change and progress, is the fundamental condition of neurosis. This inertia is in fact most peculiar ; it is not a general one, but is highly specialized ; it is not even all-powerful within its own scope, but fights against tendencies towards progress and reconstruction which remain active even after the formation of neurotic symptoms. If we search for the starting-point of this specialized inertia, we discover that it is the expression of a conjunction of instincts with impressions and with the objects connected with these impressions. This conjunction has been effected very early, is very hard to resolve, and has the effect of bringing the development of the instincts concerned to a standstill. Or in other words, this specialized 'psychic inertia' is only a different term, though hardly a better one, for what in psychoanalysis we are accustomed to call a *fixation*.

XV

A CONNECTION BETWEEN A SYMBOL AND A SYMPTOM [1]

(1916)

THE hat has been adequately established as a symbol of the genital organ, most frequently the male, through analyses of dreams. It cannot be said, however, that this symbol is at all an intelligible one. In phantasies and in numerous symptoms the head also appears as a symbol of the male genitals, or, if one prefers to put it so, as a representation of them. Many analysts will have noticed that certain patients suffering from obsessions express an abhorrence of and indignation against the penalty of beheading, feelings which are far more pronounced as regards this than any other form of capital punishment, and will in consequence have had to explain to them that they treat being beheaded as a substitute for being castrated. Dreams of young people or dreams occurring during the period of youth which concern the subject of castration, and in which there was mention of a ball which could only be interpreted as the head of the dreamer's father, have been often analysed and frequently published. I have recently been able to solve a ceremonial carried out by a patient before going to sleep, which consisted in laying a small pillow diamond-wise on a larger one so that the sleeper's head would rest exactly in the long diameter of the diamond. The diamond had the meaning that is familiar to us from drawings on walls, the head was to represent the male organ.

[1] First published in *Zeitschrift*, Bd. IV., 1916; reprinted in *Sammlung*, Vierte Folge. [Translated by Douglas Bryan.]

It may be that the symbolic meaning of the hat is derived from that of the head, in so far as the hat can be considered as a continuation of the head, though detachable. In this connection I call to mind a symptom of obsessional neurotics by means of which they manage to ensure themselves continual torment. When they are in the street they are constantly watching to see whether some acquaintance will salute them first, by taking off his hat, or whether he seems to wait for their salute ; and they give up a number of their acquaintances who they imagine no longer salute them or do not return their salute properly. There is no end to their perplexities on the point ; they find them everywhere as their mood and fancy dictate. It makes no difference to their behaviour when we tell them, what they all know already, that the salute by taking off the hat signifies an abasement before the saluted person, that a Spanish grandee, for example, enjoyed the privilege of being in the presence of the king with his head covered, and that their sensitiveness to saluting has therefore the meaning of not being willing to show themselves as of less importance than the other person thinks himself to be. The resistance of their sensitiveness to such an explanation suggests the activity of a motive less present to consciousness, and the source of this excess of feeling can easily be found in relation to the castration complex.

XVI

ON THE TRANSFORMATION OF INSTINCTS WITH SPECIAL REFERENCE TO ANAL EROTISM [1]

(1916)

MANY years ago, observations made during psycho-analysis led me to surmise that the constant co-existence in any person of the three character-traits of *orderliness, parsimony* and *obstinacy* indicated an intensification of the anal-erotic components in the sexual constitution of that person, and that these were modes of reaction specially favoured by his ego which had been established during his development in the course of the absorption of his anal erotism.[2]

In that publication my main object was to make known the fact of this definite relation : I was little concerned about its theoretical significance. Since then a general consensus of opinion has arisen that each one of the three qualities, avarice, pedantry and stubbornness, springs from anal-erotic sources—or, to express it more cautiously and more completely— draws powerful contributions from these sources. The cases in which these defects of character were combined and which in consequence bore a special stamp (the ' anal character ') were merely extreme instances, which even to superficial observation afforded illustration of the particular connection which concerns us here.

As a result of numerous impressions, and in particular of one specially cogent analytical experience,

---

[1] First published in *Zeitschrift*, Bd. IV., 1916 ; reprinted in *Sammlung*, Vierte Folge. [Translated by Edward Glover.]

[2] 'Character and Anal Erotism', 1908; see No. IV. of this volume, p. 45.

I came to the conclusion a few years later that in the development of the libido in man the phase of genital primacy must be preceded by a ' pregenital organization ' in which sadism and anal erotism play the leading parts.[1]

From that moment we had to face the following question : what becomes of anal-erotic impulses subsequently when, after the establishment of complete genital primacy, they have lost their importance in sexual life ? Do they preserve their original nature, but in a state of repression ? Are they sublimated and absorbed by transformation into character-traits ? Or do they find a place and function within the new organization of sexuality characterized by genital primacy ? Or, to put the question more accurately, since none of these three possibilities is likely to be the exclusive fate of the anal erotism, to what extent and in what way does each of them share in deciding that fate ? For the organic sources of anal erotism cannot be exhausted by the establishment of the genital organization.

One would think that there could be no lack of material from which to provide an answer, since the processes of instinctual transformation in question must have taken place in all persons undergoing analysis. Yet the material is so obscure, the abundance of ever-recurring impressions so confusing, that even now I am unable to solve the problem fully and can only contribute in part towards its solution. In this paper I shall also not neglect the opportunity to refer where connections arise to transformations of other impulses besides the anal-erotic. I need not emphasize the fact that the processes of development here described—just as the others found in psycho-analysis—have been inferred from the regressions into which they had been forced by neurotic processes.

To begin with, it would appear that in the products

---

[1] ' The Predisposition to Obsessional Neurosis ', 1913 ; see No. XI. of this volume, p. 122.

of the unconscious—spontaneous ideas, phantasies, symptoms—the conceptions *fæces* (money, gift), *child* and *penis* are seldom distinguished and are easily interchangeable. We realize, of course, that to express oneself in this way is incorrectly to apply to the sphere of the unconscious terms which belong properly to other regions of mental life ; in fact, that we have been tempted by the advantages offered by an analogy. To put the matter in a form less open to objection, these elements in the unconscious are often treated as if they were equivalent and could replace one another.

The most evident connection is that between ' child ' and ' penis '. It cannot be without significance that in the symbolic language of dreams, as well as of everyday speech, both are replaced by a single symbol ; both child and penis are called ' little one ' (*das Kleine*). It is a well-known fact that symbolic speech often ignores the difference of sex. The ' little one ', which originally meant the male genital organ, may have achieved a secondary application to the female genitals.

If we penetrate deeply into the neuroses of women, we not infrequently meet with the repressed wish to possess a penis. We call this infantile wish ' penis-envy ' and include it within the castration complex. Chance mishaps in a woman's life, mishaps which are themselves frequently the result of a very masculine disposition, have re-activated this infantile wish and, through the backward flow of libido, made it the chief vehicle of the neurotic symptoms. In other women we find no evidence of the penis-wish ; it is replaced by the wish for a child, the frustration of which in real life can lead to outbreak of a neurosis. It looks as if such women had understood (although this could not possibly have acted as a motive) that nature has given children to women as a substitute for the penis that has been denied them. From other women, again, we learn that both wishes co-existed in infancy, and that one had replaced the other. At first they had wanted a penis like a man ; then at a later, though still infantile, stage there appeared instead the wish for a child. The impression is forced upon us that this variety is caused by accidental factors during childhood, *e.g.* the presence or absence of brothers, the birth of another child at some critical time of life, so that the penis-wish and the child-wish were fundamentally identical.

We can indicate the ultimate outcome of the infantile penis-wish in those persons in whom the conditions for a neurosis in later life are absent : it changes into the wish for a *man*, accepting the man as an appendage, as it were, of the penis. A tendency hostile to the female sexual function is thus transformed into one favourable to it. Such women are capable of a love based on the masculine type of object-love, which can exist alongside the feminine one proper, which is derived from narcissism. We have already seen that in other cases the child is the first link in the transition from narcissistic self-love to object-love. In this way also, then, a child can be represented by the penis.

I have occasionally had the opportunity of hearing some dreams of women occurring after the first act of intercourse. They revealed an unmistakable wish in the woman to keep for herself the penis with which she had come in contact. Apart from their libidinal origin these dreams indicated a temporary regression from the man to the penis as an object of desire. One would certainly be inclined to trace back the wish for a man in a purely rationalistic way to the wish for a child, since a woman is bound to understand sooner or later that there can be no child without the agency of a man. It is, however, more likely that the wish for a man arises independently of the wish for a child, and that when—from obvious motives derived exclusively from ego-psychology—it does arise an unconscious reinforcement of libido from the original penis-wish becomes attached to it.

The importance of the process described lies in the fact that a part of the young woman's narcissistic masculinity is thus changed into femininity, and so can

no longer operate in a way harmful to the female
sexual function. By yet another process a part of the
erotism of the pregenital phase becomes available for
use in the phase of genital primacy. The child is
regarded as 'lumf'[1] (*Lumpf*), *i.e.* as something which
becomes detached from the body by passing through
the bowel. A certain amount of libidinal cathexis
which originally attached to the contents of the bowel
can thus be extended to the child born through it.
Linguistic evidence of this identity of child and fæces
is contained in the expression ' to *give* some one a child '.
For its fæces are the infant's first gift, a part of his
body which he will give up only on persuasion by a
loved person, to whom, indeed, he will make a spontaneous gift of it as a token of affection, since as a rule
infants do not soil strangers. (There are similar if less
intensive reactions with urine.) The process of defæcation affords the first occasion on which the child must
decide between a narcissistic and an object-loving
attitude. He either parts obediently with his fæces,
' offers them up ' to his love, or else retains them for
purposes of auto-erotic gratification and later as a
means of asserting his own will. The latter choice
constitutes the development of defiance (obstinacy), a
quality which springs, therefore, from a narcissistic
clinging to the pleasure of anal erotism.

It is probable that the first significance which fæcal
interest develops is not ' gold—money ', but ' gift '.
The child has no knowledge of money other than that
received as a gift, no idea of money earned or belonging
to it, inherited. Since its fæces constitute its first
gift, the child easily transfers interest from this
substance to the new one that meets it as the most
valuable form of gift in life. Those who question this
derivation of gifts should review their experience of
psycho-analytic treatment, study the gifts they receive
as doctors from their patients, and watch the storms of

---

[1] [A child's word for fæces. Cf. ' Analysis of a Phobia in a Five-
year-old Boy ', COLLECTED PAPERS, vol. iii.—Trans.]

transference which a gift from them can rouse in their patients.

Thus the interest in fæces is carried on partly as interest in money, partly as a wish for a child, in which latter an anal-erotic and a genital impulse (' penis-envy ') coincide. But the penis has another anal-erotic significance apart from its relation to the interest in a child. The relationship between the penis and the passage lined with mucous membrane which it fills and excites has already its prototype in the pregenital, anal-sadistic phase. The fæcal mass, or as one patient called it, the fæcal ' stick ', represents as it were the first penis, and the stimulated mucous membrane of the rectum represents that of the vagina. There are persons whose anal erotism remains vigorous and un-modified up to the age preceding puberty (ten to twelve years) ; we learn from them that already during the pregenital phase such persons had developed in phantasy and in perverse activity an organization analogous to the genital one, in which penis and vagina were represented by the fæcal stick and the rectum. In other cases (obsessional neurotics) we can observe the result of a regressive deterioration of the genital organization : all the phantasies originally conceived on the genital level are set back on to the anal level ; the penis is replaced by the fæcal mass, the vagina by the rectum.

Normally, when the interest in fæces recedes, the structural analogy we have described here effects a transference of the interest to the penis. Then if later inquiry yields the discovery that babies are born from the bowel, the greater part of the anal erotism becomes transferred to the baby, as chief heir, so to speak, of the anal erotism ; the penis, however, has been its predecessor in this as well as in another sense.

I feel sure that by this time the manifold inter-relations of the series, fæces, penis, child, have become utterly confused ; so I will attempt to remedy this defect by presenting them diagramatically, and in considering the diagram we can review the same material in a different order. Unfortunately, this technical device is not sufficiently plastic for our purpose, or possibly we have not yet learned to use it with effect. In any case we ask the reader not to expect too much from it.

Defiance springs from anal erotism and serves narcissistic purposes, forming an important ego-reaction against demands made by others. Interest in fæces is carried over first to interest in gifts, then to interest

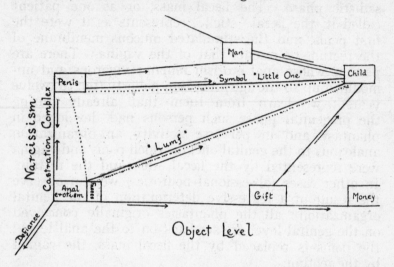

in money. In girls, the discovery of the penis gives rise to penis-envy, which later changes into the wish for a man as the possessor of a penis. At an earlier stage the wish for a penis was changed into the wish for a child, or the latter replaced the former. An organic analogy between penis and child (dotted line) is expressed by the existence of a symbol ('little one') common to both. A rational wish (double line) leads from the wish for a child to the wish for a man : we have already appreciated the importance of this instinctual transformation.

A different series of relations can be observed much

more distinctly in the male. It is formed when the boy's sexual curiosity leads him to discover the absence of a penis in women. He concludes that the penis must be a detachable part of the body, something analogous to fæces, the first bodily substance the child had to part with. Thus the original anal defiance enters into the composition of the castration complex. The structural analogy which enabled the intestinal contents to be the forerunner of the penis during the pregenital phase cannot come into account as a motive, but a substitute in the mind for it is provided by sexual investigation.

When a baby appears on the scene it is labelled ' lumf ', in accordance with the conclusions arrived at by sexual investigation, and becomes invested with powerful anal-erotic interest. When social experiences teach that a baby is to be regarded as a love-token, a gift, the wish for a child is reinforced from the same source. Fæces, penis and child are all three solid bodies : they all three, by forcible entry or expulsion, stimulate a membranous passage, i.e. the rectum and the vagina, the latter being as it were ' rented ' from the rectum, as Lou Andreas-Salome aptly remarks.[1] Infantile inquiry into sexual matters can only lead to the conclusion that the child comes down by the same route as the fæcal mass : the function of the penis is not usually discovered by it. But it is interesting to note that after so many vicissitudes an organic correspondence re-appears in the mental sphere as an unconscious identity.

[1] Lou Andreas-Salome, ' Anal ' und ' Sexual '.

XVII

'A CHILD IS BEING BEATEN'[1]

A Contribution to the Study of the Origin of Sexual Perversions

(1919)

I

IT is surprising how frequently people who come to be analysed for hysteria or an obsessional neurosis confess to having indulged in the phantasy: 'A child is being beaten'. Very probably it occurs even more often with other people who have not been obliged to come to this decision by manifest illness.

The phantasy has feelings of pleasure attached to it, and on their account it has been reproduced on innumerable occasions in the past or is even being reproduced still. At the climax of the imaginary situation there is almost invariably an onanistic gratification, that is to say, a gratification in the genitals. At first this takes place in accordance with the will of the person in question, but later on it does so in spite of his efforts, and with the characteristics of an obsession.

It is only with hesitation that this phantasy is confessed to. Its first appearance is recollected with uncertainty. The analytic treatment of the subject is met by unmistakable resistance. Shame and a sense of guilt are perhaps more strongly excited in this connection than when similar accounts are given of memories of the beginnings of sexual life.

Eventually it becomes possible to establish that the first phantasies of the kind were entertained very early

---

[1] First published in *Zeitschrift*, Bd. V., 1919; reprinted in *Sammlung*, Fünfte Folge. [Translated by Alix and James Strachey.]

in life : certainly before school age, and not later than in the fifth or sixth year. When the child was at school and saw other children being beaten by the teacher, then, if the phantasies had become dormant, this experience called them up again, or, if they were still present, it reinforced them, and noticeably modified their content. From that time forward it was ' an indefinite number ' of children that were being beaten. The influence of the school was so clear that the patients concerned were at first tempted to trace back their beating-phantasies exclusively to these impressions of school life, which dated from later than their sixth year. But it was never possible for them to maintain this position ; the phantasies had already been in existence before.

Though the children were no longer beaten in the higher forms at school, the influence of such occasions was replaced and more than replaced by the effects of reading, of which the importance was soon to be felt. In my patient's *milieu* it was almost always the same books whose contents gave a new stimulus to the beating-phantasies : those accessible to young people, such as the so-called ' *Bibliothèque rose* ', *Uncle Tom's Cabin*, etc. The child began to compete with these works of fiction by producing its own phantasies and by constructing a wealth of situations, and even whole institutions, in which children were beaten or were punished and disciplined in some other way because of their naughtiness and bad behaviour.

This phantasy — ' a child is being beaten '—was invariably charged with a high degree of pleasure and had its issue in an act of pleasurable, auto-erotic gratification ; it might therefore be expected that the sight of another child being beaten at school would also be a source of similar enjoyment. But as a matter of fact this was never so. The experience of real scenes of beating at school produced in the child who witnessed them a peculiarly excited feeling which was probably of a mixed character and in which repugnance had a

large share. In a few cases the real experience of the
scenes of beating was felt to be intolerable. Moreover,
it was always a condition even of the elaborated phantasies of later years that the punishment should do the
children no serious injury.

The question was bound to arise of what relation
there might be between the importance of the beating-
phantasies and the part that real corporal punishment
might have played in the education of the child at
home. It was impossible, on account of the one-
sidedness of the material, to confirm the first suspicion
that the relation was an inverse one. The individuals
from whom the data for these analyses were derived
were very seldom beaten in their childhood, or were at
all events not brought up by the help of the rod.
Naturally, however, each of these children was bound
to have become aware at one time or another of the
superior physical strength of its parents or educators ;
the fact that in every nursery the children themselves
at times come to blows requires no special emphasis.

As regards the early and simple phantasies which
could not obviously be traced to the influence of school
impressions or of scenes taken from books, further
information would have been welcome. Who was the
child that was being beaten ? The one who was himself
producing the phantasy or another ? Was it always
the same child or as often as not a different one ? Who
was it that was beating the child ? A grown-up
person ? And if so, who ? Or did the child imagine
that he himself was beating another one ? Nothing
could be ascertained that threw any light upon all
these questions—only the one timid reply : ' I know
nothing more about it : a child is being beaten '.

Inquiries as to the sex of the child that was being
beaten met with more success, but none the less brought
no enlightenment. Sometimes the answer was :
' Always boys ', or ' Only girls ' ; more often it was :
' I don't know ', or ' It doesn't matter which '. But
the point to which the questions were directed, the

discovery of some constant relation between the sex of the child producing the phantasy and that of the child that was being beaten, was never established. Now and again another characteristic detail of the content of the phantasy came to light : ' A little child is being beaten on its naked bottom '.

In these circumstances it was impossible at first even to decide whether the pleasure attaching to the beating-phantasy was to be described as sadistic or masochistic.

II

A phantasy of this kind, arising, perhaps from some accidental cause, in early childhood and retained for the purpose of auto-erotic gratification, can, in the light of our present knowledge, only be regarded as a primary trait of perversion. One of the components of the sexual function has, it seems, developed in advance of the rest, has made itself prematurely independent, has undergone fixation and in consequence been withdrawn from the later processes of development, and has in this way given evidence of a peculiar and anomalous constitution in the individual. We know that an infantile perversion of this sort need not persist for a whole life-time ; later on it can be subjected to repression, be replaced by a reaction-formation, or be transformed by sublimation. (It is possible, however, that sublimation arises out of some special process which would be kept in the background by repression.) But if these events do not take place, then the perversion persists to maturity ; and whenever we find a sexual aberration in adults—perversion, fetishism, inversion—we are justified in expecting that anamnestic investigation will reveal some experience in the nature of a fixation in childhood. Indeed, long before the days of psycho-analysis, observers like Binet were able to trace the strange sexual aberrations of maturity back to similar impressions and to precisely the same period of childhood, namely, the fifth or

sixth year. But at this point the inquiry was brought
up against the limitations of our knowledge ; for the
impressions that brought about the fixation were
without any traumatic force. They were for the most
part commonplace and unexciting to other people. It
was impossible to say why the sexual impulse had
undergone fixation particularly upon them. It was
possible, however, to look for their significance in the
fact that they provided an opportunity of fixation
(even though it was an accidental one) for precisely
that sexual component which was prematurely developed and was ready to spring forward. We had in
any case to be prepared to find a provisional end somewhere or other to the chain of causal connection ;
and the congenital constitution seemed exactly to
correspond with what was required for a stopping-
place of that kind.

If the sexual component which has broken loose
prematurely is the sadistic one, then we may expect,
on the basis of knowledge derived from other sources,
that a disposition to an obsessional neurosis will result
from its subsequent repression. This expectation
cannot be said to be contradicted by the results of
inquiry. The present short paper is based upon the
exhaustive study of six cases (four female and two
male). Of these, two were cases of obsessional
neurosis ; one extremely severe and incapacitating, the
other of moderate severity and quite well accessible
to influence. There was also a third case which at
all events exhibited clearly marked individual traits
of obsessional neurosis. The fourth case, it must be
admitted, was one of straightforward hysteria, with
pains and inhibitions ; and the fifth patient, who had
come to be analysed merely on account of lack of
decision in life, would not have been classified at all by
coarse clinical diagnosis, or would have been dismissed
as ' psychasthenic '. There is no need for feeling
disappointed over these statistics. In the first place,
we know that not every disposition is necessarily

developed into a disorder; in the second place, we ought to be content to explain the facts before us, and ought as a rule to avoid the additional task of making it clear why something has *not* taken place.

The present state of our knowledge would allow us to make our way so far and no farther towards the comprehension of beating-phantasies. But in the mind of the analytical physician there remains an uneasy suspicion that this is not a final solution of the problem. He is obliged to admit to himself that to a great extent these phantasies subsist apart from the rest of the content of the neurosis, and find no proper place in its structure. But impressions of this kind, as I know from my own experience, are only too easily put on one side.

III

Strictly considered—and why should this question not be considered with all possible strictness?—analytic work deserves to be recognized as genuine psycho-analysis only when it has succeeded in removing the amnesia which conceals from the adult his knowledge of his childhood from its beginning (that is, from about the second to the fifth year). This cannot be said among analysts too emphatically or repeated too often. The motives for disregarding this reminder are, indeed, intelligible. It would be desirable to obtain practical results in a shorter time and with less trouble. But at the present time theoretical knowledge is still far more important to all of us than therapeutic success, and anyone who neglects childhood analysis is bound to fall into the most disastrous errors. The emphasis which is laid here upon the importance of the earliest experiences does not imply any underestimation of the influence of later ones. But the later impressions of life speak loudly enough through the mouth of the patient, while it is the physician who has to raise his voice on behalf of the claims of childhood.

It is in the years of childhood between the ages of

two and four or five that the congenital libidinal factors are first awakened by actual experiences and become attached to certain complexes. The beating-phantasies which are now under discussion show themselves only towards the end of this period or after its termination. So it may quite well be that they have an earlier history, that they go through a process of development, that they represent an end-product and not an initial manifestation.

This suspicion is confirmed by analysis. A systematic application of it shows that beating-phantasies have an historical development which is by no means simple, and in the course of which they are changed in most respects more than once—as regards their relation to the author of the phantasy, and as regards their object, their content, and their significance.

In order to make it easier to follow these transformations in beating-phantasies I shall venture to confine my descriptions to the female cases, who, since they are four as against two, in any case constitute the greater part of my material. Moreover, beating-phantasies among men are connected with another subject, which I shall leave on one side in this paper. In my description I shall be careful to avoid being more schematic than is inevitable in presenting an average case. If then upon further observation a greater complexity of circumstances should come to light, I shall nevertheless be sure of having secured a typical occurrence and not one of an uncommon kind.

The first phase of beating-phantasies among girls must therefore belong to a very early period of childhood. Some features remain curiously indefinite, as though they were a matter of indifference. The scanty information given by the patients in their first statement, ' a child is being beaten ', seems to be justified in respect to this phase. But another of their features can be established with certainty, and to the same effect in every case. The child being beaten is never the one producing the phantasy, but is invariably another child, most often a brother or a sister if there is any. Since this other child may be a boy or a girl, there is no constant relation between the sex of the child producing the phantasy and that of the child being beaten. The phantasy, then, is certainly not masochistic. It would be tempting to call it sadistic, but one cannot neglect the fact that the child producing the phantasy is never doing the beating himself. The actual identity of the person beating remains obscure at first. Only this much can be established : it is not a child but an adult. Later on this indeterminate grown-up person becomes recognizable clearly and unambiguously as the (girl's) *father*.

This first phase of the beating-phantasy is therefore completely represented by the phrase : '*My father is beating the child*'. I am betraying a great deal of what is to be brought forward later when instead of this I say : '*My father is beating the child whom I hate*'. Moreover, one may hesitate to say whether the characteristics of a ' phantasy ' can yet be ascribed to this first step towards the later beating-phantasy. It is perhaps rather a question of recollections of events which have been witnessed, or of desires which have arisen on various occasions. But these doubts are of no importance.

Profound transformations have taken place between this first phase and the next. It is true that the person beating remains the same (that is, the father) ; but the child who is beaten has been changed into another one and is now invariably the child producing the phantasy. The phantasy is accompanied by a high degree of pleasure, and has now acquired a significant content, with the origin of which we shall be concerned later. Now, therefore, the wording runs : '*I am being beaten by my father*'. It is of an unmistakably masochistic character.

This second phase is the most important and the most momentous of all. But we may say of it in a certain sense that it has never had a real existence.

It is never remembered, it has never succeeded in becoming conscious. It is a construction of analysis, but it is no less a necessity on that account.

The third phase once more resembles the first. It has the wording which is familiar to us from the patient's statement. The person beating is never the father, but is either left undetermined just as in the first phase, or turns in a characteristic way into a representative of the father, such as a teacher. The figure of the child who is producing the beating-phantasy no longer itself appears in it. In reply to pressing inquiries the patients only declare : ' I am probably looking on '. Instead of the one child that is being beaten, there are now a number of children present as a rule. Most frequently it is boys who are being beaten (in girls' phantasies), but none of them is personally known to the subject. The situation of being beaten, which was originally simple and monoton-ous, may go through the most complicated alterations and elaborations ; and punishments and humiliations of another kind may be substituted for the beating itself. But the essential characteristic which dis-tinguishes even the simplest phantasies of this phase from those of the first, and which establishes the connection ·with the intermediate phase, is this : the phantasy now has strong and unambiguous sexual excitement attached to it, and so provides a means for onanistic gratification. But this is precisely what is puzzling. By what path has the phantasy of strange and unknown boys being beaten (a phantasy which has by this time become sadistic) found its way into the permanent possession of the little girl's libidinal tendencies ?

Nor can we conceal from ourselves that the inter-relations and sequence of the three phases of the beating-phantasy, as well as all its other peculiarities, have so far remained quite unintelligible.

IV

If the analysis is traced through the early period to which the beating-phantasies are referred and from which they are recollected, it shows us the child involved in the agitations of its parental complex.

The affections of the little girl are fixed upon her father, who has probably done all he could to win her love, and in this way has sown the seeds of an attitude of hatred and rivalry towards her mother. This attitude exists side by side with a current of affectionate dependence upon her, and as years go on it may be destined to come into consciousness more and more clearly and forcibly, or to give an impetus to an excessive reaction of devotion to her. But it is not with the girl's relation to her mother that the beating-phantasy is connected. There are other children in the nursery, only a few years older or younger, who are disliked on all sorts of other grounds, but chiefly because the parents' love has to be shared with them, and for this reason they are repulsed with all the wild energy characteristic of the emotional life of those years. If it is a younger brother or sister (as in three of my four cases) it is despised as well as hated ; yet it attracts to itself the share of affection which the blinded parents are always ready to give to the youngest child, and this is a spectacle the sight of which cannot be avoided. One soon learns that being beaten, even if it does not hurt very much, signifies a deprivation of love and a humiliation. And many children who believed themselves securely enthroned in the unshakable affection of their parents have by a single blow been cast down from all the heavens of their imaginary omnipotence. The idea of the father beating this hateful child is therefore an agreeable one, quite apart from whether he has actually been seen doing it. It means : ' My father does not love this other child, *he loves only me* '.

This then is the content and meaning of the

beating-phantasy in its first phase. The phantasy
obviously gratifies the child's jealousy and is dependent
upon the erotic side of its life, but it is also powerfully
reinforced by its egoistic interests. It remains doubtful,
therefore, whether it ought to be described as purely
' sexual ', nor can one venture to call it ' sadistic '.
As is well known, all the signs upon which we are
accustomed to base our distinctions tend to melt as
we come nearer to the source. So perhaps we may
say in words like those of the promise given by the
three Witches to Banquo : ' Not clearly sexual, not
in itself sadistic, but yet the stuff from which both
will later come '. In any case, however, there is no
ground for suspecting that in this first phase the
phantasy is already at the service of an excitement
which involves the genitals and finds its outlet in an
onanistic act.

It is clear that the sexual life of the child has
reached the stage of genital organization, now that its
incestuous love has achieved this premature object-
choice. This can be demonstrated more easily in the
case of boys, but is also indisputable in the case of
girls. Something like a premonition of what are later
to be the final and normal sexual aims governs the
libidinal tendencies of a child ; we may justly wonder
why this should be so, but we may regard it as a proof
of the fact that the genitals have already taken on their
share in the process of excitation. With boys the
wish to beget a child from their mother is never absent,
with girls the wish to have a child by their father is
equally constant ; and this in spite of their being
completely incapable of forming any clear idea of the
means for fulfilling these wishes. The child seems to
be convinced that the genitals have something to do
with the matter, even though in its constant brooding
it may look for the essence of the presumed intimacy
between its parents in relations of another sort, such
as in their sleeping together, micturating in each
other's presence, etc. ; and material of the latter kind

can be more easily apprehended in verbal images than the mystery that is connected with the genitals.

But the time comes when this early blossoming is nipped by the frost. None of these incestuous loves can avoid the fate of repression. They may succumb to it on the occasion of some discoverable external event which leads to disillusionment—such as unexpected slights, the unwelcome birth of a new brother or sister (which is felt as faithlessness), etc. ; or the same thing may happen owing to internal conditions apart from any such events, perhaps simply because their yearning remains unsatisfied too long. It is unquestionably true that the events are not the effective causes, but that these love-affairs are bound to be wrecked sooner or later, though we cannot say upon what. Most probably they pass because their time is over, because the children have entered upon a new phase of development in which they are compelled to recapitulate from the history of mankind the repression of an incestuous object-choice, just as at an earlier stage they were obliged to effect an object-choice of that very sort.[1] Nothing that is unconsciously present as a mental product of the incestuous love-impulses is taken over by consciousness in the new phase ; and whatever has already come into consciousness is expelled from it. At the same time as this process of repression takes place, a sense of guilt appears. This is also of unknown origin, but there is no doubt whatever that it is connected with the incestuous wishes, and that it is justified by the persistence of those wishes in the unconscious.

The phantasy of the period of incestuous love had said : 'He (my father) loves only me, and not the other child, for he is beating it '. The sense of guilt can discover no punishment more severe than the reversal of this triumph : 'No, he does not love you, for he is beating you '. In this way the phantasy of the second phase, that of being beaten by the father, is a

[1] Cf. the part played by Fate in the myth of Oedipus.

direct expression of the sense of guilt, to which the love for the father is now subordinated. The phantasy, therefore, has become masochistic. So far as I know, this is always so ; a sense of guilt is invariably the factor that transforms sadism into masochism. But this is certainly not the whole content of masochism. The sense of guilt cannot have won the field alone ; a share must also fall to the love-impulse. We must remember that we are dealing with children in whom the sadistic component was able for constitutional reasons to develop prematurely and in isolation. We need not abandon this point of view. It is precisely such children who find it particularly easy to hark back to the pregenital, sadistic-anal organization of their sexual life. If the genital organization, when it has scarcely been effected, is met by repression, it not only follows that every mental counterpart of the incestuous love becomes unconscious, or remains so, but there is another result as well : a regressive debasement of the genital organization itself to a lower level. ' My father loves me ' was meant in a genital sense ; owing to the regression it is turned into ' My father is beating me (I am being beaten by my father) '. This being beaten is now a meeting-place between the sense of guilt and sexual love. *It is not only the punishment for the forbidden genital relation, but also the regressive substitute for it*, and from this latter source it derives the libidinal excitation which is from this time forward attached to it, and which finds its outlet in onanistic acts. Here for the first time we have the essence of masochism.

This second phase—the child's phantasy of being itself beaten by its father—remains as a rule unconscious, probably in consequence of the intensity of the repression. I cannot explain why nevertheless in one of my six cases, that of a male, it was consciously remembered. This man, now grown up, had preserved the fact clearly in his memory that he used to employ the idea of being beaten by his mother for the purpose of onanism, though to be sure he soon substituted for his own mother the mothers of his school-fellows or other women who in some way resembled her. It must not be forgotten that when a boy's incestuous phantasy is transformed into the corresponding masochistic one, one more reversal has to take place than in the case of a girl, namely the substitution of passivity for activity ; and this additional degree of distortion may save the phantasy from having to remain unconscious as a result of repression. In this way the sense of guilt would be satisfied by regression instead of by repression. In the female cases the sense of guilt, in itself perhaps more exacting, could be appeased only by a combination of the two.

In two of my four female cases an artistic super-structure of day-dreams, which was of great significance for the life of the person concerned, had grown up over the masochistic beating-phantasy. The function of this superstructure was to make possible a feeling of gratified excitation, even though the onanistic act was abstained from. In one of these cases the content—being beaten by the father—was allowed to venture again into con-sciousness, so long as the subject's own ego was made unrecognizable by a thin disguise. The hero of these stories was invariably beaten (or later only punished, humiliated, etc.) by his father.

I repeat, however, that as a rule the phantasy remains unconscious, and can only be reconstructed in the course of the analysis. This fact perhaps vindicates patients who say they remember that with them onanism made its appearance before the third phase of the beating-phantasy (shortly to be discussed), and that this phase was only a later addition, made perhaps under the impression of scenes at school. Every time we have given credit to these statements we have felt inclined to assume that the onanism was at first under the dominion of unconscious phantasies and that conscious ones were substituted for them later.

We look upon the beating-phantasy in its familiar third phase, which is its final form, as a substitute of this sort.   Here the child who produces the phantasy appears at most as a spectator, while the father persists in the shape of a teacher or some other person in authority. The phantasy, which now resembles that of the first phase, seems to have become sadistic once more.   It appears as though in the phrase, ' My father is beating the other child, he loves only me ', the stress has been shifted back on to the first part after the second part has undergone repression.   But only the form of this phantasy is sadistic ; the gratification which is derived from it is masochistic.   Its significance lies in the fact that it has taken over the libidinal cathexis of the repressed portion and at the same time the sense of guilt which is attached to its content.   All of the many indeterminate children who are being beaten by the teacher are, after all, nothing more than substitutes for the child itself.

We find here for the first time too something like a constant relation of sex among the persons who play a part in the phantasy.   The children who are being beaten are almost invariably boys, in the phantasies of boys just as much as in those of girls.   This characteristic is naturally not to be explained by any rivalry between the sexes, as otherwise of course in the phantasies of boys it would be girls who were being beaten ; and it has nothing to do with the sex of the child who was hated in the first phase ; but it points to a complication in the case of girls.   When they turn away from their incestuous love for their father, with its genital significance, they easily abandon their feminine rôle.   They spur their ' masculinity complex ' (v. Ophuijsen) into activity, and from that time forward only want to be boys.   For that reason the whipping-boys who represent them are boys too.   In both the cases of day-dreaming—one of which almost rose to the level of a work of art—the heroes were always young men ; indeed women used not to come into these creations at all, and only made their first appearance after many years, and then in minor parts.

V

I hope I have brought forward my analytic observations in sufficient detail, and I should only like to add that the six cases I have mentioned so often do not exhaust my material. Like other analysts, I have at my disposal a far larger number of cases which have been investigated less thoroughly. These observations can be made use of along various lines : for elucidating the genesis of the perversions in general and of masochism in particular, and for estimating the part played by difference of sex in the dynamics of neurosis.

The most obvious result of such a discussion is its application to the origin of the perversions. The view which brought into the foreground in this connection the constitutional reinforcement or premature growth of a single sexual component is not shaken, indeed ; but it is seen not to comprise the whole truth. The perversion is no longer an isolated fact in the child's sexual life, but falls into its place among the typical, not to say normal, processes of development which are familiar to us. It is brought into relation with the child's incestuous object-love, with its Oedipus-complex. It first comes into prominence in the sphere of this complex, and after the complex has broken down it remains over, often quite by itself, the inheritor of its charge of libido, and weighed down by the sense of guilt that was attached to it. The abnormal sexual constitution, finally, has shown its strength by forcing the Oedipus-complex into a particular direction, and by compelling it to leave an unusual residue behind.

A perversion in childhood, as is well known, can become the basis for the construction of a perversion having a similar sense and persisting throughout life, one which consumes the subject's whole sexual life. On the other hand the perversion can be broken off and remain in the background of a normal sexual development, from which, however, it continues to withdraw a certain amount of energy. The former case is the one

which was already known before the days of analysis,
but the gulf between the two is almost filled up by the
analytic investigation of fully developed perversions of
this sort. For we find often enough with these perverts
that they too made an attempt at developing normal
sexual activity, usually at the age of puberty. But
their attempt had not enough force in it and was abandoned in the face of the first obstacles which inevitably
arise, whereupon they fell back upon their infantile
fixation once and for all.

It would naturally be important to know whether
the origin of infantile perversions from the Oedipus-
complex can be asserted as a general principle. While
this cannot be decided without further investigation, it
does not seem impossible. When we recall the anamneses which have been obtained in adult cases of perversion we cannot fail to notice that the decisive impression, the 'first experience', of all these perverts,
fetishists, etc., is scarcely ever referred back to a time
earlier than the sixth year. At this time, however, the
supremacy of the Oedipus-complex is already over ;
the experience which is recalled, and which has been
effective in such a puzzling way, may very well have
represented the legacy of that complex. The connections
between the experience and the complex which is by
this time repressed are bound to remain obscure so long
as analysis has not thrown any light on the time before
the first 'pathogenic' impression. So it may be
imagined how little value is to be attached, for instance,
to an assertion that a case of homosexuality is congenital,
when the ground given for this belief is that ever since
his eighth or sixth year the person in question has felt
inclinations only towards his own sex.

If, however, the derivation of perversions from the
Oedipus-complex can be generally established, our estimate of its importance will have gained added strength.
For in our opinion the Oedipus-complex is the actual
nucleus of neuroses, and the infantile sexuality which
culminates in this complex is the true determinant of

neuroses. What remains of the complex in the unconscious represents the disposition to the later development of neuroses in the adult. In this way the beating-
phantasy and other analogous perverse fixations would
also only be precipitates of the Oedipus-complex, scars,
so to say, after the process is completed, just as the
notorious 'sense of inferiority' corresponds to a narcissistic scar of the same sort. In taking this view of
the matter I must express my unreserved agreement
with Marcinowski, who has recently put it forward
most happily.[1] As is well known, this neurotic delusion
of inferiority is only a partial one, and is completely
compatible with the existence of a self-overestimation
derived from other sources. The origin of the Oedipus-
complex itself, and the destiny which compels man,
probably alone among all animals, to begin his sexual
life twice over, first like all other creatures in his early
childhood, and then after a long interruption once more
at the age of puberty—all the problems that are connected with man's 'archaic inheritance'—have been
discussed by me elsewhere, and I have no intention of
going into them in this place.

Little light is thrown upon the genesis of masochism
by our discussion of the beating-phantasy. To begin
with, there seems to be a confirmation of the view that
masochism is not the manifestation of a primary
instinct, but originates from sadism which has been
turned round and directed upon the self, that is to
say, by means of regression from an object to the ego.[2]
Instincts with a passive aim must be taken for granted
as existing, especially among women. But passivity is
not the whole of masochism. The characteristic of
'pain' [Unlust] belongs to it as well,—a bewildering
accompaniment to the gratification of an instinct. The
transformation of sadisr into masochism appears to be
due to the influence of the sense of guilt concerned in

---

[1] Die erotischen Quellen der Minderwertigkeitsgefühle, 1918.
[2] Cf. 'Instincts and their Vicissitudes,' 1918, COLLECTED PAPERS,
vol. iv.

the act of repression. Repression, therefore, is operative here in three ways : it renders the consequences of the genital organization unconscious, it compels that organization itself to regress to the earlier sadistic-anal stage, and it transforms the sadism of this stage into masochism, which is passive and again in a certain sense narcissistic. The second of these three effects is made possible by the weakness of the genital organization, which must be presupposed in these cases. The third becomes necessary because the sense of guilt takes as much objection to sadism as to incestuous object-choice genitally conceived. Again, the analyses do not tell us the origin of the sense of guilt itself. It seems to be brought along by the new phase upon which the child is entering, and if it afterwards persists it seems to correspond to a scar-like formation similar to the sense of inferiority. According to our present orientation in the structure of the ego, which is as yet uncertain, we should assign it to that institution in the mind which sets itself up as a critical conscience over against the rest of the ego, which produces Silberer's functional phenomenon in dreams, and which cuts itself loose from the ego in delusions of observation.

We may note too in passing that the analysis of the infantile perversion dealt with here is also of help in solving an old riddle—one which, it is true, has always troubled those who have not accepted psycho-analysis more than analysts themselves. Yet quite recently even E. Bleuler regarded it as a remarkable and inexplicable fact that neurotics make onanism the central point of their sense of guilt. We have long assumed that this sense of guilt relates to the onanism of early childhood and not to that of puberty, and that in the main it is to be connected not with the act of onanism but with the phantasy which, although unconscious, lies at its root—that is to say, with the Oedipus-complex.

As regards the third and apparently sadistic phase of the beating-phantasy, I have already discussed the

significance that it gains from carrying with it an excitation impelling towards onanism; and I have shown
how it arouses activities of phantasy which on the one
hand continue the phantasy along the same line, and
on the other hand neutralize it by way of compensation. Nevertheless the second phase, the unconscious
and masochistic one, in which the child itself is being
beaten by its father, is incomparably the more important.
Not only because it continues to operate through the
agency of the phase that takes its place; but we can also
detect effects upon the character which are directly
derived from its unconscious setting. People who
harbour phantasies of this kind develop a special sensitiveness and irritability towards anyone whom they
can put among the class of fathers. They allow themselves to be easily offended by a person of this kind,
and in that way (to their own sorrow and cost) bring
about the realization of the imagined situation of being
beaten by their father. I should not be surprised if it
were one day possible to prove that the same phantasy
is the basis of the delusional litigiousness of paranoia.

VI

It would have been quite impossible to give a clear
survey of infantile beating-phantasies if I had not
limited it, except in one or two connections, to the state
of things in women. I will briefly recapitulate the
conclusions. The little girl's beating-phantasy goes
through three phases, of which the first and third are
consciously remembered, the middle one remaining
unconscious. The two conscious phases appear to be
sadistic, whereas the middle and unconscious one is
undoubtedly of a masochistic nature; its content
consists in being beaten by the father, and it carries
with it the libidinal cathexis and the sense of guilt. In
the first and third phantasies the child who is being
beaten is always someone else; in the middle phase it
is only the child itself; in the third phase it is almost

invariably only boys who are being beaten. The person beating is from the first the father, but is later on a substitute taken from the class of fathers. The unconscious phantasy of the middle phase had primarily a genital significance and developed by means of repression and regression out of an incestuous wish to be loved by the father. Another fact, though its connection with the rest does not appear to be close, is that between the second and third phases the girls change their sex, for in the phantasies of the latter phase they turn into boys.

I have not been able to get so far in my knowledge of beating-phantasies among boys, perhaps because my material was unfavourable. I naturally expected to find a complete analogy between the state of things in the case of boys and in that of girls, the mother taking the father's place in the phantasy. This expectation seemed to be fulfilled; for the content of the boy's phantasy which was taken to be the corresponding one was actually his being beaten by his mother (or later on by a substitute for her). But this phantasy, in which the boy's own self was retained as the object, differed from the second phase in girls in that it was able to become conscious. It on this account, however, an attempt was made to draw a parallel between it and the third phase of the girl's phantasy, a new difference was found, for the boy's own person was not replaced by many, unknown, and undetermined children, least of all by many girls. Therefore the expectation of a complete parallelism was mistaken.

My male cases with an infantile beating-phantasy comprised only a few who did not exhibit some other gross injury to their sexual activities, but on the other hand they included a fairly large number of persons who would have to be described as true masochists in the sense of being sexual perverts. They were either people who obtained their sexual satisfaction exclusively from onanism accompanied by masochistic phantasies; or they were people who had succeeded in combining masochism with their genital activity in such a way as to bring about erection and emission, or to carry out normal coitus with the help of masochistic contrivances and under similar conditions. In addition to this there was the rarer case in which a masochist is interfered with in his perverse activities by the appearance of obsessional ideas of unbearable intensity. Now perverts who can obtain satisfaction rarely have occasion to come in search of analysis. But as regards the three classes of masochists that have been mentioned there may be strong motives to induce them to go to an analyst. The masochistic onanist finds that he is absolutely impotent if after all he does attempt coitus with a woman ; and the man who has hitherto effected coitus with the help of a masochistic idea or contrivance may suddenly make the discovery that the alliance which was so convenient for him has broken down, his genital organs no longer reacting to the masochistic stimulus. We are accustomed confidently to promise recovery to psychically impotent patients who come to us for treatment ; but we ought to be more guarded in making this prognosis so long as the dynamics of the disturbance are unknown to us. It comes as a disagreeable surprise if the analysis reveals the cause of the 'merely psychical' impotence to be a typically masochistic attitude, perhaps deeply embedded since infancy.

As regards these masochistic men, however, a discovery is made at this point which warns us not to pursue the analogy between their case and that of women any further at present, but to judge the matter independently. For the fact emerges that in their masochistic phantasies, as well as in the contrivances they adopt for their realization, they invariably transfer themselves into the part of a woman ; that is to say, their masochistic attitude coincides with a *feminine* one. This can easily be demonstrated from details of the phantasies ; but many patients are even aware of it themselves, and give expression to it as a subjective conviction. It makes no difference if in a fanciful embellishment of the masochistic scene they keep up the fiction that a mischievous boy, or page, or apprentice is going to be punished. On the other hand the persons who administer chastisement are always women, both in the phantasies and in the contrivances. This is confusing enough ; and the further question must be asked whether this feminine attitude already forms the basis of the masochistic element in the infantile beating-phantasy.

Let us therefore leave aside consideration of the state of things in cases of adult masochism, which it is so hard to clear up, and turn to the infantile beating-phantasy in the male sex. Analysis of the earliest years of childhood once more allows us to make a surprising discovery in this field. The phantasy which has as its content being beaten by the mother, and which is conscious or can become so, is not a primary one. It possesses a preceding stage which is invariably unconscious and has as its content : ' *I am being beaten by my father* '. This preliminary stage, then, really corresponds to the second phase of the phantasy in the girl. The familiar and conscious phantasy : ' I am being beaten by my mother ', takes the place of the third phase in the girl, in which, as has been mentioned already, unknown boys are the objects that are being beaten. I was not able to demonstrate among boys a preliminary stage of a sadistic nature that could be set beside the first phase of the phantasy in girls, but I will not now express any final disbelief in its existence, for I can readily see the possibility of meeting with more complicated types.

In the male phantasy—as I shall call it briefly, and, I hope, without any risk of being misunderstood—the being beaten also stands for being loved (in a genital sense), though this has been debased to a lower level owing to regression. So the original form of the unconscious male phantasy was not the provisional one that we have hitherto given : ' I am being beaten by my father ', but rather : ' *I am loved by my father* '. The phantasy has been transformed by the processes with which we are familiar into the conscious phantasy : ' *I am being beaten by my mother* '. The boy's beating-phantasy is therefore passive from the very beginning, and is derived from a feminine attitude towards his father. It corresponds with the Oedipus-complex just as the feminine one (that of the girl) does ; only the parallel relation which we expected to find between the two must be given up in favour of a common character of another kind. *In both cases the beating-phantasy has its origin in an incestuous attachment to the father.*

It will help to make matters clearer if at this point I enumerate the other similarities and differences between beating-phantasies in the two sexes. In the case of the girl the unconscious masochistic phantasy starts from the normal Oedipus attitude ; in that of the boy it starts from the inverted attitude, in which the father is taken as the object of love. In the case of the girl there is a first step towards the phantasy (the first phase), in which the beating bears no special significance and is performed upon a person who is viewed with jealous hatred. Both of these features are absent in the case of the boy, but this is precisely a difference which might be removed by more fortunate observation. In her transition to the conscious phantasy which takes the place of the unconscious one the girl retains the figure of her father, and in that way keeps unchanged the sex of the person beating ; but she changes the figure and sex of the person being beaten, so that eventually a man is beating male children. The boy, on the contrary, changes the figure and sex of the person beating, by putting his mother in the place of his father ; but he retains his own figure, with the result that the person beating and the person being beaten are of opposite sexes. In the case of the girl the situation, which was originally masochistic (passive), is transformed into a sadistic one by means of repression, and its sexual quality is effaced. In the case of the boy the situation remains masochistic, and shows a greater resemblance to the original phantasy with its genital significance, since there is a difference of sex between the person beating and the person being beaten. The boy evades his homosexuality by repressing and remodelling his unconscious phantasy ; and the remarkable thing about his later conscious phantasy is that it has for its content a feminine attitude without a homosexual object-choice. By the same process, on the other hand, the girl escapes from the demands of the erotic side of her life altogether. She turns herself in phantasy into a man, without herself becoming active in a masculine way, and is no longer anything but a spectator of the event which takes the place of a sexual act.

We are justified in assuming that no great change is effected by the *repression* of the original unconscious phantasy. Whatever is repressed from consciousness or replaced in it by something else remains intact and potentially operative in the unconscious. The effect of *regression* to an earlier stage of the sexual organization is quite another matter. As regards this we are led to believe that the state of things changes in the unconscious as well : so that in both sexes the masochistic phantasy of being beaten by the father, though not the passive phantasy of being loved by him, lives on in the unconscious after repression has taken place. There are, besides, plenty of indications that the repression has only very incompletely attained its object. The boy, who has tried to escape from a homosexual object-choice, and who has not changed his sex, nevertheless feels like a woman in his conscious phantasies, and endows the women who are beating him with masculine attributes and characteristics. The girl, who has even renounced her sex, and who has upon the whole accomplished a more thoroughgoing work of repression, nevertheless does not become freed from her father ; she does not venture to do the beating herself; and since she has herself become a boy, it is principally boys whom she causes to be beaten.

I am aware that the differences that I have here described between the two sexes in regard to the nature of the beating-phantasy have not been cleared up sufficiently. But I shall not make the attempt to unravel these complications by tracing out their dependence upon other factors, as I do not consider that the material for observation is exhaustive. So far as it goes, however, I should like to make use of it as a test for two theories. These theories stand in opposition to each other, though both of them deal with the relation between repression and sexual character, and each, according to its own view, represents the relation as a very intimate one. I may say at once that I have always regarded both theories as incorrect and misleading.

The first of these theories is anonymous. It was brought to my notice many years ago by a colleague with whom I was at that time on friendly terms. The theory is so attractive on account of its simplicity and comprehensiveness that the only wonder is that it should not hitherto have found its way into the literature of the subject except in a few scattered allusions. It is based upon the fact of the bisexual constitution of human beings, and asserts that the motive force of repression in each individual is a struggle between the two sexual characters. The dominant sex of the person, that which is the more strongly developed, has repressed the mental representation of the subordinated sex into the unconscious. Therefore the nucleus of the unconscious (that is to say, the repressed) is in each human being that side of him which belongs to the opposite sex. Such a theory as this can only have an intelligible meaning if we assume that a person's sex is to be determined by the formation of his genitals ; for otherwise it would not be certain which is the stronger sex of a person, and we should run the risk of reaching from the results of our inquiry the very fact which has to serve as its point of departure. To put the theory briefly : with men, what is unconscious and repressed can be reduced to feminine instinctual impulses; and conversely with women.

The second theory is of more recent origin. It is in agreement with the first one in so far as it too represents the struggle between the two sexes as being the decisive cause of repression. In other respects it comes into conflict with the former theory; moreover, it looks for support to sociological rather than biological sources. According to this theory of the ' masculine protest ', formulated by Alfred Adler, every individual makes efforts not to remain on the inferior ' feminine line of development ' and struggles towards the masculine line of development, from which gratification can alone be derived. Adler makes the masculine protest responsible for the whole formation both of character and of neuroses. Unfortunately he makes so little distinction between the two processes, which certainly have to be kept separate, and sets altogether so little store in general by the fact of repression, that to attempt to apply the doctrine of the masculine protest to repression brings with it the risk of being misunderstood. In my opinion such an attempt could only lead us to infer that the masculine protest, the desire to break away from the feminine line of development, was in every case the motive force of repression. The repressing agency, therefore, would always be a masculine instinctual impulse, and the repressed would be a feminine one. But symptoms would also be the result of a feminine impulse, for we cannot discard the characteristic feature of symptoms —that they are substitutes for the repressed, substitutes that have made their way out in spite of repression.

Now let us take these two theories, which may be said to have in common a sexualization of the process of repression, and test them by applying them to the example of the beating-phantasies which we have been studying. The original phantasy, ' I am being beaten by my father ', corresponds, in the case of the boy, to a feminine attitude, and is therefore an expression of that part of his disposition which belongs to the opposite sex. If this part of him undergoes repression, the first theory seems shown to be correct ; for this theory set it up as a rule that what belongs to the opposite sex is identical with the repressed. It scarcely answers to our expectations, it is true, when we find that the conscious phantasy, which arises after repression has been accomplished, nevertheless exhibits the feminine attitude once more, though this time directed towards the mother. But we will not go into these doubtful points, when the whole question can be so quickly decided. There can be no doubt that the original phantasy in the case of the girl, ' I am being beaten (*i.e.* I am loved) by my father ', represents a feminine attitude, and corresponds to her dominant and manifest sex ; according to the theory, therefore, it ought to escape repression, and there would be no need for its becoming unconscious. But as a matter of fact it does become unconscious, and is replaced by a conscious phantasy which disavows the girl's manifest sexual character. The theory is therefore useless as an explanation of beating-phantasies, and is contradicted by the facts. It might be objected that it is precisely in unmanly boys and unwomanly girls that these beating-phantasies appeared and went through these vicissitudes ; or that it was a trait of femininity in the boy and of masculinity in the girl which must be made responsible—that is, for the production of a passive phantasy in the boy, and its repression in the girl. We should be inclined to agree with this view, but it would be none the less impossible to defend the supposed relation between manifest sexual character and the choice of what is destined for repression. In the last resort we can only see that both in male and female individuals masculine as well as feminine instinctual impulses are found, and that each can equally well undergo repression and so become unconscious.

The theory of the masculine protest seems to

maintain its ground very much better on being tested in regard to the beating-phantasies. In the case of both boys and girls the beating-phantasy corresponds with a feminine attitude—one, that is, in which the individual is lingering upon the feminine line of development—and both sexes hasten to get free from this attitude by repressing the phantasy. Nevertheless, it seems to be only with the girl that the masculine protest is attended with complete success, and in that instance, indeed, an ideal example is to be found of the operation of the masculine protest. With the boy the result is not entirely satisfactory ; the feminine line of development is not given up, and the boy is certainly not ' on the top ' in his conscious masochistic phantasy. It would therefore agree with the expectations derived from the theory if we were to recognize that this phantasy was a symptom which had come into existence through the failure of the masculine protest. It is a disturbing fact, to be sure, that the girl's phantasy, which owes its origin to the forces of repression, should also have the value and meaning of a symptom. In this instance, where the masculine protest has completely achieved its object, surely the determining condition for the formation of a symptom must be absent.

Before we are led by this difficulty to a suspicion that the whole conception of the masculine protest is inadequate to meet the problem of neuroses and perversions, and that its application to them is unfruitful, we will for a moment leave the passive beating-phantasies and turn our attention to other instinctual manifestations of infantile sexual life—manifestations which have equally undergone repression. No one can doubt that there are also wishes and phantasies which keep to the masculine line of development from their very nature, and which are the expression of masculine instinctual impulses—sadistic tendencies, for instance, or a boy's lustful feelings towards his mother arising out of the normal Oedipus-complex. It is no less certain that these impulses are also overtaken by repression. If the masculine protest is to be taken as having satisfactorily explained the repression of passive phantasies (which later become masochistic), then it becomes for that very reason totally inapplicable to the opposite case of active phantasies. That is to say, the doctrine of the masculine protest is altogether incompatible with the fact of repression. Unless we are prepared to throw away all that has been acquired in psychology since Breuer's first cathartic treatment and through its agency, we cannot expect that the principle of the masculine protest will acquire any significance in the elucidation of the neuroses and perversions.

The theory of psycho-analysis (a theory based upon observation) holds firmly to the view that the motive forces of repression must not be sexualized. Man's archaic inheritance forms the nucleus of the unconscious mind ; and whatever part of that inheritance has to be left behind in the advance to later phases of development, because it is useless or incompatible with what is new and harmful to it, falls a victim to the process of repression. This selection is made more successfully with one group of instincts than with the other. In virtue of special circumstances which have often been pointed out already, the latter group, that of the sexual instincts, are able to defeat the intentions of repression, and to enforce their representation by substitute-formations of a disturbing kind. For this reason infantile sexuality, which is held under repression, acts as the chief motive force in the formation of symptoms ; and the essential part of its content, the Oedipus-complex, is the nuclear complex of neuroses. I hope that in this paper I have raised an expectation that the sexual aberrations of childhood, as well as those of mature life, are ramifications of the same complex.

XVIII

THE PSYCHOGENESIS OF A CASE OF HOMOSEXUALITY IN A WOMAN [1]

(1920)

I

HOMOSEXUALITY in women, which is certainly not less common than in men, although much less glaring, has not only been ignored by the law, but has also been neglected by psycho-analytic research. The narration of a single case, not too pronounced in type, in which it was possible to trace its origin and development in the mind with complete certainty and almost without a gap may, therefore, have a certain claim to attention. If this presentation of it furnishes only the most general outlines of the various events concerned and of the conclusions reached from a study of the case, while suppressing all the characteristic details on which the interpretation is founded, this limitation is easily to be explained by the medical discretion necessary in discussing a recent case.

A beautiful and clever girl of eighteen, belonging to a family of good standing, had aroused displeasure and concern in her parents by the devoted adoration with which she pursued a certain lady ' in society ' who was about ten years older than herself. The parents asserted that, in spite of her distinguished name, this lady was nothing but a *cocotte*. It was said to be well known that she lived with a married woman as her friend, having intimate relations with her, while at the same time she carried on promiscuous affairs with a number of men. The girl did not contradict

---

[1] First published in *Zeitschrift*, Bd. VI., 1920 ; reprinted in *Sammlung*, Fünfte Folge. [Translated by Barbara Low and R. Gabler.]

these evil reports, but neither did she allow them to
interfere with her worship of the lady, although she
herself was by no means lacking in a sense of decency
and propriety. No prohibitions and no supervision
hindered the girl from seizing every one of her rare
opportunities of being together with her beloved, of
ascertaining all her habits, of waiting for her for hours
outside her door or at a tram-halt, of sending her gifts
of flowers, and so on. It was evident that this one
interest had swallowed up all others in the girl's mind.
She did not trouble herself any further with educational
studies, thought nothing of social functions or girlish
pleasures, and kept up relations only with a few girl
friends who could help her in the matter or serve as
confidantes. The parents could not say to what
lengths their daughter had gone in her relations with the
questionable lady, whether the limits of devoted admiration had already been exceeded or not. They had never
remarked in their daughter any interest in young men,
nor pleasure in their attentions, while, on the other
hand, they were sure that her present attachment to a
woman was only a continuation, in a more marked
degree, of a feeling she had displayed of recent years
for other members of her own sex which had already
aroused her father's suspicion and anger.

There were two details of her behaviour, in apparent
contrast with each other, that most especially vexed
her parents. On the one hand, she did not scruple to
appear in the most frequented streets in the company
of her questionable friend, being thus quite neglectful
of her own reputation ; while, on the other hand, she
disdained no means of deception, no excuses and no
lies that would make meetings with her possible and
cover them. She thus showed herself too brazen in
one respect and full of deceitfulness in the other. One
day it happened, indeed, as was sooner or later inevitable in the circumstances, that the father met his
daughter in the company of the lady. He passed
them by with an angry glance which boded no good.

Immediately after, the girl rushed off and flung herself
over a wall down the side of a cutting on to a railway
line. She paid for this undoubtedly serious attempt at
suicide with a considerable time on her back in bed,
though fortunately little permanent damage was done.
After her recovery she found it easier to get her own
way than before. The parents did not dare to oppose
her with so much determination, and the lady, who up
till then had received her advances coldly, was moved
by such an unmistakable proof of serious passion and
began to treat her in a more friendly manner.

About six months after this episode the parents
sought medical advice and entrusted the physician
with the task of bringing their daughter back to a
normal state of mind. The girl's attempted suicide
had evidently shown them that the instruments of
domestic discipline were powerless to overcome the
existing disorder. Before going further it will be
desirable, however, to deal separately with the attitude
of her father and of her mother to the matter. The
father was an earnest, worthy man, at bottom very
tender-hearted, but he had to some extent estranged
his children by the sternness he had adopted towards
them. His treatment of his only daughter was too
much influenced by consideration for his wife. When
he first came to know of his daughter's homosexual
tendencies he flared up in rage and tried to suppress
them by threatening her ; at that time perhaps he
hesitated between different, though equally painful,
views—regarding her either as vicious, as degenerate,
or as mentally afflicted. Even after the attempted
suicide he did not achieve the lofty resignation shown
by one of our medical colleagues who remarked of a
similar irregularity in his own family, ' It is just a misfortune like any other '. There was something about
his daughter's homosexuality that aroused the deepest
bitterness in him, and he was determined to combat it
with all the means in his power ; the low estimation
in which psycho-analysis is so generally held in Vienna

did not prevent him from turning to it for help. If this way failed he still had in reserve his strongest counter-measure ; a speedy marriage was to awaken the natural instincts of the girl and stifle her unnatural tendencies. The mother's attitude towards the girl was not so easy to grasp. She was still a youngish woman, who was evidently unwilling to relinquish her own claim to find favour by means of her beauty. All that was clear was that she did not take her daughter's passion so tragically as did the father, nor was she so incensed at it. She had even for a long time enjoyed her daughter's confidence concerning the love-affair, and her opposition to it seemed to have been aroused mainly by the harmful publicity with which the girl displayed her feelings. She had herself suffered for some years from neurotic troubles and enjoyed a great deal of consideration from her husband ; she was quite unfair in her treatment of her children, decidedly harsh towards her daughter and over-indulgent to her three sons, the youngest of whom had been born after a long interval and was then not yet three years old. It was not easy to ascertain anything more definite about her character, for, owing to motives that will only later become intelligible, the patient was always reserved in what she said about her mother, whereas in regard to her father she showed no feeling of the kind.

To a physician who was to undertake psycho-analytic treatment of the girl there were many grounds for a feeling of discomfort. The situation he had to deal with was not the one that analysis demands, in which alone it can demonstrate its effectiveness. As is well known, the ideal situation for analysis is when someone who is otherwise master of himself is suffering from an inner conflict which he is unable to resolve alone, so that he brings his trouble to the analyst and begs for his help. The physician then works hand in hand with one part of the personality which is divided against itself, against the other partner in the conflict. Any situation but this is more or less unfavourable for psycho-analysis and adds fresh difficulties to those already present. Situations like that of a proprietor who orders an architect to build him a villa according to his own tastes and desires, or of a pious donor who commissions an artist to paint a picture of saints, in the corner of which is to be a portrait of himself worshipping, are fundamentally incompatible with the conditions of psycho-analysis. It constantly happens, to be sure, that a husband informs the physician as follows, ' My wife suffers from nerves, so that she gets on badly with me ; please cure her, so that we may lead a happy married life again '. But often enough it turns out that such a request is impossible to fulfil, *i.e.* that the physician cannot bring about the result for which the husband sought the treatment. As soon as the wife is freed from her neurotic inhibitions she sets about dissolving the marriage, for her neurosis was the sole condition under which maintenance of the marriage was possible. Or else parents expect one to cure their nervous and unruly child. By a healthy child they mean one who never places his parents in difficulties, but only gives them pleasure. The physician may succeed in curing the child, but after that it goes its own way all the more decidedly, and the parents are now far more dissatisfied than before. In short, it is not a matter of indifference whether someone comes to analysis of his own accord or because he is brought to it, whether he himself desires to be changed, or only his relatives, who love him (or who might be expected to love him), desire this for him.

Further unfavourable features in the present case were the facts that the girl was not in any way ill— she did not suffer from anything in herself, nor did she complain of her condition—and that the task to be carried out did not consist in resolving a neurotic conflict but in converting one variety of the genital organization of sexuality into the other. The removal of genital inversion or homosexuality is in my experience never an easy matter. On the contrary, I have found success possible only under specially favourable circumstances, and even then the success essentially consisted in being able to open to those who are restricted homosexually the way to the opposite sex, which had been till then barred, thus restoring to them full bisexual functions. After that it lay with themselves to choose whether they wished to abandon the other way that is banned by society, and in individual cases they have done so. One must remember that normal sexuality also depends upon a restriction in the choice of object ; in general, to undertake to convert a fully developed homosexual into a heterosexual is not much more promising than to do the reverse, only that for good practical reasons the latter is never attempted.

In actual numbers the successes achieved by psychoanalytic treatment of the various forms of homosexuality, which, to be sure, are manifold, are not very striking. As a rule the homosexual is not able to give up the object of his pleasure, and one cannot convince him that if he changed to the other object he would find again the pleasure that he has renounced. If he comes to be treated at all, it is mostly through the pressure of external motives, such as the social disadvantages and dangers attaching to his choice of object, and such components of the instinct of self-preservation prove themselves too weak in the struggle against the sexual impulses. One then soon discovers his secret plan, namely, to obtain from the striking failure of his attempt the feeling of satisfaction that he has done everything possible against his abnormality, to which he can now resign himself with an easy conscience. The case is somewhat different when consideration for beloved parents and relatives has been the motive for his attempt to be cured. Then there really are libidinal tendencies present which may put forth energies opposed to the homosexual choice of object, though their strength is rarely sufficient. It is only where the homosexual fixation has not yet become strong enough, or where there are considerable rudiments and vestiges of a heterosexual choice of object, *i.e.* in a still oscillating or in a definitely bisexual organization, that one may make a more favourable prognosis for psycho-analytic therapy.

For these reasons I declined altogether holding out to the parents any prospect of their wish being fulfilled. I merely said I was prepared to study the girl carefully for a few weeks or months, so as then to be able to pronounce how far a continuation of the analysis might influence her. In quite a number of cases, indeed, the analysis divides itself into two clearly distinguishable stages : in the first, the physician procures from the patient the necessary information, makes him familiar with the premises and postulates of psycho-analysis, and unfolds to him the reconstruction of the genesis of his disorder as deduced from the material brought up in the analysis. In the second stage the patient himself lays hold of the material put before him, works on it, recollects what he can of the apparently repressed memories, and behaves as if he were living the rest over again. In this way he can confirm, supplement, and correct the inferences made by the physician. It is only during this work that he experiences, through over-coming resistances, the inner change aimed at, and acquires for himself the convictions that make him independent of the physician's authority. These two stages in the course of the analytic treatment are not always sharply divided from each other ; this can only happen when the resistance maintains certain conditions. But when this is so, one may institute a comparison with two stages of a journey. The first comprises all the necessary preparations, to-day so complicated and hard to effect, before, ticket in hand, one can at last go on to the platform and secure a seat in the train. One then has the right, and the possibility, of travelling into a distant country, but after all these preliminary exertions one is not yet there—indeed, one is not a single mile nearer to one's goal. For this to happen one has to make the journey itself from one station to the other, and this part of the performance may well be compared with the second stage in the analysis.

The analysis of the patient I am discussing took this course of two stages, but it was not continued beyond the beginning of the second stage. A special constellation of the resistance made it possible, never-theless, to gain full confirmation of my inferences, and to obtain an adequate insight on broad lines into the way in which her inversion had developed. But before relating the findings of the analysis I must deal with a few points which have either been touched upon already by myself or which will have roused special interest in the reader.

I had made the prognosis partly dependent on how far the girl had succeeded in satisfying her passion. The information I gleaned during the analysis seemed favourable in this respect. With none of the objects of her adoration had the patient enjoyed anything beyond a few kisses and embraces ; her genital chastity, if one may use such a phrase, had remained intact. As for the lady who led a double life, and who had roused the girl's most recent and by far her strongest emotions, she had always treated her coldly and had never allowed any greater favour than kissing her hand. Probably the girl was making a virtue of necessity when she kept insisting on the purity of her love and her physical repulsion against the idea of any sexual intercourse. But perhaps she was not altogether wrong when she vaunted of her wonderful beloved that, aristocrat as she was, forced into her present position only by adverse family circumstances, she had preserved, in spite of her situation, a great deal of nobility. For the lady used to recommend the girl every time they met to withdraw her affection from herself and from women in general, and she had persistently rejected the girl's advances up to the time of the attempted suicide.

A second point, which I at once tried to investigate, concerned any possible motives in the girl herself

which might serve to support a psycho-analytic treatment. She did not try to deceive me by saying that
she felt any urgent need to be freed from her homosexuality. On the contrary, she said she could not
conceive of any other way of being in love, but she
added that for her parents' sake she would honestly
help in the therapeutic endeavour, for it pained her
very much to be the cause of so much grief to them.
I had to take this as a propitious sign to begin with ;
I could not divine the unconscious affective attitude
that lay behind it. What came to light later in this
connection decisively influenced the course taken by
the analysis and determined its premature conclusion.

Readers unversed in psycho-analysis will long have
been awaiting an answer to two other questions. Did
this homosexual girl show physical characteristics
plainly belonging to the opposite sex, and did the
case prove to be one of congenital or acquired (later
developed) homosexuality ?

I am aware of the importance attaching to the first
of these questions. Only one should not exaggerate
it and obscure in its favour the fact that sporadic
secondary characteristics of the opposite sex are very
often present in normal individuals, and that well-
marked physical characteristics of the opposite sex
may be found in persons whose choice of object has
undergone no change in the direction of inversion ; in
other words, that in both sexes *the degree of physical
hermaphroditism is to a great extent independent of the
psychical hermaphroditism*. In modification of this
statement it must be added that this independence is
more evident in men than women, where bodily and
mental traits belonging to the opposite sex are apt to
coincide in their incidence. Still I am not in a position
to give a satisfactory answer to the first of our questions
about my patient ; the psycho-analyst customarily
forgoes thorough bodily examination of his patients
in certain cases. Certainly there was no obvious
deviation from the feminine physical type, nor any

menstrual disturbance. The beautiful and well-developed girl had, it is true, her father's tall figure, and her facial features were sharp rather than soft and girlish, traits which might be regarded as indicating a physical masculinity. Some of her intellectual attributes also could be connected with masculinity : for instance, her acuteness of comprehension and her lucid objectivity, in so far as she was not dominated by her passion ; though these distinctions are conventional rather than scientific. What is certainly of greater importance is that in her behaviour towards her love-object she had throughout assumed the masculine part : that is to say, she displayed the humility and the sublime over-estimation of the sexual object so characteristic of the male lover, the renunciation of all narcissistic satisfaction, and the preference for being lover rather than beloved. She had thus not only chosen a feminine love-object, but had also developed a masculine attitude towards this object.

The second question, whether this was a case of inherited or acquired homosexuality, will be answered by the whole history of the patient's abnormality and its development. The study of this will show how fruitless and inappropriate this question is.

II

After an introduction which digresses in so many directions, the sexual history of the case under consideration can be presented quite concisely. In childhood the girl had passed through the normal attitude characteristic of the feminine Oedipus-complex[1] in a way that was not at all remarkable, and had later also begun to substitute for her father a brother slightly older than herself. She did not remember any sexual traumata in early life, nor were any discovered by

---

[1] I do not see any progress or advantage in the introduction of the term ' Electra-complex ', and do not advocate its use.

the analysis. Comparison of her brother's genital organs and her own, which took place about the beginning of the latency period (at five years old or perhaps a little earlier), left a strong impression on her and had far-reaching after-effects. There were only slight hints pointing to infantile onanism, or else the analysis did not go deep enough to throw light on this point. The birth of a second brother when she was between five and six years old left no special influence upon her development. During the pre-pubertal years at school she gradually became acquainted with the facts of sex, and she received this knowledge with mixed feelings of fascination and frightened aversion, in a way which may be called normal and was not exaggerated in degree. This amount of information about her seems meagre enough, nor can I guarantee that it is complete. It may be that the history of her youth was much richer in experiences ; I do not know. As I have already said, the analysis was broken off after a short time, and therefore yielded an anamnesis not much more reliable than the other anamneses of homosexuals, which there is good cause to question. Further, the girl had never been neurotic, and came to the analysis without even one hysterical symptom, so that opportunities for investigating the history of her childhood did not present themselves so readily as usual.

At the age of thirteen to fourteen she displayed a tender and, according to general opinion, exaggeratedly strong affection for a small boy, not quite three years old, whom she used to see regularly in a playground in one of the parks. She took to the child so warmly that in consequence a permanent friendship grew up between herself and his parents. One may infer from this episode that at that time she was possessed of a strong desire to be a mother herself and to have a child. However, after a short time she grew indifferent to the boy, and began to take an interest in mature, but still youthful, women ; the manifestations of this in her soon led her father to administer a mortifying chastisement to her.

It was established beyond all doubt that this change occurred simultaneously with a certain event in the family, and one may therefore look to this for some explanation of the change. Before it happened, her libido was focussed on motherhood, while afterwards she became a homosexual attracted to mature women, and has remained so ever since. The event which is so significant for our understanding of the case was a new pregnancy of her mother's, and the birth of a third brother when she was about sixteen.

The network of causes and effects that I shall now proceed to lay bare is not a product of my gift for combination ; it is based on such trustworthy analytic evidence that I can claim objective validity for it ; it was in particular a series of inter-related dreams, easy of interpretation, that proved decisive in this respect.

The analysis revealed beyond all shadow of doubt that the beloved lady was a substitute for—the mother. It is true that she herself was not a mother, but then she was not the girl's first love. The first objects of her affection after the birth of her youngest brother were really mothers, women between thirty and thirty-five whom she had met with their children during summer holidays or in the family circle of acquaintances in town. Motherhood as a ' condition of love ' was later on given up, because it was difficult to combine in real life with another one, which grew more and more important. The specially intensive bond with her latest love, the ' Lady ', had still another basis which the girl discovered quite easily one day. On account of her slender figure, regular beauty, and off-hand manner, the lady reminded her of her own brother, a little older than herself. Her latest choice corresponded, therefore, not only with her feminine but also with her masculine ideal ; it combined gratification of the homosexual tendency with that of the heterosexual one. It is well known that analysis of male homosexuals has in numerous cases revealed the same combination, which should warn us not to form too simple a conception of the nature and genesis of inversion, and to keep in mind the extensive influence of the bisexuality of mankind.[1]

But how are we to understand the fact that it was just the birth of a child who came late in the family, at a time when the girl herself was already mature and had strong wishes of her own, that moved her to bestow her passionate tenderness upon her who gave birth to this child, *i.e.* her own mother, and to express that feeling towards a substitute for her mother ? From all that we know we should have expected just the opposite. In such circumstances mothers with daughters of about a marriageable age usually feel embarrassed in regard to them, while the daughters are apt to feel for their mothers a mixture of compassion, contempt and envy which does nothing to increase their tenderness for them. The girl we are considering, however, had altogether little cause to feel affection for her mother. The latter, still youthful herself, saw in her rapidly developing daughter an inconvenient competitor ; she favoured the sons at her expense, limited her independence as much as possible, and kept an especially strict watch against any close relation between the girl and her father. A yearning from the beginning for a kinder mother would, therefore, have been quite intelligible, but why it should have flamed up just then, and in the form of a consuming passion, is not comprehensible.

The explanation is as follows : The girl was just experiencing the revival of the infantile Oedipus-complex at puberty when she suffered a great disappointment. She became keenly conscious of the wish to have a child, and a male one ; that it was her father's child and his image that she desired, her consciousness was not allowed to know. And then— it was not she who bore the child, but the unconsciously

[1] Cf. J. Sadger, *Jahresbericht über sexuelle Perversionen.*

hated rival, her mother. Furiously resentful and embittered, she turned away from her father, and from men altogether. After this first great reverse she forswore her womanhood and sought another goal for her libido.

In doing so she behaved just as many men do who after a first painful experience turn their backs for ever upon the faithless female sex and become woman-haters. It is related of one of the most attractive and unfortunate princes of our time that he became a homosexual because the lady he was engaged to marry betrayed him with a stranger. I do not know whether this is true historically, but much psychological truth lies behind the rumour. In all of us, throughout life, the libido normally oscillates between male and female objects ; the bachelor gives up his men friends when he marries, and returns to club-life when married life has lost its savour. Naturally, when the swing-over is fundamental and final, we suspect some special factor which has definitely favoured one side or the other, and which perhaps only waited for the appropriate moment in order to turn the choice of object finally in its direction.

After her disappointment, therefore, this girl had entirely repudiated her wish for a child, the love of a man, and womanhood altogether. Now it is evident that at this point the developments open to her were very manifold ; what actually happened was the most extreme one possible. She changed into a man, and took her mother in place of her father as her love-object.[1] Her relation to her mother had certainly been ambivalent from the beginning, and it proved easy to revive her earlier love for her mother and with its help to bring about an over-compensation for her current hostility towards her. Since there was little to be done with the

---

[1] It is by no means rare for a love-relation to be broken off by means of a process of identification on the part of the lover with the loved object, a process equivalent to a kind of regression to narcissism. After this has been accomplished, it is easy in making a fresh choice of object to direct the libido to a member of the sex opposite to that of the earlier choice.

real mother, there arose from the conversion of feeling described the search for a mother-substitute to whom she could become passionately attached.[1]

In her actual relations with her mother there was a practical motive furthering the change of feeling which might be called an ' advantage through illness '. The mother herself still attached great value to the attentions and the admiration of men. If, then, the girl became homosexual and left men to her mother (in other words, ' retired in favour of ' the mother), she removed something which had hitherto been partly responsible for her mother's disfavour.[2]

---

[1] The displacements of the libido here described are doubtless familiar to every analyst from investigation of the anamneses of neurotics. With the latter, however, they occur in early childhood, at the beginning of the love-life ; with our patient, who was in no way neurotic, they took place in the first years following puberty, though, by the way, they were just as completely unconscious. Perhaps one day this temporal factor may turn out to be of great importance.

[2] As ' retiring in favour of someone else ' has not previously been mentioned among the causes of homosexuality, or in the mechanism of libido-fixation in general, I will adduce here another analytical observation of the same kind which has a special feature of interest. I once knew two twin brothers, both of whom were endowed with strong libidinal impulses. One of them was very successful with women, and had innumerable affairs with women and girls. The other went the same way at first, but it became unpleasant for him to be trespassing on his brother's beat, and, owing to the likeness between them, to be mistaken for him on intimate occasions, so he got out of the difficulty by becoming homosexual. He left the women to his brother, and thus ' retired ' in his favour. Another time I treated a young man, an artist, unmistakably bisexual in disposition, in whom the homosexual trend had come to the fore simultaneously with a disturbance in his work. He fled from both women and work together. The analysis, which was able to bring him back to both, showed that the fear of the father was the most powerful psychic motive for both the disturbances, which were really renunciations. In his imagination all women belonged to the father, and he sought refuge in men out of submission, so as to ' retire from ' the conflict in favour of the father. Such a motivation of the homosexual object-choice must be by no means uncommon ; in the primeval ages of the human race all women presumably belonged to the father and head of the primal horde.

Among brothers and sisters who are not twins this ' retirement ' plays a great part in other spheres as well as in that of the love-choice. For example, an elder brother studies music and is admired for it ; the younger, far more gifted musically, soon gives up his own musical studies, in spite of his longing, and cannot be persuaded to touch an instrument again. This is one example of a very frequent occurrence, and investigation of the motives leading to this ' retirement ' rather than to open rivalry discloses very complicated conditions in the mind.

The attitude of the libido thus adopted was greatly reinforced as soon as the girl perceived how much it displeased her father.   Once she had been punished for an over-affectionate overture made to a woman she realized how she could wound her father and take revenge on him.   Henceforth she remained homosexual out of defiance against her father.   Nor did she scruple to lie to him and to deceive him in every way.   Towards her mother, indeed, she was only so far deceitful as was necessary to prevent her father from knowing things.   I had the impression that her behaviour followed the principle of the talion : ' Since you have betrayed me, you must put up with my betraying you '.   Nor can I come to any other conclusion about the striking lack of caution displayed by this otherwise ingenious and clever girl.   She *wanted* her father to know occasionally of her intercourse with the lady, otherwise she would be deprived of satisfaction of her keenest desire—namely, revenge.   So she saw to this by showing herself openly in the company of her adored one, by walking with her in the streets near her father's place of business, and the like. This maladroitness was by no means unintentional. It was remarkable, by the way, that both parents behaved as though they understood the secret psychology of their daughter.   The mother was tolerant, as though she appreciated the favour of her daughter's 'retirement' from the arena ; the father was furious, as though he realized the deliberate revenge directed against himself.

The girl's inversion, however, received its final reinforcement when she found in her ' Lady ' an object which promised to satisfy not only her homosexual tendency, but also that part of her heterosexual libido still attached to her brother.

III

Consecutive presentation is not a very adequate means of describing complicated mental processes going on in different layers of the mind.   I am therefore obliged to pause in the discussion of the case and treat more fully and deeply some of the points brought forward above.

I mentioned the fact that in her behaviour to her adored lady the girl had adopted the characteristic masculine type of love. Her humility and her tender lack of pretensions, ' *che poco spera e nulla chiede* ', her bliss when she was allowed to accompany the lady a little way and to kiss her hand on parting, her joy when she heard her praised as beautiful—while any recognition of her own beauty by another person meant nothing at all to her—her pilgrimages to places once visited by the loved one, the oblivion of all more sensual wishes : all these little traits in her resembled the first passionate adoration of a youth for a celebrated actress whom he regards as far above him, to whom he scarcely dares lift his bashful eyes. The correspondence with the ' type of object-choice in men ' that I have described elsewhere, whose special features I traced to the attachment to the mother,[1] held good even to the smallest details. It may seem remarkable that she was not in the least repelled by the evil reputation of her beloved, although her own observations sufficiently confirmed the truth of such rumours. She was after all a well-brought-up and modest girl, who had avoided sexual adventures for herself, and who regarded coarsely sensual gratification as unæsthetic. But already her first passions had been for women who were not celebrated for specially strict propriety. The first protest her father made against her love-choice had been evoked by the pertinacity with which she sought the company of a cinematograph actress at a summer resort. Moreover, in all these affairs it had never been a question of women who had any reputation for homosexuality, and who might, therefore, have offered her some prospect of homosexual gratification ; on the contrary, she illogically courted women who were coquettes in the ordinary sense of the word, and she rejected without hesitation the willing

[1] COLLECTED PAPERS, vol. iv.

advances made by a homosexual friend of her own age.
The bad reputation of her 'Lady', however, was
positively a 'condition of love' for her, and all that
is enigmatical in this attitude vanishes when we remember that in the case of the masculine type of object-choice
derived from the mother it is also an essential condition
that the loved object should be in some way or other
'of bad repute' sexually, one who really may be called
a 'light woman'. When the girl learnt later on how
far her adored lady deserved to be called by this title
and that she lived simply by giving her bodily favours,
her reaction took the form of great compassion and of
phantasies and plans for 'rescuing' her beloved from
these ignoble circumstances. We have been struck by
the same endeavours to 'rescue' in the men of the
type referred to above, and in my description of it
I have tried to give the analytical derivation of this
tendency.

We are led into quite another realm of explanation
by the analysis of the attempt at suicide, which I must
regard as seriously intended, and which, by the way,
considerably improved her position both with her
parents and with the lady she loved. She went for a
walk with her one day in a part of the town and at an
hour at which she was not unlikely to meet her father
on his way from his office. So it turned out. Her
father passed them in the street and cast a furious look
at her and her companion, whom he had by that time
come to know. A few moments later she flung herself
on to the railway cutting. Now the explanation she
gave of the immediate reasons determining her resolution
sounded quite plausible. She had confessed to the lady
that the man who had given them such an irate glance
was her father, and that he had absolutely forbidden
their friendship. The lady became incensed at this and
ordered the girl to leave her then and there, and never
again to wait for her or to address her—the affair must
now come to an end. In her despair at having thus
lost her loved one for ever, she wanted to put an end to

herself. The analysis, however, was able to disclose another and deeper interpretation behind the one she gave, which was confirmed by the evidence of her own dreams. The attempted suicide was, as might have been expected, determined by two other motives besides the one she gave : it was a ' punishment fulfilment' (self-punishment), and a wish-fulfilment. As a wish-fulfilment it signified the attainment of the very wish which, when frustrated, had driven her into homo-sexuality—namely, the wish to have a child by her father, for now she ' fell ' [1] through her father's fault.[2] The fact that at this moment the lady had spoken to the same effect as the father, and had uttered the same prohibition, forms the connecting link between this deeper interpretation and the superficial one of which the girl herself was conscious. From the point of view of self-punishment the girl's action shows us that she had developed in her unconscious strong death-wishes against one or other of her parents : perhaps against her father, out of revenge for impeding her love, but, more likely, also against her mother when she was pregnant with the little brother. For analysis has explained the enigma of suicide in the following way : probably no one finds the mental energy required to kill himself unless, in the first place, he is in doing this at the same time killing an object with whom he has identified himself, and, in the second place, is turning against himself a death-wish which had been directed against someone else. Nor need the regular discovery of these uncon-scious death-wishes in those who have attempted suicide surprise us as strange (any more than it need make an impression as confirming our deductions), since the unconscious of all human beings is full enough of such

---

[1] [In the text there is a play on the word *niederkommen*, which means both ' to fall ' and ' to be delivered of a child '. There is also in English a colloquial use of the verb ' to fall ', meaning pregnancy or childbirth.—Trans.]

[2] That the various means of suicide can represent sexual wish-fulfilments has long been known to all analysts. (To poison oneself = to become pregnant ; to drown = to bear a child ; to throw oneself from a height = to be delivered of a child.)

death-wishes, even against those we love.[1] The girl's identification of herself with her mother, who ought to have died at the birth of the child denied to herself, makes this ' punishment-fulfilment ' itself again into a ' wish-fulfilment '. Lastly, a discovery that several quite different motives, all of great strength, must have co-operated to make such a deed possible is only in accord with what we should expect.

In the girl's account of her conscious motives the father did not figure at all ; there was not even any mention of fear of his anger. In the motivation laid bare by the analysis he played the principal part. Her relation to her father had this same decisive importance for the course and outcome of the analytic treatment, or rather, analytic exploration. Behind her pretended consideration for her parents, for whose sake she had been willing to make the attempt to be transformed, lay concealed her attitude of defiance and revenge against her father which held her fast to her homosexuality. Secure under this cover, the resistance allowed a considerable degree of freedom to the analytic investigation. The analysis went forward almost without any signs of resistance, the patient participating actively with her intellect, though absolutely tranquil emotionally. Once when I expounded to her a specially important part of the theory, one touching her nearly, she replied in an inimitable tone, ' How very interesting ', as though she were a *grande dame* being taken over a museum and glancing through her lorgnon at objects to which she was completely indifferent. The impression one had of her analysis was not unlike that of an hypnotic treatment, where the resistance has in the same way withdrawn to a certain limit, beyond which it then proves to be unconquerable. The resistance very often pursues similar tactics—Russian tactics, as they might be called [2]—in cases of the obsessional neurosis,

---

[1] Cf. ' Reflections upon War and Death ', COLLECTED PAPERS, vol. iv.

[2] [A reference to the European War, 1914-18.—Trans.]

which for this reason yield the clearest results for a time
and permit of a penetrating inspection of the causation
of the symptoms. One begins to wonder how it is that
such marked progress in analytic understanding can be
unaccompanied by even the slightest change in the
patient's compulsions and inhibitions, until at last one
perceives that everything accomplished had been admitted only under the mental reservation of doubt,[1]
and behind this protective barrier the neurosis may feel
secure. ' It would be all very fine ', thinks the patient,
often quite consciously, ' if I were obliged to believe
what the man says, but there is no question of that, and
so long as that is not so I need change nothing.' Then,
when one comes to close quarters with the motivation
of this doubt, the fight with the resistances breaks forth
in earnest.

In the case of our patient, it was not doubt, but the
affective factor of revenge against her father that made
her cool reserve possible, that divided the analysis into
two distinct stages, and rendered the results of the first
stage so complete and perspicuous. It seemed, further,
as though nothing resembling a transference to the
physician had been effected. That, however, is of
course absurd, or, at least, is a loose way of expressing it ;
for some kind of relation to the analyst must come about,
and this is usually transferred from an infantile one. In
reality she transferred to me the deep antipathy to men
which had dominated her ever since the disappointment
she had suffered from her father. Bitterness against
men is as a rule easy to gratify upon the analyst ; it need
not evoke any violent emotional manifestations, it
simply expresses itself in rendering futile all his endeavours and in clinging to the neurosis. I know from
experience how difficult it is to make the patient
understand just this mute kind of symptomatic
behaviour and to make him aware of this latent, and
often exceedingly strong, hostility without endangering

---

[1] [*I.e.* believed on condition that it is regarded as not certain.—
Trans.]

the treatment. So as soon as I recognized the girl's attitude to her father, I broke off the treatment and gave the advice that, if it was thought worth while to continue the therapeutic efforts, it should be done by a woman. The girl had in the meanwhile promised her father that at any rate she would not communicate with the 'Lady', and I do not know whether my advice, the motive for which is evident, will be followed.

Only once in the course of this analysis did anything appear which I could regard as a positive transference, a greatly weakened revival of the original passionate love for the father. Even this manifestation was not quite free from other motives, but I mention it because it brings up, in another direction, an interesting problem of analytic technique. At a certain period, not long after the treatment had begun, the girl brought a series of dreams which, distorted as is customary and couched in the usual dream-language, could nevertheless be easily translated with certainty. Their content, when interpreted, was, however, remarkable. They anticipated the cure of the inversion through the treatment, expressed her joy over the prospects in life then opened before her, confessed her longing for a man's love and for children, and so might have been welcomed as a gratifying preparation for the desired change. The contradiction between them and the girl's utterances in waking life at the time was very great. She did not conceal from me that she meant to marry, but only in order to escape from her father's tyranny and to follow her true inclinations undisturbed. As for the husband, she remarked rather contemptuously, she would easily deal with him, and besides, one could have sexual relations with a man and a woman at one and the same time, as the example of the adored lady showed. Warned through some slight impression or other, I told her one day that I did not believe these dreams, that I regarded them as false or hypocritical, and that she intended to deceive me just as she habitually deceived her father. I was right; after this exposition this kind of dream ceased. But I still believe that, beside the intention to mislead me, the dreams partly expressed the wish to win my favour ; they were also an attempt to gain my interest and my good opinion—perhaps in order to disappoint me all the more thoroughly later on.

I can imagine that to point out the existence of lying dreams of this kind, destined to please the analyst, will arouse in some readers who call themselves analysts a real storm of helpless indignation. ' What ! ' they will exclaim, ' so the unconscious, the real centre of our mental life, the part of us that is so much nearer the divine than our poor consciousness, so that too can lie ! Then how can we still build on the interpretations of analysis and the accuracy of our findings ? ' To which one must reply that the recognition of these lying dreams does not constitute an astounding novelty. I know, indeed, that the craving of mankind for mysticism is ineradicable, and that it makes ceaseless efforts to win back for mysticism the playground it has been deprived of by the *Traumdeutung*, but in the case under consideration surely everything is simple enough. A dream is not the ' unconscious ' itself ; it is the form into which a thought from the preconscious, or even from waking conscious life, can, thanks to the favouring conditions of sleep, be recast. During sleep this thought has been reinforced by unconscious wish-excitations and thus has experienced distortion through the ' dream-work ', which is determined by the mechanisms valid for the unconscious. With our dreamer, the intention to mislead me, just as she did her father, certainly emanated from the preconscious, or perhaps even from consciousness ; it could come to expression by entering into connection with the unconscious wish-impulse to please the father (or father-substitute), and in this way it created a lying dream. The two intentions, to betray and to please the father, originate in the same complex ; the former resulted from the repression of the latter, and the later one was reduced by the dream-work to the earlier one. There can therefore be no question of any devaluation of the unconscious, nor of a shaking of our confidence in the results of our analysis.

I will not miss this opportunity of expressing for once my astonishment that human beings can go through such great and momentous phases of their love-life without heeding them much, sometimes even, indeed, without having the faintest suspicion of them : or else that, when they do become aware of these phases, they deceive themselves so thoroughly in their judgement of them. This happens not only with neurotics, where we are familiar with the phenomenon, but seems also to be common enough in ordinary life. In the present case, for example, a girl develops a devotion for women, which her parents at first find merely vexatious and hardly take seriously ; she herself knows quite well that her feelings are greatly engaged, but still she is only slightly aware of the sensations of intense love until a certain disappointment is followed by an absolutely excessive reaction, which shows everyone concerned that they have to do with a consuming passion of elemental strength. Even the girl herself had never perceived anything of the conditions necessary for the outbreak of such a mental upheaval. In other cases we come across girls or women in a state of severe depression, who on being asked for a possible cause of their condition tell us that they have, it is true, had a little feeling for a certain person, but that it was nothing deep and that they soon got over it when they had to give up hope. And yet it was this renunciation, apparently so easily borne, that became the cause of serious mental disturbance. Again, we have to do with men who have passed through casual love-affairs and then realize only from the subsequent effects that they had been passionately in love with someone whom they had apparently regarded lightly. One is also amazed at the unexpected results that may follow an artificial abortion which

had been decided upon without remorse and without
hesitation. One must agree that the poets are right
who are so fond of portraying people in love without
knowing it, or uncertain whether they do love, or who
think that they hate when in reality they love. It
would seem that the knowledge received by our
consciousness of what is happening to our love-instincts
is especially liable to be incomplete, full of gaps, or
falsified. Needless to say, in this discussion I have
not omitted to allow for the part played by subsequent failures of memory.

IV

I now come back, after this digression, to the
consideration of my patient's case. We have made a
survey of the forces which led the girl's libido from the
normal Oedipus attitude into that of homosexuality,
and of the paths thus traversed by it in the mind.
Most important in this respect was the impression made
by the birth of her little brother, and we might from
this be inclined to classify the case as one of late
acquired inversion.

But at this point we become aware of a state of
things which also confronts us in many other instances
in which light has been thrown by psycho-analysis on
a mental process. So long as we trace the development
from its final stage backwards, the connection appears
continuous, and we feel we have gained an insight
which is completely satisfactory or even exhaustive.
But if we proceed the reverse way, if we start from the
premises inferred from the analysis and try to follow
these up to the final result, then we no longer get the
impression of an inevitable sequence of events which
could not be otherwise determined. We notice at once
that there might have been another result, and that
we might have been just as well able to understand
and explain the latter. The synthesis is thus not so
satisfactory as the analysis; in other words, from a

knowledge of the premises we could not have foretold the nature of the result.

It is very easy to account for this disturbing state of affairs. Even supposing that we thoroughly know the ætiological factors that decide a given result, still we know them only qualitatively, and not in their relative strength. Some of them are so weak as to become suppressed by others, and therefore do not affect the final result. But we never know beforehand which of the determining factors will prove the weaker or the stronger. We only say at the end that those which succeeded must have been the stronger. Hence it is always possible by analysis to recognize the causation with certainty, whereas a prediction of it by synthesis is impossible.

We do not, therefore, mean to maintain that every girl who experiences a disappointment of this kind, of the longing for love that springs from the Oedipus attitude during puberty, will necessarily on that account fall a victim to homosexuality. On the contrary, other kinds of reaction to this trauma are probably commoner. Then, however, there must have been present in this girl special factors that turned the scale, factors outside the trauma, probably of an internal nature. Nor is there any difficulty in pointing them out.

It is well known that even in the normal person it takes a certain time before a decision in regard to the sex of the love-object is finally achieved. Homo-sexual enthusiasms, unduly strong friendships tinged with sensuality, are common enough in both sexes during the first years after puberty. This was also so with our patient, but in her these tendencies un-doubtedly showed themselves to be stronger, and lasted longer, than with others. In addition, these presages of later homosexuality had always occupied her conscious life, while the attitude arising from the Oedipus-complex had remained unconscious and had appeared only in such signs as her tender fondling of the little boy. As a school-girl she was for a long time in love with a strict and unapproachable mistress, obviously a mother-substitute. A long time before the birth of her brother and still longer before the first reprimand at the hands of her father, she had taken a specially keen interest in various young mothers. From very early years, therefore, her libido had flowed in two streams, the one on the surface being one that we may unhesitatingly designate homosexual. This latter was probably a direct and unchanged continuation of an infantile mother-fixation. Possibly the analysis described here actually revealed nothing more than the process by which, on an appropriate occasion, the deeper heterosexual libido-stream was also deflected into the manifest homosexual one.

The analysis showed, further, that the girl had suffered from childhood from a strongly marked ' masculinity complex '. A spirited girl, always ready to fight, she was not at all prepared to be second to her slightly older brother ; after inspecting his genital organs she had developed a pronounced envy of the penis, and the thoughts derived from this envy still continued to fill her mind. She was in fact a feminist ; she felt it to be unjust that girls should not enjoy the same freedom as boys, and rebelled against the lot of woman in general. At the time of the analysis the idea of pregnancy and child-birth was disagreeable to her, partly, I surmise, on account of the bodily disfigurement connected with them. Her girlish narcissism had betaken itself to this refuge,[1] and ceased to express itself as pride in her good looks. Various clues indicated that she must formerly have taken great pleasure in exhibitionism and scoptophilia. Anyone who is anxious that the claims of environment in ætiology should not come short, as opposed to those of heredity, will call attention to the fact that the girl's behaviour, as described above, was exactly what would follow from the combined effect in a person with a strong mother-fixation of the two influences of her mother's indifference and of her

---

[1] Cf. Kriemhilde's confession in the *Nibelungenlied*.

comparison of her genital organs with her brother's. It is possible here to trace back to the impression of an effective external influence in early life something which one would have been ready to regard as a constitutional peculiarity. But a part even of this acquired disposition, if it has really been acquired, has to be ascribed to the inborn constitution. So we see in practice a continual mingling and blending of what in theory we should try to separate into a pair of opposites—namely, inherited and acquired factors.

An earlier, more tentative conclusion of the analysis might have led to the view that this was a case of late-acquired homosexuality, but deeper consideration of the material undertaken later impels us to conclude that it is rather a case of inborn homosexuality which, as usual, became fixed and unmistakably manifest only in the period following puberty. Each of these classifications does justice only to one part of the state of affairs ascertainable by observation, but neglects the other. It would be best not to attach too much value to this way of stating the problem.

Publications on homosexuality usually do not distinguish clearly enough between the questions of the choice of object, on the one hand, and of the sexual characteristics and sexual attitude of the subject, on the other, as though the answer to the former necessarily involved the answers to the latter. Experience, however, proves the contrary : a man with predominantly male characteristics and also masculine in his love-life may still be inverted in respect to his object, loving only men instead of women. A man in whose character feminine attributes evidently predominate, who may, indeed, behave in love like a woman, might be expected, from this feminine attitude, to choose a man for his love-object ; but he may nevertheless be heterosexual, and show no more inversion in respect of his object than an average normal man. The same is true of women ; here also mental sexual character and object-choice do not necessarily coincide. The mystery of homosexuality is therefore by no means so simple as it is commonly depicted in popular expositions, *e.g.* a feminine personality, which therefore has to love a man, is unhappily attached to a male body ; or a masculine personality, irresistibly attracted by women, is unfortunately cemented to a female body. It is instead a question of three series of characteristics, namely—

Physical sexual characteristics—Mental sexual characteristics
(physical hermaphroditism)   (masculine, or feminine, attitude)
Kind of object-choice

which, up to a certain point, vary independently of one another, and are met with in different individuals in manifold permutations. Tendencious publications have obscured our view of this inter-relationship by putting into the foreground, for practical reasons, the third feature (the kind of object-choice), which is the only one that strikes the layman, and in addition by exaggerating the closeness of the association between this and the first feature. Moreover, they block the way leading to a deeper insight into all that is uniformly designated homosexuality by rejecting two fundamental facts which have been revealed by psycho-analytic investigation. The first of these is that homosexual men have experienced a specially strong fixation in regard to the mother ; the second, that, in addition to their manifest heterosexuality, a very considerable measure of latent or unconscious homosexuality can be detected in all normal people. If these findings are taken into account, then, to be sure, the supposition that nature in a freakish mood created a ' third sex ' falls to the ground.

It is not for psycho-analysis to solve the problem of homosexuality. It must rest content with disclosing the psychical mechanisms that resulted in determination of the object-choice, and with tracing the paths leading from them to the instinctual basis of the disposition. There its work ends, and it leaves the rest to biological research, which has recently brought to light, through

Steinach's [1] experiments, such very important results concerning the influence exerted by the first factor mentioned above on the second and third. Psycho-analysis has a common basis with biology, in that it presupposes an original bisexuality in human beings (as in animals). But psycho-analysis cannot elucidate the intrinsic nature of what in conventional or in biological phraseology is termed 'masculine' and 'feminine': it simply takes over the two concepts and makes them the foundation of its work. When we attempt to reduce them further, we find masculinity vanishing into activity and femininity into passivity, and that does not tell us enough. In what has gone before I have tried to explain how far we may reasonably expect, or how far experience has already proved, that the elucidations yielded by analysis furnish us with the means for altering inversion. When one compares the extent to which we can influence it with the remarkable transformations that Steinach has effected in some cases by his operations, it does not make a very imposing impression. Thus it would be premature, or a harmful exaggeration, if at this stage we were to indulge in hopes of a 'therapy' of inversion that could be generally used. The cases of male homosexuality in which Steinach has been successful fulfilled the condition, which is not always present, of a very patent physical 'herma-phroditism'. Any analogous treatment of female homo-sexuality is at present quite obscure. If it were to consist in removing the probably hermaphroditic ovaries, and in implanting others, which would, it is hoped, be of a single sex, there would be little prospect of its being applied in practice. A woman who has felt herself to be a man, and has loved in masculine fashion, will hardly let herself be forced into playing the part of a woman when she must pay for this transformation, which is not in every way advantageous, by renouncing all hope of motherhood.

[1] Cf. A. Lipschütz, *Die Pubertätsdrüse und ihre Wirkungen*.

CERTAIN NEUROTIC MECHANISMS IN JEALOUSY, PARANOIA AND HOMO-SEXUALITY [1]

(1922)

A. JEALOUSY is one of those affective states, like grief, that may be described as normal. If anyone appears to be without it, the inference is justified that it has undergone severe repression and consequently plays all the greater part in his unconscious mental life. The instances of abnormally intense jealousy met with in analytic work reveal themselves as constructed of three layers. The three layers or stages of jealousy may be described as (1) *competitive* or normal, (2) *projected*, and (3) *delusional* jealousy.

There is not much to be said from the analytic point of view about normal jealousy. It is easy to see that essentially it is compounded of grief, the pain caused by the thought of losing the loved object, and of the narcissistic wound, in so far as this is distinguishable from the other wound ; further, of feelings of enmity against the successful rival, and of a greater or lesser amount of self-criticism which tries to hold the person himself accountable for his loss. Although we may call it normal, this jealousy is by no means completely rational, that is, derived from the actual situation, proportionate to the real circumstances and under the complete control of the conscious ego ; for it is rooted deep in the unconscious, it is a continuation of the earliest stirrings of the child's affective life, and it originates in the Oedipus or family complex of the first sexual period. Moreover, it is noteworthy that in many

[1] First published in *Zeitschrift*, Bd. VIII., 1922. [Translated by Joan Riviere.]

persons it is experienced bisexually; that is to say, in a
man, beside the suffering in regard to the loved woman
and the hatred against the male rival, grief in regard
to the unconsciously loved man and hatred of the
woman as a rival will add to its intensity. I even know
of a man who suffered exceedingly during his attacks
of jealousy and who, according to his own account,
went through unendurable torments by consciously
imagining himself in the position of the faithless woman.
The sensation of helplessness which then came over
him, the images he used to describe his condition—
exposed to the vulture's beak like Prometheus, or cast
fettered into a serpent's den—he himself referred to
the impressions received during several homosexual
aggressions to which he had been subjected as a boy.

The jealousy of the second layer, the *projected*, is
derived in both men and women either from their own
actual unfaithfulness in real life or from impulses
towards it which have succumbed to repression. It is
a matter of everyday experience that fidelity, especially
that degree of it required in marriage, is only maintained
in the face of continual temptation. Anyone who
denies this in himself will nevertheless be impelled so
strongly in the direction of infidelity that he will be
glad enough to make use of an unconscious mechanism
as an alleviation. This relief—more, absolution by
his conscience—he achieves when he projects his own
impulses to infidelity on to the partner to whom he
owes faith. This weighty motive can then make use
of the material at hand (perception-material) by which
the unconscious impulses of the partner are likewise
betrayed, and the person can justify himself with the
reflection that the other is probably not much better
than he is himself.[1]

Social conventions have taken this universal state
of things into account very adroitly, by granting a

---

[1] Cf. Desdemona's song :

> ' I called my love false love; but what said he then?
> If I court moe women, you'll couch with moe men.'

certain amount of latitude to the married woman's thirst to find favour in men's eyes and the married man's thirst to capture and possess, in the expectation that this inevitable tendency to unfaithfulness will thus find a safety-valve and be rendered innocuous. Convention has laid down that neither partner is to hold the other accountable for these little excursions in the direction of unfaithfulness, and it achieves the result on the whole that the desire awakened by the new love-object is gratified by a kind of turning-back to the object already possessed. The jealous person, however, does not recognize this convention of tolerance ; he does not believe in any such thing as a halt or a turning-back once the path has been trod, nor that a social ' flirtation ' may be a safeguard against actual infidelity. In the treatment of a jealous person like this one must refrain from disputing with him the material on which he bases his suspicions ; one can only aim at bringing him to regard the matter in a different light.

The jealousy that arises from this projection has, it is true, an almost delusional character ; it is, however, amenable to the analytic work of exposing the unconscious phantasies of personal infidelity. The jealousy of the third layer, the true *delusional* type, is worse. It also has its origin in repressed impulses towards unfaithfulness—the object, however, in these cases is of the same sex as the subject. Delusional jealousy represents an acidulated homosexuality, and rightly takes its position among the classical forms of paranoia. As an attempt at defence against an unduly strong homosexual impulse it may, in a man, be described in the formula : ' Indeed I do not love him, *she* loves him ! ' [1] In a delusional case one will be prepared to find the jealousy arising in all three layers, never in the third alone.

B. Paranoia.—Cases of paranoia are for well-known reasons not usually amenable to analytic investigation.

---

[1] Cf. Freud, ' Psycho-Analytic Notes upon an Autobiographical Account of a Case of Paranoia ', COLLECTED PAPERS, vol. iii.

I have recently been able, nevertheless, by an intensive study of two paranoiacs, to discover something new to me.

The first case was that of a youngish man with a fully developed paranoia of jealousy, the object of which was his impeccably faithful wife. A stormy period in which the delusion had possessed him uninterruptedly already lay behind him. When I saw him he was still subject only to clearly defined attacks, which lasted for several days and, curiously enough, regularly appeared on the day following an act of intercourse, which was, incidentally, satisfying to both of them. The inference is justified that after every satiation of the heterosexual libido the homosexual component, likewise stimulated by the act, forced for itself an outlet in the attack of jealousy.

The jealousy of the attack drew its material from his observation of the smallest possible indications, in which the utterly unconscious coquetry of the wife, unnoticeable to any other person, had betrayed itself to him. She had unintentionally touched the man sitting next her with her hand ; she had turned too much towards him, or she had smiled more pleasantly than when alone with her husband. To all these manifestations of her unconscious feelings he paid extraordinary attention, and always knew how to interpret them correctly, so that he really was always in the right about it, and could justify his jealousy still more by analytic interpretation. His abnormality really reduced itself to this, that he watched his wife's unconscious mind much more closely and then regarded it as far more important than anyone else would have thought of doing.

We are reminded that sufferers from persecutory paranoia act in just the same way. They, too, cannot regard anything in others as indifferent, and into their ' delusions of reference ' they, too, take up the smallest possible indications which these others, strangers, offer them. The meaning of their delusion of reference is that they expect from every stranger something like love ; these ' others ' show them nothing of the kind, however—they laugh to themselves, fiddle with their sticks, even spit on the ground as they go by—and one really does not do these things while anyone in whom one takes a friendly interest is near. One does them only when one is quite indifferent to the passer-by, when one can treat him like air ; and when we consider the fundamental kinship of the words ' stranger ' and ' enemy ', the paranoiac is not so far wrong in regarding this indifference as hate, in comparison with his claim for love.

We begin to see that we describe the behaviour of both jealous and persecuted paranoiacs very inadequately by saying that they project outwards on to others what they do not wish to recognize in themselves. Certainly they do this ; but they do not project it into the sky, so to speak, where there is nothing of the sort already. They let themselves be guided by their knowledge of the unconscious, and displace to the unconscious minds of others the attention which they have withdrawn from their own. Our jealous husband perceives his wife's unfaithfulness instead of his own ; by becoming conscious of hers and magnifying it enormously he succeeds in keeping unconscious his own. If we accept his example as typical, we may infer that the enmity which the persecuted paranoiac sees in others is the reflection of his own hostile impulses against them. Since we know that with the paranoiac it is precisely the most loved person of his own sex that becomes his persecutor, the question arises where this reversal of affect takes its origin ; the answer is not far to seek—the ever-present ambivalence of the feelings provides its source and the unfulfilment of his claim for love strengthens it. This ambivalence thus serves the same purpose for the persecuted paranoiac as jealousy serves for our patient—that of a defence against homosexuality.

The dreams of my jealous patient contained a great surprise for me. They were not simultaneous with the outbreaks of the attacks, though they occurred within the period influenced by the delusion ; they were completely free from the delusion and showed themselves based on homosexual tendencies which were disguised no more strictly than usual. In view of my slight knowledge of the dreams of paranoiacs I was inclined to suppose at that time that the disease did not penetrate into dreams.

The homosexuality of this patient was easily surveyed. He had made no friendships and developed no social interests ; one had the impression that the delusion had constituted the first actual development of his relations with men, as if it had taken over a piece of work that had been neglected. The fact that his father was of no great importance in the family life, combined with a humiliating homosexual trauma in early childhood, had forced his homosexuality into repression and barred the way to its sublimation. The whole of his youth was governed by a strong attachment to his mother. Of all her many sons he was her declared favourite, and he developed marked jealousy of the normal type in regard to her. When later he made his choice of a wife—mainly prompted by the impulse to enrich his mother—his longing for a virgin mother expressed itself in obsessive doubts about his wife's virginity. The first years of his marriage were free from jealousy. Then he became unfaithful to his wife and entered upon an intimate relationship with another woman that lasted for a considerable time. Startled by a certain suspicion, he at length made an end of this love affair, and not until then did the jealousy of the second, projected type break out, by means of which he was able to assuage his self-reproaches about his own unfaithfulness. It was soon complicated by an accession of homosexual impulses, of which his father-in-law was the object, and became a fully formed jealousy paranoia.

My second case would probably not have been classified as persecutory paranoia without analysis ;

but I had to recognize the young man as a candidate for this termination of the illness. In his attitude to his father there existed an ambivalence which in its range was quite extraordinary. On the one hand, he was the most pronounced rebel imaginable, and had developed manifestly in every direction in opposition to his father's wishes and ideals ; on the other hand, at a deeper level he was still the most utterly abject son, in loving remorse after his father's death denying himself all enjoyment of women. His actual relations with men were clearly dominated by suspiciousness ; his keen intellect easily rationalized this attitude ; and he knew how to bring it about that both friends and acquaintances deceived and exploited him. The new thing I learned from studying him was that classical persecution-ideas may be present without finding belief or acceptance. They flashed up occasionally during the analysis, but he regarded them as unimportant and invariably scoffed at them. This may occur in many cases of paranoia ; it may be that the delusions which we regard as new formations when the disease breaks out have already long been in existence.

It seems to me that this is an important recognition —namely, that the qualitative factor, the presence of certain neurotic formations, has less practical significance than the quantitative factor, the degree of attention, or more correctly, the measure of cathexis that these formations engage. Our consideration of the first case, the jealousy paranoia, led to a similar estimate of the importance of the quantitative factor, by showing that there also the abnormality essentially consisted in the hyper-cathexis of the interpretations of another's unconscious behaviour. We have long known of an analogous fact in the analysis of hysteria. The pathogenic phantasies, derivatives of repressed instinctual trends, are for a long time tolerated alongside the normal life of the mind, and have no pathogenic effect until by a revolution in the libido-economy they undergo hyper-cathexis ; not till then does the conflict which leads to symptom-formation break out. Thus as our knowledge increases we are ever being impelled to bring the *economic* point of view into the foreground. I should also like to throw out the question whether this quantitative factor that I am now dwelling on does not suffice to cover the phenomena for which Bleuler and others have lately wished to introduce the term ' switching '. One need only assume that increased resistance in one direction of the psychical currents results in hyper-cathexis along some other path and thus causes the whole current to be switched into this path.

The dreams of my two cases of paranoia showed an instructive contrast. Whereas those of the first case were free from delusion, as has already been said, the other patient produced great numbers of persecution-dreams, which may be regarded as forerunners or substitutive formations of the delusional ideas. The pursuer, from whom he managed to escape only in terror, was usually a powerful bull or some other male symbol which even in the dream itself he sometimes recognized as representing his father. One day he produced a very characteristic paranoiac transference-dream. He saw me shaving in front of him, and from the scent of the soap he realized that I was using the same soap as his father had used. I was doing this in order to induce in him a father-transference on to myself. The choice of this incident out of which the dream was formed unmistakably betrays the patient's depreciatory attitude to his paranoiac phantasies and his disbelief in them ; for his own eyes could tell him every day that I never require to avail myself of shaving-soap and that therefore there was in this respect nothing to which a father-transference could attach itself.

A comparison of the dreams of the two patients shows, however, that the question whether or not paranoia (or any other psychoneurosis) can penetrate into dreams is based on a false conception of dreams. Dreams are distinguishable from waking thought in that for their content they can draw from material (belonging to the region of the unconscious) which cannot emerge in waking thought. Apart from this, dreams are merely a *form of thinking*, a transformation of preconscious thought-material by the dream-work and its conditions. Our terminology of the neuroses is not applicable to repressed material ; this cannot be called hysterical, nor obsessional, nor paranoiac. The other part of the material which is woven into the structure of a dream, the preconscious thoughts, may be normal or may bear the character of any neurosis ; they may be the effects of all those pathogenic processes in which the essence of neurosis lies. It is not evident why any such morbid idea should not become woven into dreams. A dream may therefore quite simply represent an hysterical phantasy, an obsessional idea, or a delusion, that is, may reveal it upon interpretation. Observation of the two paranoiacs shows that the dreams of the one were quite normal while he was subject to his delusion, and that those of the other were paranoiac in content while he treated his delusional ideas with contempt. In both cases, therefore, the dream took up the material that was at the time being forced into the background in waking life. This too, however, need not necessarily be an invariable rule.

C. Homosexuality.—Recognition of the organic factor in homosexuality does not relieve us of the obligation of studying the psychical processes of its origin. The typical process, already established in innumerable cases, is that a few years after the termination of puberty the young man, who until this time has been strongly fixated to his mother, turns in his course, identifies himself with his mother, and looks about for love-objects in whom he can re-discover himself, and whom he wishes to love as his mother loved him. The characteristic mark of this process is that usually for several years one of the ' conditions of love ' is that the male object shall be of the same age as he himself was when the change took place. We know of various factors contributing to this result, probably in different degrees. First there is the fixation on the mother, which renders passing on to another woman difficult. The identification with the mother is an outcome of this attachment, and at the same time in a certain sense it enables the son to keep true to her, his first object. Then there is the inclination towards a narcissistic object-choice, which lies in every way nearer and is easier to put into effect than the move towards the other sex. Behind this factor there lies concealed another of quite exceptional strength, or perhaps it coincides with it : the high value set upon the male organ and the inability to tolerate its absence in a love-object. Depreciation of women, and aversion from them, even horror of them, are generally derived from the early discovery that women have no penis. We subsequently discovered, as another powerful motive urging towards the homosexual object-choice, regard for the father or fear of him ; for the renunciation of women means that all rivalry with him (or with all men who may take his place) is avoided. The two last motives, the clinging to the condition of a penis in the object as well as the retiring in favour of the father, may be ascribed to the castration complex. Attachment to the mother, narcissism, fear of castration— these are the factors (which by the way have nothing specific about them) that we have hitherto found in the psychical ætiology of homosexuality ; and on them is superimposed the effect of any seduction bringing about a premature fixation of the libido, as well as the influence of the organic factor favouring the passive rôle in love.

We have, however, never regarded this analysis of the origin of homosexuality as complete ; and I can now point to a new mechanism leading to homosexual object-choice, although I cannot say how large a part it plays in the formation of the extreme, manifest and exclusive type of homosexuality. Observation has directed my attention to several cases in which during early childhood feelings of jealousy derived from the mother-complex and of very great intensity arose against rivals, usually older brothers. This jealousy led to an exceedingly hostile aggressive attitude against brothers (or sisters) which might culminate in actual death-wishes, but which could not survive further development. Under the influences of training—and certainly not uninfluenced also by their own constant powerlessness—these feelings yielded to repression and to a transformation, so that the rivals of the earlier period became the first homosexual love-objects. Such an outcome of the attachment to the mother shows various interesting relations with other processes known to us. First of all it is a complete contrast to the development of persecutory paranoia, in which the person who has before been loved becomes the hated persecutor, whereas here the hated rivals are transformed into love-objects. It represents, too, an exaggeration of the process which, according to my view, leads to the birth of social instincts in the individual.[1] In both processes there is first the presence of jealous and hostile feelings which cannot achieve gratification ; and then both the personal affectionate and the social identification feelings arise as reaction-formations against the repressed aggressive impulses.

This new mechanism in the homosexual object-choice, its origin in rivalry which has been overcome and in aggressive impulses which have become repressed, is often combined with the typical conditions known to us. In the history of homosexuals one often hears that the change in them took place after the mother had praised another boy and set him up as a model. The tendency to a narcissistic object-choice was thus stimulated, and after a short phase of keen jealousy the rival became a love-object. Otherwise, however, the new mechanism is a separate one, in that the change

[1] Cf. Freud, *Group Psychology and the Analysis of the Ego.*

takes place at a much earlier period, and the identification with the mother recedes into the background. Moreover, in the cases I have observed, it led only to homosexual attitudes, which did not exclude heterosexuality and did not involve a horror of women.

It is well known that a good number of homosexual persons is distinguished by a special development of the social instincts and by a devotion to the interests of the community. It would be tempting, as a theoretical explanation of this, to say that the behaviour towards men in general of a man who sees in other men potential love-objects must be different from that of a man who looks upon other men first as rivals in regard to women. Against this there is only the objection that jealousy and rivalry play their part in homosexual love also, and that the community of men also includes these potential rivals. Apart from this speculative explanation, however, the fact that the homosexual object-choice not rarely proceeds from an early conquest of the rivalry in regard to men cannot be unimportant for the connection between homosexuality and social feeling.

In the light of psycho-analysis we are accustomed to regard social feeling as a sublimation of homosexual attitudes towards objects. In the homosexual person with marked social interests, the detachment of social feeling from object-choice has not been fully carried through.

THE INFANTILE GENITAL ORGANIZATION OF THE LIBIDO

A Supplement to the Theory of Sexuality [1]

(1923)

IT is indicative of the difficulties which beset the work of psycho-analytic research that it is possible, in spite of unremitting observation extending over periods of years, to overlook quite broad general features and typical situations, until at last they confront one in a completely unmistakable guise. The remarks that follow are intended to retrieve a lapse of this sort in the field of infantile sexuality.

Readers of my *Drei Abhandlungen zur Sexualtheorie* (1905) will be aware that I have never undertaken any thorough alteration of this work for later editions, but have preserved the original arrangement and have fulfilled the claims of later advances in our knowledge by supplementing and correcting the text. Thus it may well be that the old and the new do not admit of fusion without indications of contradiction. In the beginning, for instance, the emphasis fell upon pointing out the fundamental difference between the sexual life of children and of adults ; later on the pregenital organizations of the libido swung into the foreground, together with the remarkable and significant fact of the double thrust of sexual development, twice making a start at separate periods. Finally, the curiosity of the child engaged our interest ; and from this proceeded the recognition of the far-reaching similarity between the last stages of infantile sexuality (about the fifth

[1] First published in *Zeitschrift*, Bd. IX., 1923. [Translated by Joan Riviere.]

year) and the final form to which it develops in the
adult.   In the last edition of the *Sexualtheorie* (1922)
I left things at this point.

I stated there (on p. 63) that ' often, or perhaps
regularly, complete object-choice is established in
early childhood, of the kind that we have inferred to
be characteristic of the pubertal phase of development,
namely, such as occurs when all the sexual trends
become directed towards one single person, and in that
person seek to reach their aims.   This constitutes the
most complete approximation possible in childhood to
the definitive form taken by sexual life after puberty.
The sole difference from the latter is that the coalescence
of the component-impulses and their concentration
under the primacy of the genital organs is not effected
in childhood, or only very imperfectly.   The institution
of this primacy is, therefore, the last phase which the
sexual organization undergoes.'

I am to-day no longer satisfied with the statement
that the primacy of the genitals is not effected in the
early period of childhood, or only very imperfectly.
The approximation of childhood-sexuality to that of
the adult goes much farther and is not limited solely
to the establishment of an object-attachment.   Even
if perfect concentration of the component-impulses
under the primacy of the genitals is not attained, at any
rate at the height of the development of childhood-
sexuality the functioning of the genitals and the
interest in them reaches predominant significance,
which comes little short of that reached in maturity.
The *difference* between the two—the ' infantile genital
organization ' and the final genital organization of the
adult—constitutes at the same time the main characteristic of the infantile form, namely, that for both sexes
in childhood only one kind of genital organ comes into
account—the male.   The primacy reached is, therefore,
not a primacy of the *genital*, but of the *phallus*.

Unfortunately we can describe this state of things
only as it concerns the male child ; the corresponding

processes in the little girl are not sufficiently known to us. The little boy undoubtedly perceives the distinction between men and women, but to begin with he has no occasion to connect it with any difference in the genitals. It is natural for him to assume that all living beings, persons and animals, possess a genital organ like his own ; indeed we know that he investigates inanimate objects with a view to discovering something like his member in them.[1] This part of the body, so easily excitable and changeable, and so rich in sensation, occupies the boy's interest to a high degree, and never ceases to provide new problems for his epistemophilic impulse. He wants to see the same thing in other people, so as to compare it with his own ; he behaves as if he had a dim idea that this member might be and should be larger. The driving force which this male portion of his body will generate later at puberty expresses itself in childhood essentially as an impulsion to inquire into things—as sexual curiosity. Many of those deeds of exhibitionism and aggression which children commit, and which in later years would be judged without hesitation to be manifestations of sensual passion, prove on analysis to be experiments undertaken in the search for sexual knowledge.

In the course of these investigations the child makes the discovery that the penis is not one of the possessions common to all creatures who are like himself. The accidental sight of the genitals of a little sister or a little playmate is the occasion of this. In unusually intelligent children the sight of girls urinating arouses the suspicion even earlier that something is different here ; for they will have noticed the different position adopted and the different sound heard, and have taken steps to repeat their observations in such a way as to find out the truth. We know how they react to their

---

[1] It is remarkable, by the way, what a small degree of interest the other part of the male genitals, the little sac with its contents, arouses in the child. From all one hears in analyses one could not guess that the male genitals consist of anything more than the penis.

first perception of the absence of the penis. They deny its absence, and believe they do see a penis all the same ; the discrepancy between what they see and what they imagine is glossed over by the idea that the penis is still small and will grow ; gradually they come to the conclusion, so fraught with emotion, that at least it had been there and had at some time been taken away. The absence of the penis is thought to be the result of a castration, and then the child is faced with the task of dealing with the thought of a castration in relation to himself. Subsequent developments are too well known for it to be necessary to recapitulate them here. It seems to me, however, that the significance of the castration complex can only be rightly appreciated when its origin in the phase of *primacy of the phallus* is also taken into account.[1]

We know, too, to what a degree depreciation of women, loathing of women, and a disposition to homosexuality are derived from a final conviction of women's lack of a penis. Ferenczi has recently, with complete justification, traced back the mythological symbol of loathing—the head of Medusa—to the impression made by the female genitals devoid of a penis.[2]

It should not be presumed, however, that the child instantly and readily makes a generalization of its perception that many women possess no penis ; in the way of this there lies the assumption that the absence

[1] It has quite correctly been pointed out that the child acquires the idea of a narcissistic wound or deprivation of a part of its body by the experience of the loss of the nipple after suckling and of the daily production of its fæces, even already by its separation from the womb of the mother at birth. Nevertheless, the castration complex should be a term reserved for the occasion when the idea of such deprivations comes to be associated with the loss of the male organ.

[2] *Zur Symbolik des Medusenhauptes.* I will merely add that in the myth it is the genital of the mother that is represented. Athene, who carries the head of Medusa on her armour, becomes by virtue of it the unapproachable, the woman at sight of whom all thought of sexual desire is stifled.

of the penis is due to a castration performed as a punishment. On the contrary, the child imagines that only unworthy female persons have thus sacrificed their genital organ, such persons as have probably been guilty of the same forbidden impulses as he himself. Women who are regarded with respect, such as the mother, retain the penis long after this date. Not yet is being a woman the same thing to the child as having no penis.[1] Not till later, when the child takes up the problems of the origin and birth of children, and divines that only women can bear children, does the mother, too, become deprived of a penis ; and along with this quite complicated theories are constructed, so as to account for the exchange of a penis in return for a child. At the same time the real female genitals never seem to be discovered. As we know, the baby is supposed to live in the mother's body (bowels) and to be born through the bowel passage. These last theories take us up to the end of the period of infantile sexuality or beyond.

It is well, further, to bear in mind the transformations which the familiar polarity of the sexes goes through in the course of the sexual development of childhood. A first contrast is introduced with object-choice, which of course presupposes a subject and an object. At the level of the pregenital sadistic-anal organization nothing is yet heard of any maleness and femaleness ; the dominant antithesis is that between active and passive.[2] In the following stage of the infantile genital organization *maleness* has come to life, but no femaleness. The antithesis runs : a male genital organ or a castrated condition. Not until completion of development at the time of puberty does the polarity of sexuality coincide with *male* and *female*.

---

[1] From the analysis of a young woman I learnt that, having no father and several aunts, until quite late in the latency-period she clung to a belief that her mother and some of her aunts possessed a penis. One of the aunts, however, was weak-minded, and she was regarded by the child as castrated like herself.

[2] Cf. *Drei Abhandlungen zur Sexualtheorie.* Fünfte Auflage, S. 62.

In maleness is concentrated subject, activity, and the possession of a penis ; femaleness carries on the object, and passivity. The vagina becomes valued henceforth as an asylum for the penis ; it comes into the inheritance of the mother's womb.

XXI

NEUROSIS AND PSYCHOSIS [1]

(1924)

IN my booklet *Das Ich und das Es*,[2] which appeared recently, I suggested that the mental apparatus should be subdivided in such a way as to allow of a series of relationships being represented in a simple and synoptic fashion. In other matters—for instance, concerning the origin and function of the super-ego—a good deal remained insufficiently elucidated. Now one may reasonably expect that a proposition of the kind should prove itself useful and helpful in other directions as well, even if it only enables us to see from another angle what we already know, to group it differently and to describe it more convincingly. By applying it in this. way we might also reap the advantage of turning away from the greyness of theory back to the ever-green realm of observation.

The essay referred to describes the various allegiances the ego owes, its mediate position between the outer world and the *id*, and its struggles to serve all its masters at one and the same time. Now it so happened that a train of thought suggested elsewhere, which had to do with the causes giving rise to the psychoses and with prevention of them, furnished me with a simple formula concerning what is perhaps the most important genetic difference between neurosis and psychosis : *Neurosis is the result of a conflict between*

[1] First published in *Zeitschrift*, Bd. X., 1924. [Translated by Joan Riviere.]

[2] [*The Ego and the Id*, shortly to appear in translation. To translate the German ' *es* ', which means ' *it* ' and thus implies the *impersonality* of the mind apart from its ego, the Latin ' *id* ' has been selected.—ED.]

the ego and its id, *whereas psychosis is the analogous outcome of a similar disturbance in the relation between the ego and its environment (outer world).*

To be suspicious of such simple solutions of problems is undoubtedly a piece of justifiable caution. Moreover, the most that we should expect from it would not be more than that this formula should prove itself correct in rough outline. But even that would be something. Also one recalls immediately a whole series of conclusions and discoveries which seem to support our proposition. All our analyses go to show that the transference neuroses originate from the ego's refusing to accept a powerful instinctual impulse existing in its *id* and denying it motor discharge, or disputing the object towards which it is aimed. The ego then defends itself against the impulse by the mechanism of repression ; the repressed impulse struggles against this fate, and finds ways which the ego cannot control to create for itself substitutive gratification (a symptom), which is forced upon the ego in the form of a compromise ; the ego finds its unity menaced and injured by this interloper, pursues against the symptom the struggle it had formerly maintained against the original impulse, and all this together produces the clinical picture of a neurosis. It is no matter that in undertaking the repression the ego is at bottom following the dictates of its super-ego, which dictates originated in influences of the same kind from the real environment that subsequently found representation in the super-ego. The fact remains that the ego takes sides with these powers that be, that their demands are stronger in it than the claims of instinct from the *id,* and that the force which sets repression to work against that part of the *id* and fortifies it by the anti-cathexis of resistance is the ego. In the service of its super-ego and of reality the ego has come into conflict with its *id,* and this state of affairs is found in all the transference neuroses.

It is just as easy, on the other hand, from what we

already know of the mechanism of the psychoses, to quote examples from them pointing to a disturbance in the relation between the ego and its environment. In Meynert's amentia,[1] the acute hallucinatory confusion which is perhaps the most extreme and striking form of psychosis, the outer world is either not perceived in the very least or else any perception of it remains absolutely without effect. Normally, indeed, the outer world commands the ego in two ways : first, by current perceptions which it is constantly able to engender afresh, and secondly, by the store of memories of former perceptions which, as its 'inner world', has become the possession and a constituent part of the ego. Now in amentia not only is acceptance denied to fresh perceptions, but the importance (cathexis) of the inner world—that inner world which formerly reflected the outer world as an image of it—is withdrawn too; the ego creates for itself in a lordly manner a new outer and inner world; and there is no doubt about two facts, that this new world is constructed after the pattern of the impulses in the *id*, and that the motive of this collapse of the ego's relation with the outer world is a severe frustration by reality of a wish, a frustration which seemed too unendurable to be borne. The close affinity of this psychosis with normal dreams is unmistakable. A pre-condition of dreaming, however, is a state of sleep, and complete abandonment of perceptive capacity and of the outer world is one of the features of sleep.

We know that other forms of psychosis, the schizophrenias, incline to end in affective hebetude, that is, to lose all interest in the outer world. In regard to the genesis of delusions, a number of analyses have taught us that the delusion is found like a patch on the spot where originally there was a rent in the relation between ego and outer world. If the condition of a conflict with the outer world is not still more striking

---

[1] [To be distinguished, of course, from the common English use of the term, meaning feeble-mindedness.—Ed.]

than it seems to us now, this is due to the fact
that in the clinical picture of the psychoses manifestations of the pathogenic process are often overlaid
by those resulting from an attempt at cure or at
reconstruction.

There always remains as a common feature in the
ætiology both of the psychoneuroses and the psychoses
the factor of frustration—the lack of fulfilment of one
of those eternal uncontrollable childhood's wishes that
are so deeply rooted in our composition, phylogenetically
fore-ordained as it is.   In the last resort this frustration
is always an outer one ; in the individual case it may
proceed from that internal institution (in the super-
ego) which has taken over the part played by the
demands of reality.   Now the pathogenic effect depends
on whether, in the tension of such a conflict, the ego
remains true in its allegiance to the outer world and
endeavours to subjugate the *id*, or whether it allows
itself to be overwhelmed by the *id* and thus torn away
from reality.   In this apparently simple situation,
however, a complication is introduced by the existence
of the super-ego, which, in some connection not yet
clear to us, combines in itself influences from the *id*
as well as from the outer world, and is to some extent
an ideal prototype of that state towards which all the
ego's endeavours are bending, a reconciliation of its
manifold allegiances.   The attitude of the super-ego
should be taken into account, as has not hitherto been
done, in all forms of mental disorder.   For the moment,
however, we can postulate that there must be diseases
founded on a conflict between ego and super-ego.
Analysis gives us the right to infer that melancholia is
the model of this group, and then we should put in a
claim for the name of ' narcissistic psychoneuroses '
for these disorders.   It does not fit in badly with our
impressions if we find reasons for distinguishing conditions such as melancholia from the other psychoses.
We then observe, however, that we were able to complete our simple genetic formula without abandoning

it. A transference neurosis corresponds to a conflict between ego and *id*, a narcissistic neurosis to that between ego and super-ego, and a psychosis to that between ego and outer world. To be sure, we can hardly say at a glance whether this really represents new knowledge or is merely an addition to our list of formulas ; but I think that after all its capacity for application must give us courage to keep in mind this dissection of the mental apparatus that I have proposed, namely, into ego, super-ego and *id*.

The proposition that neuroses and psychoses originate in the ego's conflicts with the various powers ruling it, that is, that they correspond with a failure in the function of the ego, which after all is straining to reconcile all these different claims with one another, requires supplementing in a further point. One would like to know in what circumstances and by what means the ego succeeds in surviving such conflicts, which are undoubtedly always present, without falling ill. Now this is a new field for research in which the most various factors will certainly demand consideration. Two of them, however, can be indicated at once. The outcome of such situations will assuredly depend upon economic conditions, upon the relative strength of the forces striving with one another. And further, it is always possible for the ego to avoid a rupture in any of its relations by deforming itself, submitting to forfeit something of its unity, or in the long run even to being gashed and rent. Thus the illogicalities, eccentricities and follies of mankind would fall into a category similar to their sexual perversions, for by accepting them they spare themselves repressions.

In conclusion there remains to be considered the question what that mechanism analogous to repression may be by which the ego severs itself from the outer world. This is not to be answered, in my opinion, without fresh investigations, but, like repression, the content of this mechanism must include a withdrawal of the cathexes emanating from the ego.

XXII

THE ECONOMIC PROBLEM IN MASOCHISM [1]

(1924)

WE have a right to describe the existence of the masochistic trend in the life of the human instincts as from the economic point of view mysterious. For if mental processes are governed by the pleasure-principle, so that avoidance of 'pain' and obtaining pleasure is their first aim, masochism is incomprehensible. If physical pain and feelings of distress [2] can cease to be signals of danger and be ends in themselves, the pleasure-principle is paralysed, the watchman of our mental life is to all intents and purposes himself drugged and asleep.

In this light, masochism appears to us as a great danger, which is in no way true of sadism, its counterpart. We feel tempted to call the pleasure-principle the watchman of our lives, instead of only the watchman of our mental life. But then the question of the relation of the pleasure-principle to the two varieties of instincts that we have distinguished, the death-instincts and the erotic (libidinal) life-instincts, demands investigation, and we can reach no further conclusion about the problem of masochism till we have answered this call.

As will be remembered,[3] we have conceived the principle which governs all mental processes as a special case of Fechner's *tendency to stability*, and consequently have ascribed to the mental apparatus the aim of extinguishing, or at least of maintaining at as low a level as possible, the quantities of excitation flowing

---

[1] First published in *Zeitschrift*, Bd. X., 1924. [Translated by Joan Riviere.]

[2] [*Unlust*, usually translated by 'pain'.—Trans.]

[3] Freud, *Beyond the Pleasure-Principle*.

into it. For this tendency that has been presumed by us Barbara Low has suggested the name Nirvana-principle, which we accept. But we have unquestioningly identified the pleasure-pain-principle with this Nirvana-principle. From this it would follow that every 'pain' coincides with a heightening, every pleasure with a lowering, of the stimulus-tension existing in the mind ; the Nirvana-principle (and the pleasure-principle which is assumed to be identical with it) would be entirely in the service of the death-instincts (the aim of which is to lead our throbbing existence into the stability of an inorganic state) and would have the function of warning us against the claims of the life-instinct, of the libido, which tries to disturb the course life endeavours to take. Unfortunately, this view cannot be correct. It seems that we experience the ebb and flow of quantities of stimuli directly in perceptions of tension which form a series, and it cannot be doubted that there is such a thing as both pleasurable tension and 'painful' lowering of tension. The condition of sexual excitement is the most striking example of a pleasurable increase in tension of this kind, but it is certainly not the only one. Pleasure and 'pain' cannot, therefore, be referred to a quantitative increase or decrease of something which we call stimulus-tension, although they clearly have a great deal to do with this factor. It seems as though they do not depend on this quantitative factor, but on some peculiarity in it which we can only describe as qualitative. We should be much farther on with psychology if we knew what this qualitative peculiarity was. Perhaps it is something rhythmic, the periodical duration of the changes, the risings and fallings of the volume of stimuli ; we do not know.

Whatever it is, we must perceive that the Nirvana-principle, which belongs to the death-instincts, underwent a modification in the living organism through which it became the pleasure-principle, and henceforth we shall avoid regarding the two principles as one. It is not difficult to infer what force it was that effected this modification, that is, if one has any interest at all in following this argument. It can only be the life-instinct, the libido, which has thus wrested a place for itself alongside the death-instinct in regulating the processes of life. In this way we obtain a series, a small but an interesting one : the *Nirvana*-principle expresses the tendency of the death - instincts, the *pleasure*-principle represents the claims of the libido and that modification of it, the *reality*-principle, the influence of the outer world.

None of these three principles can actually be put out of action by another. As a rule they know how to tolerate one another, although conflicts must occasionally arise from the various aims towards which each strives—a quantitative reduction of the stimulus-pressure on one side, on another side some qualitative feature in it, and lastly a postponement of the discharge of tension and a temporary acquiescence in ' painful ' tension.

The conclusion to be derived from these considerations is that a description of the pleasure-principle as the watchman over our lives cannot be altogether put aside.

Let us return to masochism. It comes under our observation in three shapes : as a condition under which sexual excitation may be roused ; as an expression of feminine nature ; and as a norm of behaviour. According to this one may distinguish an *erotogenic*, a *feminine*, and a *moral* type of masochism. The first, the erotogenic masochism, the lust of pain, is also to be found at bottom in the other forms ; the concept of it can be supported on biological and constitutional grounds ; it remains incomprehensible unless one can bring oneself to make certain assumptions about matters that are wrapt in obscurity. The third, in certain respects the most important form in which masochism appears, has only lately, as a sense of guilt that is for the most part unconscious, been properly appreciated by psycho-analysis ; it already admits, however, of full explanation and of co-ordination into our previous knowledge. Feminine masochism, on the other hand, is the form most accessible to observation, least mysterious, and is comprehensible in all its relations. We may begin our discussion with it.

In men (to whom for reasons connected with the material I shall limit my remarks) we know this kind of masochism sufficiently well from the phantasies of masochistic persons, who are often in consequence impotent ; their phantasies either terminate in an onanistic act or else themselves constitute the sexual gratification. These phantasies are in complete accord with the real conditions sought by masochistic perverts, whether these situations are enacted as an end in themselves or serve to induce potency and lead up to sexual intercourse. In both cases—for the real situations are in fact only a kind of make-believe performance of the phantasies—the manifest content is of being pinioned, bound, beaten painfully, whipped, in some way mishandled, forced to obey unconditionally, defiled, degraded. Far more rarely some kind of mutilation is also included in their content, but then only in a very restricted manner. The obvious interpretation, which is easily arrived at, is that the masochist wants to be treated like a little, helpless, dependent child, but especially like a naughty child. It is unnecessary to adduce case-material in this connection, for it is all so very much alike and is accessible to any observer, even to non-analysts. But if one has an opportunity of studying cases in which the masochistic phantasies have undergone specially rich elaboration, one easily discovers that in them the subject is placed in a situation characteristic of womanhood, *i.e.* they mean that he is being castrated, is playing the passive part in coitus, or is giving birth. For this reason I have called this form of masochism *a potiori* feminine, although so many of its features point to childish life. This stratification in superimposed layers of the infantile and the feminine will later find a simple explanation. Castration, or the blinding which represents it, often leaves a negative trace in these phantasies by the condition that just the genitals or the eyes are not to be injured in any way. (Incidentally, masochistic tortures seldom convey an impression of such seriousness as the brutalities—phantasied or actual—of sadists.) Moreover, in the manifest content of the masochistic phantasies a feeling of guilt comes to expression, it being assumed that the subject has committed some crime (the nature of which is left uncertain) which is to be expiated by his undergoing the pain and torture. This looks like a superficial rationalization of the masochistic content of the phantasy, but behind it there lies a relation to infantile masturbation. On the other hand, this element of guilt takes us to the third, the moral type of masochism.

The feminine type of masochism described is based entirely on the primary erotogenic type, on the ' lust of pain ', which cannot be explained without going very far back.

In my *Drei Abhandlungen zur Sexualtheorie*, in the section on the sources of infantile sexuality, I put forward the proposition that sexual excitation arises as an accessory effect of a large series of internal processes as soon as the intensity of these processes has exceeded certain quantitative limits ; indeed, that perhaps nothing very important takes place within the organism without contributing a component to the excitation of the sexual instinct. According to this, an excitation of physical pain and feelings of distress would surely also have this effect. This libidinal sympathetic excitation accompanying the tension of physical pain and feelings of distress would be an infantile physiological mechanism which ceases to operate later on. It would reach a varying degree of development in different sexual constitutions ; in any case it would provide the physiological foundation on which the structure of erotogenic masochism is subsequently erected in the mind.

The inadequacy of this explanation is seen, however, in that it throws no light on the regular and close connection of masochism with sadism, its counterpart in the life of the instincts. If we go a step further back to our hypothesis of the two varieties of instincts which we believe to be active in animate beings, we come to another conclusion which, however, does not contradict the one just mentioned. In the multicellular living organism the libido meets the death or destruction instinct which holds sway there, and which tries to disintegrate this cellular being and bring each elemental primary organism into a condition of inorganic stability (though this again may be but relative). To the libido falls the task of making this destructive instinct harmless, and it manages to dispose of it by directing it to a great extent and early in life—with the help of a special organic system, the musculature—towards the objects of the outer world. It is then called the instinct of destruction, of mastery, the will to power. A section of this instinct is placed directly in the service of the sexual function, where it has an important part to play : this is true sadism. Another part is not included in this displacement outwards ; it remains within the organism and is ' bound ' there libidinally with the help of the accompanying sexual excitation mentioned above : this we must recognize as the original erotogenic masochism.

We are entirely without any understanding of the physiological ways and means by which this subjugation of the death-instinct by the libido can be achieved. In the psycho-analytical world of ideas we can only assume that a very extensive coalescence and fusion, varying according to conditions, of the two instincts takes place, so that we never have to deal with pure life-instincts and death-instincts at all, but only with combinations of them in different degrees. Corresponding with the fusion of instincts there may under certain influences occur a ' *de*fusion ' of them. How large a part of the death-instincts may refuse to be subjugated in this way by becoming attached to libidinal quantities is at present not possible to ascertain.

If one is willing to disregard a certain amount of inexactitude, it might be said that the death-instinct active in the organism—the primal sadism—is identical with masochism. After the chief part of it has been directed outwards towards objects, there remains as a residuum within the organism the true erotogenic masochism, which on the one hand becomes a component of the libido and on the other still has the subject itself for an object. So that this masochism would be a witness and a survival of that phase of development in which the amalgamation, so important for life afterwards, of death-instinct and Eros took place. We should not be astonished to hear that under certain conditions the sadism or destruction instinct which has been directed outwards can be introjected, turned inward again, regressing in this way to its earlier condition. It then provides that secondary masochism which supplements the original one.

The erotogenic type of masochism passes through all the developmental stages of the libido, and from them it takes the changing shapes it wears in the life of the mind. The fear of being devoured by the totem-animal (father) is derived from the primitive oral stage of libido-organization ; the desire to be beaten by the father from the next-following sadistic-anal stage ; castration, although it is subsequently denied, enters into the content of masochistic phantasies as a residue from the phallic stage [1] ; and from the final genital stage are derived of course the situations characteristic of womanhood, namely, the passive part in coitus and the act of giving birth. The part played by the nates in masochism is also easily intelligible, apart from its obvious foundation in reality. The

[1] See No. XX. of this volume, p. 244.

nates are the special erotogenic bodily regions which have preference in the sadistic-anal stage, as the nipple in the oral stage and the penis in the genital stage.

The third form of masochism, the moral type, is chiefly remarkable for having loosened its connection with what we recognize to be sexuality. To all other masochistic sufferings there still clings the condition that it should be administered by the loved person ; it is endured at his command ; in the moral type of masochism this limitation has been dropped. It is the suffering itself that matters ; whether the sentence is cast by a loved or by an indifferent person is of no importance ; it may even be caused by impersonal forces or circumstances, but the true masochist always holds out his cheek wherever he sees a chance of receiving a blow. One is much tempted, in explaining this attitude, to leave the libido out of account and to confine oneself to an assumption that here the instinct of destruction is again turned inwards and is now raging against the self ; yet there should be some meaning in the usage of speech, which has not ceased to connect this norm of behaviour in life with erotism and calls these maimers of themselves masochists too.

True to a habit which has grown out of our technique, let us first consider the extreme, undeniably pathological form of this masochism. I have described elsewhere [1] how in analytic treatment we come across patients whose behaviour in regard to the effects of the analysis compels us to ascribe to them an ' unconscious ' feeling of guilt. I there mentioned the trait by which these people are recognized (the ' negative therapeutic reaction '), and I did not conceal the fact that a strong feeling of this kind amounts to one of the most difficult resistances and the greatest menace to the success of our medical or educative aims. The gratification of this unconscious sense of guilt is perhaps

[1] *Das Ich und das Es.*

the strongest item in the whole ' advantage through illness ' (which is as a rule composed of many different gains), *i.e.* in the sum-total of the forces which oppose the cure and struggle against relinquishing the neurosis ; the suffering that the neurosis involves is the very element which makes it of value to the masochistic trend. It is instructive, too, to find, against all theory and expectation, that a neurosis which has defied every therapeutic effort may vanish when the person has become involved in the misery of an unhappy marriage, has lost his fortune, or has developed a dangerous organic disease. The one form of suffering has then given way to another, and all that mattered, as we see, was that a certain level of suffering should be maintained.

Patients do not easily believe what we tell them about an unconscious sense of guilt. They know well enough by what torments (pangs of conscience) a conscious feeling of guilt, the consciousness of guilt, can express itself, and so they cannot admit that they could harbour entirely analogous feelings in themselves without observing a trace of them. I think we may meet their objection by abandoning the term ' unconscious feeling of guilt ', which is in any case an incorrect one psychologically, and substitute for it a ' need for punishment ' which describes the state of things observed just as aptly. We cannot, however, let ourselves be prevented from judging and localizing this unconscious feeling of guilt in the same way as we do the conscious variety.

We have ascribed to the super-ego the function of the conscience and have recognized the consciousness of guilt as an expression of a tension between ego and super-ego. The ego reacts with feelings of anxiety (pangs of conscience) to the perception that it has failed to perform the behests of its ideal, the super-ego. Now we want to know how the super-ego came to play this exacting part and why the ego has to fear a difference of opinion with its ideal.

We have said that the function of the ego consists in uniting with one another the claims of the three powers it serves, in reconciling them ; and we can add that it has in the super-ego a model for this which it can strive to emulate. This super-ego is in fact just as much a representative of the *id* as of the outer world. It originated through the introjection into the ego of the first objects of the libidinal impulses in the *id*, namely, the two parents, by which process the relation to them was desexualized, that is, underwent a deflection from direct sexual aims. Only in this way was it possible for the child to overcome the Oedipus-complex. Now the super-ego has retained essential features of the introjected persons, namely, their power, their severity, their tendency to watch over and to punish. As has been set forth elsewhere,[1] it is quite conceivable that this severity becomes intensified through the ' defusion ' of the instincts which takes place along with this incorporation into the ego. The super-ego, the conscience at work in it, can then become harsh, cruel and inexorable against the ego which is in its charge. The categorical imperative of Kant is thus a direct inheritance from the Oedipus-complex.

These same persons, however, whose effect persists as the power of conscience after they have ceased to be objects of libidinal impulses in the *id*, belong also to the real outer world. This is where they came from ; their power, behind which lie concealed all the influences of the past and of tradition, was one of the most acutely-felt manifestations of reality. In virtue of their coincidence the super-ego, which replaces the Oedipus-complex, becomes also a representative of the real outer world and is thus a model for the ego's endeavours.

In this way the Oedipus-complex proves itself, as has already been suggested on an historical basis,[2] to

[1] *Das Ich und das Es.*
[2] Freud, *Totem und Tabu*, Abschnitt IV.

be the origin of morality in each one of us.   In the course of development through childhood which brings about an ever-increasing severance from the parents, their personal significance for the super-ego recedes. To the imagos they leave behind are then linked on the influences of teachers, authorities, of self-chosen models and heroes venerated by society ;   these persons need no longer be introjected by the ego, which has now become much more resistant.   The last figure in the series beginning with the parents is that dark supremacy of Fate, which only the fewest among us are able to conceive of impersonally.   Little can be said against the Dutch writer, Multatuli,[1] when he substitutes the divine pair Λόγος καὶ ’Ανάγκη for the Μοῖρα of the Greeks ;   but all those who transfer the guidance of the world to Providence, to God, or to God and Nature, rouse a suspicion that they still look upon these farthest and remotest powers as a parent - couple — mythologically—and imagine themselves linked to them by libidinal bonds.   In *Das Ich und das Es* I have made an attempt to derive the objective fear of death in mankind also from the same sort of parental conception of Fate.   It seems to be very difficult to free oneself from it.

After these preliminaries we can return to our consideration of the moral type of masochism.   We said that the persons in question, by their behaviour— in the treatment and in their lives—make the impression of being morally inhibited to an excessive degree, of being dominated by an especially sensitive conscience, although they are not at all conscious of any such ultra-morality.   On close inspection we can surely see the distinction which divides this kind of unconscious development of morality from the moral type of masochism.   In the first, the accent falls on the heightened sadism of the super-ego to which the ego subjects itself ;   in the last, it falls instead on the masochism in the ego itself, which seeks punishment, whether from

[1] Ed. Douwes Dekker (1820-1887).

the super-ego within or from parental authorities without. It may be excused us that we confounded them to begin with, for in both cases it is a question of a relation between the ego and the super-ego or the powers equivalent to it ; in both cases there is a craving which is satisfied by punishment and suffering. It is hardly an insignificant detail then that the sadism of the super-ego is for the most part acutely perceived consciously, while the masochistic impulse of the ego as a rule remains hidden from the person and must be inferred from his behaviour.

The unconsciousness of the moral form of masochism guides us to a near clue. We have translated the words ' unconscious feeling of guilt ' as meaning a need for punishment by some parental authority. Now we know that the wish to be beaten by the father, which is so common, is closely connected with the other wish, to have some passive (feminine) sexual relations with him, and is only a regressive distortion of the latter. If we introduce this explanation into the content of moral masochism, its hidden meaning becomes clear to us. Conscience and morality arose through overcoming, desexualizing, the Oedipus-complex ; in moral maso-chism morality becomes sexualized afresh, the Oedipus-complex is reactivated, a regression from morality back to the Oedipus-complex is under way. This is to the advantage neither of the person concerned nor of morality. An individual may, it is true, preserve the whole or a certain amount of his morality alongside his masochism, but, on the other hand, a good part of his conscience may become swallowed up by his masochism. Further, the masochism in him creates a temptation to ' sinful acts ' which must then be expiated by the reproaches of the sadistic conscience (as in so many Russian character-types) or by chastise-ment from the great parental authority of Fate. In order to provoke punishment from this last parent-substitute the masochist must do something inex-pedient, act against his own interests, ruin the prospects which the real world offers him, and possibly destroy his own existence in the world of reality.

The revulsion of sadism against the self regularly occurs under the condition of civilized suppression of the instincts, which withholds a great part of the destructive instinctual components from being exercised in life. One can imagine that this backward-flowing part of the instinct of destruction comes to expression in the ego as an intensified masochism. The manifestations of conscience allow us to infer, however, that the destructiveness rebounding from the outer world is also absorbed by the super-ego without any such transformation and increases its sadism against the ego. The sadism of the super-ego and the masochism of the ego supplement each other and combine to produce the same effects. In my opinion it is only in this way possible to understand how it is that a feeling of guilt ensues—frequently or even quite generally—from a suppression of instinct and how it is that the more anyone refrains from aggressiveness towards others the more strict and sensitive his conscience becomes. One might expect that a person who knows himself to be in the habit of avoiding aggressions that are regarded as undesirable by civilization would have a good conscience as a result and would therefore watch over his ego less suspiciously. The situation is generally represented as though the requirements of social life came first and the instinctual renunciation were its consequence. The origin of morality remains then unexplained. The actual state of things seems to be a reversal of this : the first renunciation of instinctual gratification is enforced by external powers, and it is this that creates morality, which expresses itself in conscience and exacts a further renunciation of instinct.

Moral masochism thus becomes the classical piece of evidence for the existence of ' instinctual fusion '. Its dangerousness lies in its origin in the death-instinct and represents that part of the latter which escaped deflection on to the outer world in the form of an instinct of destruction. But since, on the other hand, it has the value of an erotic component, even the destruction of anyone by himself cannot occur without gratification of the libido.

XXIII

THE PASSING OF THE OEDIPUS-COMPLEX [1]

(1924)

THE significance of the Oedipus-complex as the central phenomenon of the sexual period in early childhood reveals itself more and more. After this it disappears; it succumbs to repression, as we say, and is followed by the latency period. But it is not yet clear to us what occasions its decay; analyses seem to show that the painful disappointments experienced bring this about. The little girl who wants to believe herself her father's beloved and partner in love must one day endure a harsh punishment at his hands, and finds herself hurled to earth from her cloud-castles. The boy who regards his mother as his own property finds that her love and care for him are transferred to a new arrival. Reflection deepens the effect of these impressions by insisting that painful experiences of this kind, antagonistic to the content of the complex, are inevitable. Even when no special events such as those mentioned occur, the absence of the hoped-for gratification, the continual frustration of the wish for a child, causes the love-lorn little one to turn from its hopeless longing. According to this, the Oedipus-complex becomes extinguished by its lack of success, the result of its inherent impossibility.

Another view would put it that the Oedipus-complex must come to an end because the time has come for its dissolution, just as the milk-teeth fall out when the permanent ones begin to press forward. Although the majority of human children individually pass through

[1] First published in *Zeitschrift*, Bd. X., 1924. [Translated by Joan Riviere.]

the Oedipus-complex, yet after all it is a phenomenon determined and laid down for him by heredity, and must decline according to schedule when the next pre-ordained stage of development arrives. It is therefore not very important what the occasions are through which this happens, or whether any such occasions are discoverable at all.

One cannot dispute the justice of both these views. They are compatible with each other, moreover ; there is room for the ontogenetic alongside the more far-reaching phylogenetic one. Even at birth, indeed, the whole organism is destined to die, and an indication of what will eventually cause its death may possibly already be contained in its organic disposition. Yet after all it is of interest to follow up the way in which the innate schedule is worked out, the way in which accidental noxiae exploit the disposition.

We have lately recognized more clearly than before that the sexual development of a child advances up to a certain point, and that when it reaches this point the genital organ has already taken over the leading part. The genital organ in question, however, is the male alone, or, more exactly, the penis ; the female organ is still undiscovered. This phallic phase, which is contemporaneous with the Oedipus-complex, does not develop further into the final stage of genital organization, but becomes submerged, and is succeeded by the latency period. Its conclusion, however, is effected in a typical manner and in conjunction with happenings that recur regularly.

When the (male) child's interest turns to his genital organ, he betrays this by handling it frequently, and then he is bound to discover that grown-up people do not approve of this activity. More or less plainly and more or less brutally the threat is uttered that this highly valued part of him will be taken away. Usually it is from women that the threat emanates ; very often they seek to strengthen their authority by referring to the father or the doctor, who, as they assure the

child, will carry out the punishment. In a number of
cases women will themselves modify the threat in a
symbolic manner by warning the child that his actively
sinning hand will be removed, instead of his genital,
which is after all passive. It happens particularly often
that the little boy is threatened in this way not because
he plays with his penis with his hand, but because he
wets his bed every night and is not to be induced to
learn cleanliness. Children's attendants behave as if
this nocturnal incontinence were a result and a proof
of undue preoccupation with the penis, and are probably
right in their inference. In any case long-continued
bed-wetting is comparable to pollutions in adults—
an expression of the same excitation in the genitals
that impels the child to masturbate at this period.

Now the view we hold is that the phallic stage of
the genital organization succumbs to this threat of
castration. But not immediately, and not without
the assistance of further influences. For to begin with
the boy does not believe in the threat, nor obey it in
the least. Psycho-analysis has recently laid fresh
emphasis on two experiences which all children go
through, by which it is thought that they become
prepared for the loss of a valued part of the body—the
withdrawal from them of the mother's breast, at first
intermittently and later finally, and the daily demand
made on them to give up the contents of the bowel.
But if these experiences have an effect when the threat
of castration takes place, one sees nothing of it. Not
until yet another experience comes its way does the
child begin to reckon with the possibility of being
castrated, and then only hesitatingly, unwillingly, and
not without efforts to depreciate the significance of
what it has itself observed.

The observation that finally breaks down the child's
unbelief is the sight of the female genitalia. Some day
or other it happens that the child whose own penis is
such a proud possession obtains a sight of the genital
parts of a little girl ; he must then become convinced

of the absence of a penis in a creature so like himself. With this, however, the loss of his own penis becomes imaginable, and the threat of castration achieves its delayed effect.

We must not be so short-sighted as the child's attendant who threatens it with castration ; we cannot overlook the fact that the child's sexual life at this time is by no means exhausted by masturbation. The child is demonstrably under the influence of the Oedipus-attitude to its parents ; masturbation is only the discharge in the genital of the excitation belonging to the complex, and to this connection between the two masturbation will owe its significance to him for ever after. The Oedipus-complex offered the child two possibilities of satisfaction, an active and a passive one. It could have put itself in its father's place and had intercourse with the mother as he did, so that the father was soon felt to be an obstacle ; or else it had wanted to supplant the mother and be loved by the father, whereupon the mother became superfluous. The child may have had only the vaguest notions of what constituted the love-intercourse which serves as a gratification, but that the penis played a part in it was certain, for the feelings in his own organ were evidence of that. So far there had been no occasion for doubt about a penis in women. But now the acceptance of the possibility of castration, the recognition that women are castrated, makes an end of both the possibilities of satisfaction in the Oedipus-complex. For both of them — the male as a consequence, a punishment, and the other, the female, as a prerequisite—would indeed be accompanied by a loss of the penis. If the gratification desired in consequence of the love is to cost the child his penis, a conflict must arise between the narcissistic interest in this part of the body and the libidinal cathexis of the parent-objects. Normally, in this conflict the first of these forces triumphs ; the child's ego turns away from the Oedipus-complex.

I have described elsewhere the way by which this aversion is accomplished. The object-cathexes are given up and replaced by identification. The authority of the father or the parents is introjected into the ego and there forms the kernel of the super-ego, which takes its severity from the father, perpetuates his prohibition against incest, and so insures the ego against a recurrence of the libidinal object-cathexis. The libidinal trends belonging to the Oedipus-complex are in part desexualized and sublimated, which probably happens with every transformation into identification ; in part they are inhibited in their aim and changed into affectionate feelings. The whole process, on the one hand, preserves the genital organ, wards off the danger of losing it ; on the other hand, it paralyses it, takes away its function from it. This process introduces the latency period which now interrupts the child's sexual development.

I see no reason to deny the name of ' repression ' to the ego's turning from the Oedipus-complex, although later repressions are for the most part effected with the participation of the super-ego, which is only built up during this process. But the process described is more than a repression ; when carried out in the ideal way it is equivalent to a destruction and abrogation of the complex. It is not a great step to assume that here we have come upon the borderland between normal and pathological which is never very sharply defined. If the ego has really not achieved much more than a repression of the complex, then this latter persists unconsciously in the *id*, and will express itself later on in some pathogenic effect.

Analytic observation enables us to perceive or to infer these connections between the phallic organization, the Oedipus-complex, the threat of castration, the formation of the super-ego and the latency period. They justify the statement that the Oedipus-complex succumbs to the threat of castration. But this does not dispose of the problem ; there is room for a theoretical speculation which may overthrow the results obtained or set them in a new light. Before we traverse this path, however, we must attend to a question which was already roused during this discussion and has long been left on one side. The process described relates, as we expressly stated, only to the male child. How is the corresponding development effected in a little girl ?

Here our material—for some reason we do not understand—becomes far more shadowy and incomplete. The female sex develops an Oedipus-complex, too, a super-ego and a latency period. May one ascribe to it also a phallic organization and a castration complex ? The answer is in the affirmative, but it cannot be the same as in the boy. The feministic demand for equal rights between the sexes does not carry far here ; the morphological difference must express itself in differences in the development of the mind. ' Anatomy is Destiny ', to vary a saying of Napoleon's. The little girl's clitoris behaves at first just like a penis, but by comparing herself with a boy playfellow the child perceives that she has ' come off short ', and takes this fact as ill-treatment and as a reason for feeling inferior. For a time she still consoles herself with the expectation that later, when she grows up, she will acquire just as big an appendage as a boy. Here the woman's ' masculine complex ' branches off. The female child does not understand her actual loss as a sex characteristic, but explains it by assuming that at some earlier date she had possessed a member which was just as big and which had later been lost by castration. She does not seem to extend this conclusion about herself to other grown women, but in complete accordance with the phallic phase she ascribes to them large and complete, that is, male, genitalia. The result is an essential difference between her and the boy, namely, that she accepts castration as an established fact, an operation already performed, whereas the boy dreads the possibility of its being performed.

The castration-dread being thus excluded in her case, there falls away a powerful motive towards forming the super-ego and breaking up the infantile genital organization. These changes seem to be due in the girl far more than in the boy to the results of educative influences, of external intimidation threatening the loss of love. The Oedipus-complex in the girl is far simpler, less equivocal, than that of the little possessor of a penis ; in my experience it seldom goes beyond the wish to take the mother's place, the feminine attitude towards the father. Acceptance of the loss of a penis is not endured without some attempt at compensation. The girl passes over—by way of a symbolic analogy, one may say—from the penis to a child ; her Oedipus-complex culminates in the desire, which is long cherished, to be given a child by her father as a present, to bear him a child. One has the impression that the Oedipus-complex is later gradually abandoned because this wish is never fulfilled. The two desires, to possess a penis and to bear a child, remain powerfully charged with libido in the unconscious and help to prepare the woman's nature for its subsequent sex rôle. The comparative weakness of the sadistic component of the sexual instinct, which may probably be related to the penis-deficiency, facilitates the transformation of directly sexual trends into those inhibited in aim, feelings of tenderness. It must be confessed, however, that on the whole our insight into these processes of development in the girl is unsatisfying, shadowy and incomplete.

I have no doubt that the temporal and causal relations described between Oedipus-complex, sexual intimidation (the threat of castration), formation of the super-ego and advent of the latency period are of a typical kind ; but I do not maintain that this type is the only possible one. Variations in the sequence and the linking up of these processes must be very significant in the development of the individual.

Since the publication of Otto Rank's interesting

study on the trauma of birth, the conclusion of the present modest communication—that the boy's Oedipus-complex succumbs to the dread of castration—cannot be accepted without further discussion. It seems to me premature, however, to enter upon this discussion at the present time, and perhaps also inadvisable to begin to criticize or to assess the value of Rank's view in the present connection.

XXIV

THE LOSS OF REALITY IN NEUROSIS AND PSYCHOSIS [1]

(1924)

I HAVE recently [2] defined as follows one of the features distinguishing the neuroses from the psychoses : in the former the ego, in virtue of its allegiance to reality, suppresses a part of the *id* (the life of instinct), whereas in the psychoses the same ego, in the service of the *id*, withdraws itself from a part of reality. According to this, the excessive power of the influence of reality is decisive for neurosis, and for psychosis that of the *id*. A loss of reality must be an inherent element in psychosis ; while in neurosis, one would suppose, it would be avoided.

But now, this does not at all agree with experience, which shows us all that every neurosis in some way interferes with the patient's situation in life, that it serves him as a means whereby he can withdraw from his real situation and that in its severe forms it signifies directly a flight from real life. This contradiction appears to give grounds for thought ; it is, however, easily removed, and an explanation of it will but advance our comprehension of neurosis.

The contradiction exists only so long as we keep in mind merely the situation at the outbreak of the neurosis, when the ego undertakes, in the service of reality, to repress an instinctual impulse. This is not yet the neurosis itself, however. The latter consists much more in those processes which render compensation for the damage done to a part of the *id*, *i.e.* in the

---

[1] Here first published. [Translated by Joan Riviere.]
[2] ' Neurosis and Psychosis ', No. XXI. of this volume, p. 250.

reaction to the repression and in a miscarriage of it. The loosening of the relation to reality is then a consequence of this second step in the formation of a neurosis, and we should not be surprised if close investigation showed that the loss of reality concerned precisely that very part of reality which demanded the instinctual repression.

It is nothing new to characterize neurosis as the outcome of a repression which has miscarried. We have always said this, and only because of the new connection it has come into was it necessary to repeat it.

Incidentally, the same doubts arise again in a specially impressive manner when the neurosis in question is a case in which the exciting cause (' the traumatic scene ') is known, and in which one can see how the person averts himself from the experience and consigns it to an amnesia. I will take, for instance, a case analysed many years ago,[1] in which a young woman who was in love with her brother-in-law, and whose sister lay dying, was horrified at the thought, ' Now he is free and can marry me ' ! This scene was instantly forgotten, and thus the process of repression which led to the hysterical pains was set in motion. It is instructive to see precisely in such a case, however, the way in which a neurosis attempts to solve the conflict. It discounts the change in reality, by repressing the claim of the instinct in question, the love for the brother-in-law. The psychotic reaction would have been a denial of the fact of the sister's death.

Now one might expect that when a psychosis breaks out something analogous to the process in a neurosis happens, though of course between different institutions in the mind ; that is, that two steps may be discernible in a psychosis also, the first of which tears the ego away from reality, while the second tries to make good the damage done and re-establish the relation to reality at the expense of the *id*. And

---

[1] Breuer und Freud, *Studien über Hysterie*, 1895.

something of the kind can really be observed in a
psychosis ; there are indeed two stages in it, the
second of which bears the character of a reparation—
but then the analogy gives way to a far more extensive
similarity in the two processes. The second step in a
psychosis is also an attempt to make good the loss of
reality, not, however, at the expense of a restriction
laid on the *id*—as in neurosis at the expense of the
relation with reality—but in another, a more lordly
manner, by creating a new reality which is no longer
open to objections like that which has been forsaken.
The second step, therefore, in both neurosis and
psychosis is induced by the same tendencies ; in both
it serves the struggle for power on the part of the *id*
which will not allow reality to dictate to it. Neurosis
and psychosis are both of them an expression of the
rebellion of the *id* against the outer world, of its
' pain ', unwillingness to adapt itself to necessity—to
ἀνάγκη, or, if one prefers, of its incapacity to do so.
They are far more distinguishable from each other in
the reaction at the outbreak than in the attempt at
reparation which follows it.

The difference at the beginning comes to expression
at the end in this way : in neurosis a part of reality
is avoided by a sort of flight, but in psychosis it is
remodelled. Or one may say that in psychosis flight
at the beginning is succeeded by an active phase of
reconstruction, while in neurosis obedience at the
beginning is followed by a subsequent attempt at
flight. Or, to express it in yet another way, neurosis
does not deny the existence of reality, it merely tries to
ignore it ; psychosis denies it and tries to substitute
something else for it. A reaction which combines
features of both these is the one we call normal or
' healthy ' ; it denies reality as little as neurosis, but
then, like a psychosis, is concerned with effecting
a change in it. This expedient normal attitude
leads naturally to some active achievement in the
outer world and is not content, like a psychosis, with

establishing the alteration within itself; it is no longer *auto-plastic* but *allo-plastic*.

In a psychosis the remodelling of reality is effected by means of the residues in the mind of former relations with reality; that is, it concerns the memory-traces, ideas and judgements which have previously been formed about reality and by which reality was represented in the life of the mind. But this relation was never a final and complete one; it was perpetually being enriched and altered by new perceptions. Thus to a psychosis also there falls the task of creating perceptions of a kind corresponding with the new reality, which is accomplished most effectually by way of hallucinations. Now the falsifications of memory, the delusional systems and hallucinations in so many cases and forms of psychosis are of a most distressing character and are bound up with a development of dread, which is surely a sign that the whole process of remodelling reality is conducted in the face of most strenuous opposition. We may, for our own purposes, reconstruct the process on the model of a neurosis, which is more familiar to us. Here we see that a reaction of anxiety takes place every time the repressed instinct makes a move forward, and that the result of the conflict is after all but a compromise and as a satisfaction is incomplete. Probably in a psychosis the rejected part of reality re-asserts its claim, just as in neurosis the repressed instinct does; hence the consequences in both are the same. Elucidation of the various mechanisms in the psychoses by which the turning from reality and reconstruction of it is effected, and also of the degree of success they are able to achieve, is a task for special psychiatry which has not yet been undertaken.

There exists, therefore, a further analogy between neurosis and psychosis in that the task undertaken in the second step of each to some extent miscarries; for the repressed instinct (in neurosis) cannot create for itself a completely satisfying substitute, and the presentations of reality do not permit of being re-casted into entirely satisfying moulds (not, at least, in all forms of mental disorder). But the accent falls differently in the two cases. In a psychosis it falls exclusively on the first step, which is pathological in itself and can only lead to disease ; in neurosis, on the contrary, it falls on the second step, the miscarriage of repression, whereas the first step may succeed and does succeed on innumerable occasions within the bounds of health—even though it is not achieved free of cost and without leaving traces of the necessary expenditure of mental energy. These differences, and perhaps many others too, are the consequence of the topographical difference in the original situation at the outbreak of the pathogenic conflict—whether in this conflict the ego surrenders to its dependence on the real world or to its allegiance to the *id*.

A neurosis usually contents itself with avoiding the part of reality in question and protecting itself against coming into contact with it. The sharp distinction between neurosis and psychosis is modified, however, by the circumstance that neurosis, too, does not fail to make attempts to substitute a reality more in accord with its desires for the unsatisfactory real one. The way in which this becomes possible is through the *world of phantasy*, a realm that, at the time when the activity of the reality-principle first set in, became distinguished from the real outer world, and later on was excluded from the demands of necessity, like a kind of ' reservation ', and which, though not inaccessible to the ego, is only loosely attached to it. It is from this world of phantasy that neurosis draws the material for re-creating the world afresh according to its desires, and it finds this material there, as a rule, by way of a regression to an earlier period in real life.

It is hardly possible to doubt that the world of phantasy plays the same part in a psychosis, that for it, too, this world represents the store-chamber from which the materials or the design for constructing a new reality are obtained. But the new phantastic outer world of a psychosis attempts to set itself in place of external reality. That of neurosis, on the contrary, is glad to attach itself, like a children's game, to a part of reality—some other part than the one against which it must protect itself ; it endows it with a special meaning and a secret significance which we, not always quite correctly, call *symbolical*. Thus we see that there arises both in neurosis and in psychosis the question not only of the *loss of reality*, but of a *substitute for reality* too.

PAPERS ON TECHNIQUE

XXV

THE FUTURE PROSPECTS OF PSYCHO-ANALYTIC THERAPY [1]

An Address delivered before the Second International Psycho-analytical Congress at Nuremberg in 1910

(1910)

SINCE the objects for which we are assembled here to-day are mainly practical, I shall choose a practical theme for my introductory address and appeal to your interest in medical, not in scientific, matters. I can imagine what your opinion about the success of our therapy probably is, and I assume that most of you have already passed through the two stages which all beginners go through, that of enthusiasm at the unexpected increase in our therapeutic achievements, and that of depression at the magnitude of the difficulties which stand in the way of our efforts. Whichever of these stages in development, however, each of you may happen to be going through at the moment, my intention to-day is to show you that we have by no means come to the end of our resources for combating the neuroses, and that we may expect a substantial improvement in our therapeutic prospects before very long.

This improvement will come, I think, from three sources :

1. From internal progress.
2. From increased prestige.
3. From the general effect of our work.

[1] First published in *Zentralblatt*, Bd. I., 1910 ; reprinted in *Sammlung*, Dritte Folge. [Translated by Joan Riviere.]

1. Under ' internal progress ' I understand advances (*a*) in our analytical knowledge, (*b*) in our technique.

(*a*) Advances in our knowledge. We are, of course, still a long way from knowing all that is required for an understanding of the unconscious minds of our patients. Now it is clear that every advance in our knowledge means an increase in the power of our therapy. As long as we understood nothing, we accomplished nothing; the more we understand the more we shall achieve. At its beginning psycho-analytic treatment was inexorable and exhaustive. The patient had to say everything himself, and the physician's part consisted of urging him on incessantly. To-day things have a more friendly air. The treatment is made up of two parts, out of what the physician infers and tells the patient, and out of the patient's work of assimilation, of ' working through ', what he hears. The mechanism of our curative method is indeed quite easy to understand ; we give the patient the conscious idea of what he may expect to find (*bewusste Erwartungsvorstellung*), and the similarity of this with the repressed unconscious one leads him to come upon the latter himself. This is the intellectual help which makes it easier for him to overcome the resistances between conscious and unconscious. Incidentally, I may remark that it is not the only mechanism made use of by the analytic method ; you all know that far more powerful one which lies in the use of the ' transference '. I intend soon to undertake an exposition of these various factors, which are so important for an understanding of the cure, in a Practice of Psycho-Analysis. And, further, in speaking to you I need not rebut the objection that the way in which we practise the method to-day obscures its testimony to the correctness of our hypotheses ; you will not forget that this evidence is to be found elsewhere, and that a therapeutic procedure cannot be performed in the same way as a theoretical investigation.

Now let me refer briefly to various fields in which

we both have much to learn that is new and do actually make new discoveries daily. First of all, there is the matter of symbolism in dreams and in the unconscious —a fiercely contested subject, as you know ! It is no small credit to our colleague, W. Stekel, that, indifferent to all the objections of our opponents, he has undertaken a study of dream-symbols. In this there is indeed much still to learn ; my *Traumdeutung*, which was written in 1899, awaits important amplification from researches into symbolism.

I will say a few words about one of the symbols that has lately been recognized. Not long ago it came to my knowledge that a psychologist whose views are not too distant from ours had remarked to one of us that we undoubtedly overestimate the hidden sexual significance of dreams ; his most frequent dream was of going upstairs, and there could certainly be nothing sexual about that. Our attention being thus drawn to it, we began to study the incidence of stairs, steps and ladders in dreams, and soon could establish the fact that stairs and such things are certainly a symbol of coitus. The underlying element which the two things have in common is not difficult to discover ; one climbs an acclivity in rhythmic movements, accompanied by increasing breathlessness, and in a few rapid leaps can be down below again. Thus the rhythm of coitus reappears in climbing steps. We will not forget to adduce the usages of speech in this connection. It shows us that ' mounting ' is used quite simply as a symbol for the sexual act. In German one says ' the man is a *Steiger, nachsteigen* '. In French the steps of a stair are called ' *marches* ' ; ' *un vieux marcheur* ', *ein alter Steiger* both mean an old profligate. The dream-material from which these newly recognized symbols are derived will in due time be put before you by the committee we are about to form for collecting and studying symbols. An account of another interesting symbol, of the idea of ' rescue ' and its changes in significance, will appear in the second volume of our

Jahrbuch. However, I must break off here or I shall
not reach my other points.

Every one of you will know from his own experience
the total change in one's attitude to a new case when
once one has thoroughly mastered the structure of some
typical cases of illness. Assuming now that we had
narrowly defined the regular elements in the composition of the various forms of neurosis, just as we
have already succeeded in doing for hysterical symptom-
formation, how much more assured we should be in
our prognoses ! Just as an obstetrician knows by
examining the placenta whether it has been completely
expelled or whether noxious fragments of it still
remain, so we should be able, independently of the
success of the cure and the patient's present condition,
to say whether the work had been completely carried to
an end or whether we had to expect relapses and fresh
onsets of illness.

(*b*) I will hasten on to the innovations in the field
of technique, where indeed nearly everything still
awaits definitive settlement, and much is only now
beginning to come clear. There are now two aims in
psycho-analytic technique : to save the physician
effort and to open up for the patient the freest access
to his unconscious. You know that our technique has
been transformed in important respects. At the time
of the cathartic treatment we set ourselves the aim
of elucidating the symptoms, then we turned away
from the symptoms to discovering the ' complexes ',
to use Jung's indispensable word ; now, however, our
work is aimed directly at finding out and overcoming
the ' resistances ', and we can with justification rely
on the complexes coming to light as soon as the
resistances have been recognized and removed. Some
of you have since shown a desire to formulate and
classify these resistances. Now I beg you to examine
your material and see whether you can confirm the
following statement : In male patients the most
important resistances to the treatment seem to be

derived from the father-complex and to express themselves in fear of the father, and in defiance and
incredulity towards him.

Other innovations in technique relate to the
physician himself. We have begun to consider the
' counter-transference ', which arises in the physician
as a result of the patient's influence on his unconscious
feelings, and have nearly come to the point of requiring
the physician to recognize and overcome this counter-
transference in himself. Now that a larger number
of people have come to practise psycho-analysis and
mutually exchange their experiences, we have noticed
that every analyst's achievement is limited by what
his own complexes and resistances permit, and consequently we require that he should begin his practice
with a self-analysis and should extend and deepen
this constantly while making his observations on his
patients. Anyone who cannot succeed in this self-
analysis may without more ado regard himself as
unable to treat neurotics by analysis.

We are also now coming to the opinion that the
analytic technique must undergo certain modifications
according to the nature of the disease and the dominating instinctual trends in the patient. Our therapy
was, in fact, first designed for conversion-hysteria ;
in anxiety-hysteria (phobias) we must alter our
procedure to some extent. The fact is that these
patients cannot bring out the material necessary for
resolving the phobia so long as they feel protected
by retaining their phobic condition. One cannot, of
course, induce them to give up their protective measures
and work under the influence of anxiety from the
beginning of the treatment. One must therefore help
them by interpreting their unconscious to them until
they can make up their minds to do without the
protection of their phobia and expose themselves to a
now comparatively moderate degree of anxiety. Only
when they have done so does the material necessary
for achieving solution of the phobia become accessible.

Other modifications of technique which seem to me not yet ready for discussion will be required in the treatment of obsessional neurosis. In this connection very important questions arise, which are not yet elucidated : how far the instincts involved in the conflict in the patient are to be allowed some gratification during the treatment, and what difference it then makes whether these impulses are active (sadistic) or passive (masochistic) in nature.

I hope you have received the impression that, when all that can at present be merely glimpsed is known and when we have established all the improvements in technique to which deeper experience with our patients must lead us, then our medical practice will reach a degree of precision and certainty of success which is not to be had in all medical specialities.

2. I said that we had much to expect from the increase in prestige which must accrue to us as time goes on. I need hardly say much to you about the importance of authority. Only very few civilized persons are capable of existing without reliance on others or are even capable of coming to an independent opinion. You cannot exaggerate the intensity of man's inner irresolution and craving for authority. The extraordinary increase in the neuroses since the power of religion has waned may give you some indication of it. The impoverishment of the ego due to the tremendous effort in repression demanded of every individual by culture may be one of the principal causes of this state of things.

Hitherto the weight of authority with its enormous ' suggestive ' force has been against us. All our therapeutic successes have been achieved in spite of this suggestion ; it is surprising that any success was to be had at all in the circumstances. I will not let myself go to the extent of describing to you the agreeable things that happened during the time when I alone represented psycho-analysis. I know that when I assured my patients that I knew how to relieve them

permanently of their sufferings they looked round
my modest abode, thought of my want of fame and
honours, and regarded me like a man who possesses an
infallible system in a gambling-place, of whom people
say that if he could do what he professes he would
look very different. Nor was it really at all pleasant to
operate on people's minds while colleagues whose duty
it was to assist took a pleasure in spitting into the
field of operation, and while at the first signs of blood or
restlessness in him the patient's relatives threatened
one. An operation may surely cause reactions ; in
surgery we became used to that long ago. Nobody
believed in me, in fact, just as even to-day very few
believe in us ; under such conditions many an attempt
was bound to fail. To estimate the increase in our
therapeutic capacities that will ensue when general
recognition is accorded us, you should think of the
different positions of gynæcologists in Turkey and in
the West. All that a woman's physician may do there
is to feel the pulse of an arm which is stretched out to
him through a hole in the wall. And his curative
results are in proportion to the inaccessibility of their
object ; our opponents in the West wish to restrict
our access over our patients' minds to something very
similar. But now that the force of public opinion
drives sick women to the gynæcologist, he has become
their helper and saviour. Now do not say that, even
if the weight of public opinion comes to our aid and so
much increases our successes, that will in no way prove
the validity of our hypotheses. Suggestion is supposed
to be able to do anything, and our successes would then
be results of suggestion and not of psycho-analysis.
Public opinion is at present suggesting hydropathic
cures, diet cures, electricity cures for nervous persons,
but that does not enable these measures to remove the
neuroses. It will be seen whether psycho-analytic
treatment can accomplish more than they.

But now, to be sure, I must damp the ardour of
your expectations. The community will not hasten

to grant authority to us. It is bound to offer resistance to us, for we adopt a critical attitude towards it ; we accuse it of playing a great part itself in causing the neuroses. Just as we make any single person our enemy by discovering what is repressed in him, so the community cannot respond with sympathy to a relentless exposure of its injurious effects and deficiencies ; because we destroy illusions we are accused of endangering ideals. It seems, therefore, that the state of things from which I expect such great advantages for our therapeutic results will never arrive. And yet the situation is not so hopeless as one might think at the present time. Powerful though the feelings and the self-interest of men may be, yet intellect is a power too. It has not, perhaps, the power that makes itself felt immediately, but one that is all the more certain in the end. The most mordant verities are heard at last, after the interests they injure and the emotions they rouse have exhausted their frenzy. It has always been so, and the unwelcome truths which we psychoanalysts have to tell the world will undergo the same fate. Only it will not come very quickly ; we must be able to wait.

3. Finally, I have to explain to you what I mean by the ' general effect ' of our work, and how I come to set my hopes on it. This consists in a very remarkable therapeutic constellation which could perhaps not be repeated anywhere else and which will appear strange to you too at first, until you recognize in it something you have long been familiar with. You know, of course, that the psychoneuroses are substitutive gratifications of instincts the existence of which one is forced to deny to oneself and others. Their capacity to exist depends on this distortion and disguise. When the riddle they hold is solved and the solution accepted by the sufferers these diseases will no longer be able to exist. There is hardly anything quite like it in medicine ; in fairy-tales you hear of evil spirits whose power is broken when you can tell them their name which they have kept secret.

Now in place of a single sick person put the whole community of persons liable to neuroses, persons ill and persons well ; in place of the acceptance of the solution in the first put a general recognition in the second ; and a little reflection will show you that this substitution cannot alter the result at all.   The success which the therapy has with individuals must appear in the many too.   Diseased people cannot let their various neuroses become known — their apprehensive over-anxiousness which is to conceal their hatred, their agoraphobia which betrays disappointed ambition, their obsessive actions which represent self-reproaches for evil intentions and precautions against them— when all their relatives and every stranger from whom they wish to conceal their thoughts and feelings know the general meaning of these symptoms, and when they know themselves that the manifestations of their disease produce nothing which others cannot instantly understand.   The effect, however, will not be merely that they will conceal their symptoms—a design, by the way, which would be impossible to execute ; for this concealment will destroy the purpose of the illness. Disclosure of the secret will have attacked, at its most sensitive point, the ' ætiological equation ' from which the neuroses descend, will have made the ' advantage through illness ' illusory, and consequently in the end nothing can come of the changed situation brought about by the indiscretions of physicians but an end of producing these illnesses.

If this hope seems utopian to you, you may remember that certain neurotic phenomena have already been dispelled by this means, although only in quite isolated instances.   Think how common hallucinations of the Virgin Mary were in peasant-girls in former times.   So long as such a phenomenon brought a flock of believers and resulted perhaps in a chapel being built on the sacred spot, the visionary state of these maidens was inaccessible to influence.   To-day even the priesthood has changed its attitude to such things ; it allows police and medical men to visit the seer, and since then the Virgin appears very seldom. Or allow me to study the same processes, that I have been describing as taking place in the future, in an analogous situation which is on a smaller scale and consequently more easily appreciated. Suppose that a number of ladies and gentlemen in good society had planned a picnic at an inn in the forest one day. The ladies make up their minds that if one of them wants to relieve a natural need she will say aloud that she is going to pick flowers ; but a wicked fellow hears of this secret and has printed on the programme which is sent round to the whole party—' If the ladies wish to retire they are requested to say that they are going to pick flowers '. Of course after this no lady will think of availing herself of this flowery pretext, and other freshly devised formulas of the same kind will be seriously compromised by it. What will be the result ? The ladies will own up to their natural needs without shame and none of the men will take exception to it. Let us return to the serious aspect of our problem. A number of people who find life's conflicts too difficult to solve have taken flight into neurosis and in this way won an unmistakable, although in the end too costly, advantage through illness. What would these people have to do if their flight into illness were barred by the indiscreet revelations of psycho-analysis ? They would have to be honest, own up to the instincts that are at work in them, face the conflict, fight for what they want or go without, and the tolerance from the community which is bound to ensue as a result of psycho-analytical knowledge would help them in their task.

Let us remember, however, that it is not for us to advance upon life as fanatical hygienists or therapeutists. We must admit that this ideal prevention of all neurotic illness would not be advantageous to every individual. A good number of those who now take flight into illness would not support the conflict under the conditions we have assumed, but would rapidly succumb or would commit some outrage which would be worse than if they themselves fell ill of a neurosis. The neuroses have in fact their biological function as defensive measures and their social justification ; the ' advantage through illness ' that they provide is not always a purely subjective one. Is there one of you who has not at some time caught a glimpse behind the scenes in the causation of a neurosis and had to allow that it was the.least of the evils possible in the circumstances ? And should one really require such sacrifices in order to exterminate the neuroses, while the world is all the same full of other inextinguishable miseries ?

Should we therefore abandon our efforts to explain the hidden meaning of neurotic manifestations, regarding it as dangerous to the individual and harmful to the interests of society ; should we give up drawing the practical conclusion from a piece of scientific insight ? No ; I think that nevertheless our duty lies in the other direction. The ' advantage through illness ' provided by the neuroses is indeed on the whole and in the end detrimental to the individual as well as to society. The distress that our work of revelation may cause will but affect a few. The change to a more honest and honourable attitude in the world in general will not be bought too dearly by these sacrifices. But above all, all the energies which are to-day consumed in the production of neurotic symptoms, to serve the purposes of a world of phantasy out of touch with reality, will, even if they cannot at once be put to uses in life, help to strengthen the outcry for those changes in our civilization from which alone we can hope for better things for our descendants.

I will let you go, therefore, with the assurance that you do your duty in more than one sense by treating your patients psycho-analytically. You are not merely working in the service of science, by using the only and irreplaceable opportunity for discovering the secrets of the neuroses ; you are not only giving your patients the most efficacious remedy for their sufferings available at the present time ; but you are contributing your share to that enlightenment of the many from which we expect to gain the authority of the community in general and thus to achieve the most far-reaching prophylaxis against neurotic disorders.

OBSERVATIONS ON 'WILD' PSYCHO-ANALYSIS [1]

(1910)

A FEW days ago an elderly lady, under the protection of a female friend, called upon me for a consultation, complaining of anxiety-states. She was in the second half of the forties, fairly well preserved, and had obviously not yet finished with her womanhood. A divorce from her last husband had been the occasion exciting the anxiety-states ; but the anxiety had become greatly intensified, according to her account, since she had consulted a young physician in the suburb she lived in, for he had informed her that her sexual desires were the cause of her anxiety. He said that she could not tolerate the loss of intercourse with her husband, and so there were only three ways by which she could recover her health—she must either return to her husband, or take a lover, or satisfy herself. Since then she had been convinced that she was incurable, for she would not return to her husband, and the other two alternatives were repugnant to her moral and religious feelings. She had come to me, however, because the doctor had said that I was responsible for this new opinion, and that she had only to come and ask me to confirm what he said, and I should tell her that this and nothing else was the truth. The friend who was with her, a still older, pinched and unhealthy-looking woman, then implored me to assure the patient that the doctor was mistaken. It could not possibly be true, for she herself had been

¹ First published in *Zentralblatt*, Bd. I., 1910 ; reprinted in *Sammlung*, Dritte Folge. [Translated by Joan Riviere.]

a widow for many years, and had remained respectable without suffering from anxiety.

I will not dwell on the awkward predicament in which I was placed by this visit, but instead will consider the conduct of the practitioner who sent this lady to me. First, however, it will be as well to adopt a cautious attitude, which may possibly not be super-fluous—indeed we will hope so. Long experience has taught me—as it may others—not to accept straight away as true what patients, especially nervous patients, relate about their physician. A neurologist not only easily becomes the object of many of the patient's hostile feelings, whatever method of treatment he employs ; he must also sometimes resign himself to accepting responsibility, by a kind of projection, for the buried repressed wishes of his nervous patients. That such accusations then nowhere find more credence than among other physicians is a melancholy but a significant circumstance.

I have some grounds, therefore, for hoping that this lady gave me a tendenciously distorted account of what her physician had said, and that I do a man who is unknown to me an injustice by connecting my remarks about 'wild' psycho-analysis with this incident. But all the same, by doing so I may perhaps prevent others from acting wrongly towards their patients.

Let us suppose, therefore, that her medical prac-titioner spoke to the patient exactly as she reported of him. Everyone will at once vouchsafe the criticism that if a physician holds it necessary to discuss the question of sexuality with a woman he must do so with tact and consideration. Compliance with this demand, however, coincides with carrying out certain of the *technical* regulations of psycho-analysis ; moreover, the physician in question was ignorant of a number of the *scientific* principles of psycho-analysis or had misapprehended them, and thus showed how little understanding of its nature and purposes he had in fact acquired.

We will begin with the second of these, with his scientific errors. His advice to the lady shows clearly in what sense he understands the expression ' sexual life '—in the popular sense, namely, in which by sexual needs nothing is meant but the need for coitus or analogous acts producing orgasm and emission of sexual secretions. The physician cannot have been unaware, however, that psycho-analysis is commonly reproached with having extended the connotation of the term ' sexual ' far beyond its usual range. The fact is undisputed ; whether it may justly be used as a reproach shall not be discussed here. In psycho-analysis the term ' sexuality ' comprises far more ; it goes lower and also higher than the popular sense of the word. This extension is justified genetically ; we reckon as belonging to ' sexual life ' all expressions of tender feeling, which spring from the source of primitive sexual feelings, even when those feelings have become inhibited in regard to their original sexual aim or have exchanged this aim for another which is no longer sexual. For this reason we prefer to speak of *psycho-sexuality*, thus laying stress on the point that the mental factor should not be overlooked or under-estimated. We use the word sexuality in the same comprehensive sense as that in which the German language uses the word *lieben* (to love). And we have long known that a mental lack of satisfaction with all its consequences can exist where there is no lack of normal sexual intercourse ; as therapeutists, too, we have constantly to remember that the unsatisfied sexual trends (the substitutive satisfactions of which in the form of nervous symptoms we have to combat) can often find only very inadequate outlet in coitus or other sexual acts.

Anyone not sharing this psycho-analytical point of view has no right to call to his aid psycho-analytical theories concerned with the ætiological significance of sexuality. By emphasizing exclusively the somatic factor in sexuality he certainly simplifies the problem greatly, but he alone must bear the responsibility for what he does.

A second and equally gross misunderstanding is discernible behind the physician's advice.

It is true that psycho-analysis puts forward lack of sexual satisfaction as the cause of nervous disorders. But does it not also go much further than this ? Is its teaching to be ignored as too complicated when it declares that nervous symptoms arise from a conflict between two forces—on the one hand, the libido (which is for the most part excessive), and on the other, a too severe aversion from sexuality or a repression ? No one who remembers this second factor, which is by no means secondary in importance, can ever believe that sexual satisfaction in itself constitutes a remedy of general reliability for the sufferings of neurotics. A good number of nervous persons are, indeed, either in the actual circumstances or altogether incapable of satisfaction. If they were capable of it, if they were without their inner resistances, the strength of the instinct itself would point the way to satisfaction for them even though no physician recommended it. What is the good, therefore, of advice such as that supposed to have been given to this lady by her physician ?

Even if it could be justified scientifically, it is not advice that she can carry out. If she had had no inner resistances against onanism or against a liaison she would of course have adopted one of these measures long before. Or does the physician think that a woman of over forty has never heard of such a thing as taking a lover, or does he overestimate his influence so much as to think that she could never decide upon such a step without medical recommendation ?

All this seems very simple, and yet it must be admitted that there is one factor which often complicates the issue in forming a judgement. Some nervous states which we call the *actual* neuroses, such as typical neurasthenia and pure forms of anxiety-neurosis, obviously depend on the physical factor in sexual life, and we have no certain knowledge of the part played in them by the mental factor and by repression. In such cases it is natural that the physician should first consider some 'actual' therapy, some alteration in the physical sexual way of life, and he does so with perfect justification if his diagnosis is correct. The lady who consulted the young physician complained chiefly of anxiety-states, and so he probably assumed that she was suffering from an *anxiety-neurosis*, and felt justified in recommending an actual therapy to her. Again a convenient misapprehension ! A person suffering from anxiety is not for that reason necessarily suffering from anxiety-neurosis ; a diagnosis of it cannot be based on its name ; one has to know what manifestations are comprised in an anxiety-neurosis, and be able to distinguish it from other pathological states in which anxiety appears. My impression was that the lady in question was suffering from anxiety-hysteria, and the whole value of such nosographical distinctions, one which quite justifies them, lies in the fact that they indicate a different ætiology and a different therapy. No one who took into consideration the possibility of anxiety-hysteria in this case would have fallen into the error of neglecting the mental factors, as this physician did with his three alternatives.

Oddly enough, the three therapeutic alternatives of this would-be psycho-analyst leave no room for— psycho-analysis ! This woman can only be cured of her anxiety by returning to her husband, or by satisfying her needs by onanism or with a lover. And where does analytic treatment come in, the treatment which we regard as the first remedy in anxiety-states ?

This brings us to the *technical* errors to be remarked in the way that, according to our assumption, this physician proceeded. The idea that a neurotic is suffering from a sort of ignorance, and that if one removes this ignorance by telling him facts (about the causal connection of his illness with his life, about his experiences in childhood, and so on) he must recover, is an idea that has long been superseded, and one derived from superficial appearances. The pathological factor is not his ignorance in itself, but the root of this ignorance in his *inner resistances* ; it was they that first called this ignorance into being, and they still maintain it now. In combating these resistances lies the task of the therapy. Telling the patient what he does not know because he has repressed it, is only one of the necessary preliminaries in the therapy. If knowledge about his unconscious were as important for the patient as the inexperienced in psycho-analysis imagine, it would be sufficient to cure him for him to go to lectures or read books. Such measures, however, have as little effect on the symptoms of nervous disease as distributing menu-cards in time of famine has on people's hunger. The analogy goes even further than its obvious application, too ; for describing his unconscious to the patient is regularly followed by intensification of the conflict in him and exacerbation of his symptoms.

Since, however, psycho-analysis cannot dispense with making this disclosure to patients, it prescribes that two conditions are to be fulfilled before it is done. First, by preparatory work, the repressed material must have come very near to the patient's thoughts, and secondly, he must be sufficiently firmly attached by an affective relationship to the physician (transference) to make it impossible for him to take fresh flight again.

Only when these two conditions are fulfilled is it possible to recognize and to overcome the resistances which have led to the repression and the ignorance. Psycho-analytic measures, therefore, cannot possibly dispense with a fairly long period of contact with the patient, and attempts to bully the patient during his first consultation by brusquely telling him the hidden things one infers behind his story are technically reprehensible ; they mostly lead to their own doom, too, by inspiring a hearty dislike for the physician in the patient and putting an end to any further influence.

Besides all this, one may sometimes make a false inference, and one is never in a position to discover the whole truth. In psycho-analysis these exact technical precautions take the place of a vague demand, implying a peculiar talent, for ' medical tact '.

It is not enough, therefore, for a physician to know a little of what psycho-analysis has discovered ; he must also have familiarized himself with its technique if he wishes his medical practice to be guided by a psycho-analytic point of view. This technique is even to-day not to be learnt from books, and it is certainly not to be discovered independently without great sacrifices of time, labour and success. It is to be learnt, like other medical measures, from those who are already proficient in it. In forming a judgement on the incident that I took as a starting-point for these remarks, therefore, it is a matter of some significance that I do not know the physician who is said to have given the lady such advice and have never before heard his name.

Neither for myself nor for my friends and co-workers is it pleasant to claim in this way a monopoly in the use of psycho-analytic technique. But in face of the danger to patients and to the cause of psycho-analysis which one foresees in this ' wild ' psycho-analysis, we have no other choice. In the spring of 1910 we founded an International Psycho-Analytical Association, in which the members admit their participation by allowing publication of their names, in order to be able to repudiate responsibility for what is done by those who do not belong to us and yet call their methods ' psycho-analysis '. For as a matter of fact ' wild ' analysts of this kind do more harm to the cause of psycho-analysis than to individual patients. I have often found that a clumsy feat of a similar kind led to good results in the end, although it first produced an exacerbation of the patient's condition. Not always, but still often. When he has abused the physician enough and feels impervious enough to any further influence of the kind, his symptoms give way, or he decides to take some step leading to recovery. The final improvement then ' comes of itself,' or is ascribed to some entirely harmless treatment by another physician to whom the patient turned afterwards. In the case of the lady whose complaint against her doctor we have heard, I should say that, in spite of all, the wild psycho-analyst did more for her than some highly respected authority who might have told her she was suffering from a ' vasomotor neurosis '. He did force her attention to the real cause of her trouble, or in that direction, and in spite of all her struggles that cannot be without some favourable results. But he has done himself harm and helped to intensify the prejudices which patients feel, owing to their natural resistances, against the ways of psycho-analysts. And this can be avoided.

XXVII

THE EMPLOYMENT OF DREAM-INTERPRE-TATION IN PSYCHO-ANALYSIS [1]

(1912)

THE *Zentralblatt für Psychoanalyse* was not designed solely to keep its readers informed of the advances made in psycho-analytical knowledge, and itself to publish lesser contributions to the subject; but it aims also at presenting to the student a clear outline of what is already known, so that by means of suitable directions the beginner in analytical practice should be saved waste of time and effort. Henceforward, therefore, articles of a didactic nature and a technical content, not necessarily containing new matter, will appear in this Journal.

The question with which I now intend to deal is not that of the technique of dream-interpretation; neither the methods by which dreams may be interpreted nor the use of such interpretations when made will be considered, but merely the way in which the analyst should employ the art of dream-interpretation in the psycho-analytic treatment of patients. There are undoubtedly different ways of going to work in the matter, but then the answer to questions of technique in analysis is never a matter of course. Although there may perhaps be more than one good road to to follow, still there are very many bad ones, and a comparison of the various methods can only be illuminating, even if it should not lead to a decision in favour of any particular one.

[1] First published in the *Zentralblatt*, Bd. II., 1912; reprinted in *Sammlung*, Vierte Folge. [Translated by Joan Riviere.]
[The following six papers (omitting No. XXX.) originally formed a Series of Papers on Technique, and are reprinted together in the *Sammlung*.—Ed.]

Anyone coming from the study of dream-interpretation to analytic practice will retain his interest in the content of dreams, and his inclination will be to interpret as fully as possible every dream related by the patient. But he will soon remark that he is now working under very different conditions, and that in attempting to carry out such an intention he will come into conflict with the most immediate aims of the treatment. Even if a patient's first dream proves to be admirably suited for the introduction of the first explanations to be given, other dreams will straightway appear, so long and so obscure that the full meaning cannot be extracted from them in the limited hour of one day's work. If the physician pursues the work of interpretation throughout the next few days, fresh dreams which have been produced in the meantime will have to be put aside until he can regard the first dream as finally resolved. The supply of dreams is at times so copious, and the patient's progress towards comprehension of them so slow, that a suspicion will force itself upon the analyst that the appearance of the material in this form may be simply a manifestation of the patient's resistance perceiving and taking advantage of the inability of the method to master adequately what is so presented. Moreover, the treatment will meanwhile have fallen some way behind the present and quite lost touch with actuality. In opposition to this method stands the rule that it is of the greatest importance for the cure that the analyst should always be aware of what is chiefly occupying the surface of the patient's mind at the moment, that he should know just what complexes and resistances are active and what conscious reaction to them will govern the patient's behaviour. It is seldom if ever advisable to sacrifice this therapeutic aim to an interest in dream-interpretation.

Then if we take account of this rule how are we to proceed with interpreting dreams in analysis? More or less as follows: The interpretation which can be

obtained in an hour should be taken as sufficient and it
is not to be counted a loss if the content of a dream is
not fully revealed. On the following day, the thread
of the dream is not to be taken up again as a matter of
course, unless it is first evident that nothing has
happened meanwhile to come more into the foreground
of the patient's thoughts. Therefore no exception in
favour of uninterrupted dream-interpretation is to be
made to the rule that what first comes to the patient's
mind is first to be dealt with. If fresh dreams occur
before the others are disposed of, they must be attended
to, and no uneasiness need be felt about neglecting the
others. If the dreams become altogether too diffuse
and voluminous, all hope of completely unravelling
them should tacitly be given up at the start. One must
generally guard against displaying special interest in
the meaning of dreams, or arousing the idea that the
work would come to a standstill if no dreams were
forthcoming ; otherwise there is a danger of resistance
being directed against the production of dreams and a
risk of bringing about a cessation of them. The patient
must be brought to believe, on the contrary, that
material is always at hand for analysis, regardless of
whether or no he has dreams to report or what measure
of attention is bestowed upon them.

It will now be asked : If dreams are in practice only
to be interpreted in this restricted way, will not too
much valuable material which might throw light on
the unconscious be lost ? The answer to this is as
follows: The loss is by no means so great as might
appear from a superficial view of the matter. To
begin with, the analyst should recognize that in cases
of severe neurosis any elaborate dream-productions are
to be regarded as, theoretically and in the nature of the
case, incapable of complete solution. A dream of this
kind is often based on the entire pathogenic material of
the case, as yet unknown to both analyst and patient
(so-called descriptive and biographical dreams, etc.),
and is sometimes equivalent to a translation into

dream-language of the whole content of the neurosis. In the attempt to find the meaning of such a dream all the latent, as yet untouched resistances will be roused to activity and soon make it impossible to penetrate very far. The full interpretation of such a dream will coincide with the completion of the whole analysis ; if a note is made of it at the beginning, it may be possible to understand it at the end, after many months. In the same way as with the elucidation of a single symptom (the main symptom, perhaps), the explanation will depend upon the whole analysis, during which one must endeavour to lay hold of first this, then that, fragment of its meaning, one after another, until one can finally piece them all together. Similarly, no more can be expected of a dream in the early stages of the analysis ; one must be content with bringing a single pathogenic wish-motive to light in the attempt at interpretation.

Thus nothing that could have been attained is abandoned by relinquishing the idea of a perfect dream-interpretation ; neither is anything lost, as a rule, by breaking off from one dream to another more recent one. We have found from fine examples of fully analysed dreams that the several successive scenes of one dream may contain the same idea running through them all, perhaps with gathering distinctness, and likewise we have learnt that several dreams occurring on the same night are generally nothing more than attempts, expressed in various forms, to represent one meaning. In general, we can rest assured that every wish-impulse which creates a dream to-day will re-appear in other dreams as long as it has not been understood and withdrawn from the control of the unconscious. It often happens, therefore, that the best way to complete the interpretation of a dream is to dismiss it and to devote attention to a new dream, which may contain the same material in perhaps a more accessible form. I know that it is making a great demand, not only on the patient but also on the physician, to expect them both to put aside all thought of the conscious aim of the treatment, and to abandon themselves to promptings which, in spite of all, still seem to us so accidental. But I can answer for it that one is rewarded every time that one resolves to have faith in one's theoretical principles, and prevails upon oneself not to compete with the guidance of the unconscious towards the establishment of the connection.

I submit, therefore, that dream - interpretation should not be pursued in analytic treatment as an art for its own sake, but that its use should be subject to those technical rules that govern the conduct of the analysis throughout. Naturally, one can at times adopt the other course and give way a little to theoretical interest ; but one should always be well aware of what one is doing. Another situation to be considered is that which has arisen since we have acquired more confidence in our understanding of dream-symbolism, and in this way know ourselves to be more independent of the patient's associations. An unusually skilful interpreter will sometimes be able to see through every dream a patient brings without requiring him to go through the tedious and time-absorbing process of dissection. Such an analyst does not experience these conflicts between the demands of the cure and those of dream-interpretation. And then he will be tempted to make full use every time of his interpretations, by telling the patient all that he has seen in the dream. In so doing, however, he will be conducting the analysis in a way which departs considerably from the established method, as I shall point out in another connection. Beginners in analytic practice, at any rate, are urged against taking this exceptional case as a model.

Every analyst will be in the position of this supposed expert of ours in regard to the first dreams that his patients bring on beginning the treatment, before they have learnt anything of the process of dream-interpretation. These initial dreams are, so to speak, naïve ; they betray a great deal to the auditor, like the dreams of so-called healthy people. The question then arises whether the analyst is promptly to translate and communicate to the patient all that he himself sees in them. However, this question will not be answered here, for it obviously forms part of the wider question : at what stage in the treatment and how rapidly should the analyst guide him to the knowledge of that which lies veiled in the patient's mind ? The more the patient has learnt of the method of dream-interpretation the more obscure do his later dreams become, as a rule. All the acquired knowledge about dreams serves also as a warning to the dream-work.

In the ' scientific ' works about dreams, which in spite of their repudiation of dream-interpretation have received a new stimulus from psycho-analysis, one repeatedly finds a very superfluous care exercised about the accurate preservation of the text of the dream. This is thought necessary in order to guard it against the distortions and accretions supervening in the hours immediately after waking. Even many psycho-analysts, in giving the patient instructions to write down the dream immediately upon waking, seem not to rely consistently enough upon their knowledge of the conditions of dream-making. This direction is super-fluous in the treatment ; and the patients are glad enough to make use of it to disturb their slumbers and to display eager obedience where it cannot serve any useful purpose. Even if the substance of a dream is in this way laboriously rescued from oblivion, it is easy enough to convince oneself that nothing has thereby been achieved for the patient. The associations will not come to the text, and the result is the same as if the dream had not been preserved. The physician certainly has acquired some knowledge which he would not have done otherwise. But it is by no means the same thing whether the analyst knows something or the patient knows it ; later on the importance of this distinction in the technique of psycho-analysis will be more fully considered.

In conclusion, I will mention a particular type of dream which, in the nature of the case, occurs only in the course of psycho-analytic treatment, and may bewilder or deceive beginners in practice. These are the corroborating dreams which follow, as one may say, like ' hangers-on ' ; they are easily translated, and contain merely what has been arrived at by analysis of the previous few days' material. It looks as though the patient had had the amiability to reproduce for us in dream-form exactly what we had been ' suggesting ' to him immediately beforehand in the treatment. The more experienced analyst will certainly have some difficulty in attributing any such graciousness to the patient ; he accepts such dreams as hoped-for confirmations, and recognizes that they are only to be observed under certain conditions brought about under the influence of the treatment. The great majority of the dreams forge ahead of the analysis, so that, after subtraction of all that in them which is already known and understood, there still remains a more or less clear indication of something hitherto deeply hidden.

XXVIII

THE DYNAMICS OF THE TRANSFERENCE [1]

(1912)

THE almost inexhaustible subject of 'transference' has recently been dealt with in this Journal by W. Stekel in a descriptive manner.[2] I wish to add a few remarks in order to make clear how it happens that the transference inevitably arises during the analysis and comes to play its well-known part in the treatment.

Let us bear clearly in mind that every human being has acquired, by the combined operation of inherent disposition and of external influences in childhood, a special individuality in the exercise of his capacity to love—that is, in the conditions which he sets up for loving, in the impulses he gratifies by it, and in the aims he sets out to achieve in it.[3] This

[1] First published in the *Zentralblatt*, Bd. II., 1912 ; reprinted in *Sammlung*, Vierte Folge. [Translated by Joan Riviere.]

[2] *Zentralblatt*, Bd. II., Nr. II. S. 26.

[3] We will here provide against misconceptions and reproaches to the effect that we have denied the importanc of the inborn (constitutional) factor because we have emphasized the importance of infantile impressions. Such an accusation arises out of the narrowness with which mankind looks for causes, inasmuch as one single causal factor satisfies him, in spite of the many commonly underlying the face of reality. Psycho-Analysis has said much about the 'accidental' component in ætiology and little about the constitutional, but only because it could throw new light upon the former, whereas of the latter it knows no more so far than is already known. We deprecate the assumption of an essential opposition between the two series of ætiological factors ; we presume rather a perpetual interchange of both in producing the results observed. δαίμων καὶ τύχη determine the fate of man ; seldom, perhaps never, one of these powers alone. The relative ætiological effectiveness of each is only to be measured individually and in single instances. In a series comprising varying degrees of both factors extreme cases will certainly also be found. According to the knowledge we possess we shall estimate the parts played by the forces of heredity and of environment differently in each case, and retain the right to modify our opinion in consequence

forms a *cliché* or stereotype in him, so to speak (or even several), which perpetually repeats and reproduces itself as life goes on, in so far as external circumstances and the nature of the accessible love-objects permit, and is indeed itself to some extent modifiable by later impressions. Now our experience has shown that of these feelings which determine the capacity to love only a part has undergone full psychical development ; this part is directed towards reality, and can be made use of by the conscious personality, of which it forms part. The other part of these libidinal impulses has been held up in development, withheld from the conscious personality and from reality, and may either expend itself only in phantasy, or may remain completely buried in the unconscious so that the conscious personality is unaware of its existence. Expectant libidinal impulses will inevitably be roused, in anyone whose need for love is not being satisfactorily gratified in reality, by each new person coming upon the scene, and it is more than probable that both parts of the libido, the conscious and the unconscious, will participate in this attitude.

It is therefore entirely normal and comprehensible that the libido-cathexes, expectant and in readiness as they are in those who have not adequate gratification, should be turned also towards the person of the physician. As we should expect, this accumulation of libido will be attached to prototypes, bound up with one of the *clichés* already established in the mind of the person concerned, or, to put it in another way, the patient will weave the figure of the physician into one of the ' series ' already constructed in his mind. If the physician should be specially connected in this way with the father-imago (as Jung has happily named [1] it) it is quite in accordance with his actual

---

of new knowledge. Further, we may venture to regard the constitution itself as a residue from the effects of accidental influences upon the endless procession of our forefathers.

[1] *Symbole und Wandlungen der Libido.*

relationship to the patient ; but the transference is not bound to this prototype ; it can also proceed from the mother- or brother-imago and so on. The peculiarity of the transference to the physician lies in its excess, in both character and degree, over what is rational and justifiable—a peculiarity which becomes comprehensible when we consider that in this situation the transference is effected not merely by the conscious ideas and expectations of the patient, but also by those that are under suppression, or unconscious.

Nothing more would need to be said or would perplex us concerning this characteristic of the transference, if it were not that two points which are of particular interest to psycho-analysts still remain unexplained by it. First, it is not clear why neurotic subjects under analysis develop the transference so much more intensely than those who are not being analysed ; and secondly, it remains a mystery why in analysis the transference provides the *strongest resistance* to the cure, whereas in other forms of treatment we recognize it as the vehicle of the healing process, the necessary condition for success. Experience shows, and a test will always confirm it, that when the patient's free associations fail [1] the obstacle can be removed every time by an assurance that he is now possessed by a thought which concerns the person of the physician or something relating to him. No sooner is this explanation given than the obstacle is removed, or at least the absence of thoughts has been transformed into a refusal to speak.

It appears at the first glance to be an enormous disadvantage in psycho-analysis as compared with other methods that in it the transference, elsewhere such a powerful instrument for success, should become here the most formidable ally of the resistance. On closer consideration, however, the first of these difficulties at least will disappear. It is not the fact that the

---

[1] I mean here, when really nothing comes to his mind, and not when he keeps silence on account of some slight disagreeable feeling.

transference in psycho-analysis develops more intensely and immoderately than outside it. Institutions and homes for the treatment of nervous patients by methods other than analysis provide instances of transference in its most excessive and unworthy forms, extending even to complete subjection, which also show its erotic character unmistakably. A sensitive observer, Gabriele Reuter, depicted these facts at a time when psycho-analysis hardly existed, in a remarkable book [1] which altogether reveals great insight into the nature and causes of the neuroses. This peculiarity of the transference is not, therefore, to be placed to the account of psycho-analysis but is to be ascribed to the neurosis itself. The second problem still remains unexplained.

This problem must now be tackled at close quarters : Why does the transference in analysis confront us as resistance ? Let us call to mind the psychological situation in the treatment. One of the invariable and indispensable preliminary conditions in *every* case of psychoneurosis is the process which Jung has aptly named *introversion* of the libido.[2] This means that the quantity of libido which is capable of becoming conscious, and is directed towards reality, has become diminished, while the part which is unconscious and turned away from reality (and, although it may still nourish phantasies in the person concerned, belongs to the unconscious) is by so much increased. The libido (entirely or in part) has found its way back into regression and has re-animated the infantile imagos [3] ;

[1] *Aus guter Familie*, 1895.
[2] Although many of Jung's utterances give the impression that he sees introversion as something characteristic of dementia præcox and not observable to the same extent in the other neuroses.
[3] It would be easy to say : the libido has re-invested the infantile ' complexes '. But this would be erroneous ; it would be correct only if expressed thus : ' the unconscious part of these complexes '. The exceptional intricacy of the theme dealt with in this essay tempts one to discuss further a number of adjunct problems, which require elucidation before one can speak definitely enough about the psychical processes here described. Such problems are : The definition of the boundary between introversion and regression ; the incorporation of the complex-doctrine into the libido-theory ; the relationship of

and thither we pursue it in the analytic treatment, aiming always at unearthing it, making it accessible to consciousness and at last serviceable to reality. Wherever in our analytic delving we come upon one of the hiding-places of the withdrawn libido, there ensues a battle ; all the forces which have brought about the regression of the libido will rise up as ' resistances.' against our efforts in order to maintain the new condition. For if the introversion or regression of the libido had not been justified by some relation to the outer world (in the broadest terms, by a frustration of some desired gratification) and at the time been even expedient, it would never have taken place at all. Yet the resistances which have this origin are not the only ones, nor even the most powerful. The libido at the disposal of the personality had always been exposed to the attraction of unconscious complexes (strictly speaking, of that part of those complexes which belongs to the unconscious), and underwent regression because the attraction of reality had weakened. In order to free it, this attraction of the unconscious must now be overcome ; that is, the repression of the unconscious impulses and their derivatives, which has subsequently developed in the mind of the person concerned, must be lifted. Here arises by far the greater part of the resistances, which so often succeed in upholding the illness, even though the original grounds for the recoil from reality have now disappeared. From both these sources come the resistances with which the analysis has to struggle. Every step of the treatment is accompanied by resistance ; every single thought, every mental act of the patient's, must pay toll to the resistance, and represents a compromise between the forces urging towards the cure and those gathered to oppose it.

Now as we follow a pathogenic complex from its

---

phantasy-creation to the conscious, the unconscious, and to reality ; etc. I need not apologize for having resisted these temptations here.

representative in consciousness (whether this be a conspicuous symptom or something apparently quite harmless) back to its root in the unconscious, we soon come to a place where the resistance makes itself felt so strongly that it affects the next association, which has to appear as a compromise between the demands of this resistance and those of the work of exploration. Experience shows that this is where the transference enters on the scene. When there is anything in the complex-material (the content of the complex) which can at all suitably be transferred on to the person of the physician such a transference will be effected, and from it will arise the next association ; it will then manifest itself by the signs of resistance—for instance, a cessation in the flow of associations. We conclude from such experiences that this transferred idea is able to force itself through to consciousness in preference to all other possible associations, just *because* it also satisfies resistance. This type of incident is repeated innumerable times during an analysis. Over and over again, when one draws near to a pathogenic complex, that part of it which is first thrust forward into consciousness will be some aspect of it which can be transferred ; having been so, it will then be defended with the utmost obstinacy by the patient.[1]

Once this point is won, the elements of that complex which are still unresolved cause little further difficulty. The longer the analysis lasts, and the more clearly the patient has recognized that distortions of the pathogenic material in themselves offer no protection against disclosure, the more consistently he makes use of that variety of distortion which obviously brings him the greatest advantage, the distortion by transference.

[1] From which, however, one need not infer in general any very particular pathogenic importance in the point selected for resistance by transference. In warfare, when a bitter fight is raging over the possession of some little chapel or a single farmhouse, we do not necessarily assume that the church is a national monument, or that the barns contain the military funds. Their value may be merely tactical ; in the next onslaught they will very likely be of no importance.

These incidents all converge towards a situation in which eventually all the conflicts must be fought out on the field of transference.

Transference in analysis thus always seems at first to be only the strongest weapon of the resistance, and we are entitled to draw the inference that the intensity and duration of the transference are an effect and expression of the resistance. The mechanism of transference is indeed explained by the state of readiness in which the libido that has remained accumulated about the infantile imagos exists, but the part played by it in the process of cure is only intelligible in the light of its relation to the resistance.

How does it come about that the transference is so pre-eminently suitable as a weapon of resistance ? One might think that this could easily be answered. It is surely clear enough that it must become peculiarly difficult to own up to any particular reprehended wish when the confession must be made to the very person with whom that feeling is most concerned. To proceed at all in such situations as this necessity produces would appear hardly possible in real life. This impossibility is precisely what the patient is aiming at when he merges the physician with the object of his emotions. Yet on closer consideration we see that this apparent gain cannot supply the answer to the riddle, for, on the contrary, an attitude of affectionate and devoted attachment can surmount any difficulty in confession ; in analogous situations in real life we say : ' I don't feel ashamed with you ; I can tell you everything '. The transference to the physician might quite as well relieve the difficulties of confession, and we still do not understand why it aggravates them.

The answer to this reiterated problem will not be found by pondering it any further, but must be sought in the experience gained by examination of individual instances of transference-resistance occurring in the course of an analysis. From these one perceives eventually that the use of the transference for resistance

cannot be understood so long as one thinks simply of
' transference '. One is forced to distinguish ' positive '
transference from ' negative ' transference, the transference of affectionate feeling from that of hostile
feeling, and to deal separately with the two varieties of
the transference to the physician. Positive transference
can then be divided further into such friendly or
affectionate feelings as are capable of becoming conscious
and the extensions of these in the unconscious. Of
these last, analysis shows that they invariably rest
ultimately on an erotic basis ; so that we have to
conclude that all the feelings of sympathy, friendship,
trust and so forth which we expend in life are genetically
connected with sexuality and have developed out of
purely sexual desires by an enfeebling of their sexual
aim, however pure and non-sensual they may appear in
the forms they take on to our conscious self-perception.
To begin with we knew none but sexual objects ;
psycho-analysis shows us that those persons whom in
real life we merely respect or are fond of may be sexual
objects to us in our unconscious minds still.

So the answer to the riddle is this, that the transference to the physician is only suited for resistance in
so far as it consists in *negative* feeling or in the repressed
erotic elements of positive feeling. As we ' raise ' the
transference by making it conscious we detach only
these two components of the emotional relationship
from the person of the physician ; the conscious and
unobjectionable component of it remains, and brings
about the successful result in psycho-analysis as in all
other remedial methods. In so far we readily admit
that the results of psycho-analysis rest upon a basis of
suggestion ; only by suggestion we must be understood
to mean that which we, with Ferenczi,[1] find that it
consists of—influence on a person through and by
means of the transference-manifestations of which he
is capable. The eventual independence of the patient
is our ultimate object when we use suggestion to bring

[1] Ferenczi, *Introjection and Transference.*

him to carry out a mental operation that will necessarily result in a lasting improvement in his mental
condition.

The next question is, Why do these manifestations
of transference-resistance appear only in psycho-
analysis and not in other forms of treatment, in
institutions, for example ? The answer is that they
do appear there also, but they need to be recognized
for what they are. The outbreak of negative transference is a very common occurrence in institutions ;
as soon as he is seized by it the patient leaves, uncured
or worse. The erotic transference has not such an
inhibitory effect in institutions, since there, as otherwise
in life, it is decorously glossed over, instead of being
exposed ; nevertheless, it betrays itself unequivocally
as resistance to the cure, not, indeed, by driving the
patient out of the place—on the contrary, it binds him
to the spot—but just as certainly by keeping him away
from real life. Actually it is quite unimportant for
his cure whether or not the patient can overcome this
or that anxiety or inhibition in the institution ; what
is of importance, on the contrary, is whether or not he
will be free from them in real life.

The negative transference requires a more thorough
elucidation than is possible within the limits of this
paper. It is found in the curable forms of the psychoneuroses alongside the affectionate transference, often
both directed on to the same person at the same time,
a condition for which Bleuler has coined the useful term
ambivalence.[1] This ambivalence of the feelings appears
to be normal up to a point, but a high degree of it is
certainly a special peculiarity of neurotics. In the
obsessional neurosis an early ' splitting of the pairs of
opposites ' seems to characterize the instinctual life
and to form one of the constitutional conditions of

---

[1] E. Bleuler, *Dementia Praecox oder Gruppe der Schizophrenien*,
in Aschaffenburg's *Handbuch der Psychiatrie*, 1911 ; also a Lecture on
Ambivalence in Berne, 1910, abstracted in *Zentralblatt für Psychoanalyse*, Bd. I., S. 266. W. Stekel had previously suggested the term
bipolarity for the same phenomenon.

this disease. The ability of neurotics to make the transference a form of resistance is most easily accounted for by ambivalence in the flow of feelings. Where the capacity to transfer feeling has come to be of an essentially negative order, as with paranoids, the possibility of influence or cure ceases.

After all this investigation we have so far considered one aspect only of transference-phenomena ; some attention must be given to another side of this question. Those who have formed a true impression of the effect of an extreme transference-resistance on the patient, of the way in which as soon as he comes under its influence he is hurled out of all reality in his relation to the physician—how he then arrogates to himself freedom to ignore the psycho-analytic rule (to communicate without reserve whatever goes through his mind), how all the resolutions with which he entered upon the analysis then become obliterated, and how the logical connections and conclusions which just before had impressed him deeply then become matters of indifference to him—will need some further explanation than that supplied by the factors mentioned above to account for this effect, and these other factors are, indeed, not far to seek ; they lie again in the psychological situation in which the analysis has placed the patient.

In following up the libido that is withdrawn from consciousness we penetrate into the region of the unconscious, and this provokes reactions which bring with them to light many of the characteristics of unconscious processes as we have learnt to know them from the study of dreams. The unconscious feelings strive to avoid the recognition which the cure demands ; they seek instead for reproduction, with all the power of hallucination and the inappreciation of time characteristic of the unconscious. The patient ascribes, just as in dreams, currency and reality to what results from the awakening of his unconscious feelings ; he seeks to discharge his emotions, regardless of the reality of the situation. The physician requires of him that he shall fit these emotions into their place in the treatment and in his life-history, subject them to rational consideration, and appraise them at their true psychical value. This struggle between physician and patient, between intellect and the forces of instinct, between recognition and the striving for discharge, is fought out almost entirely over the transference-manifestations. This is the ground on which the victory must be won, the final expression of which is lasting recovery from the neurosis. It is undeniable that the subjugation of the transference-manifestations provides the greatest difficulties for the psycho-analyst ; but it must not be forgotten that they, and they only, render the invaluable service of making the patient's buried and forgotten love-emotions actual and manifest ; for in the last resort no one can be slain *in absentia* or *in effigie*.

RECOMMENDATIONS FOR PHYSICIANS ON THE PSYCHO-ANALYTIC METHOD OF TREATMENT [1]

(1912)

THE technical rules which I bring forward here have been evolved out of my own experience in the course of many years, after I had renounced other methods which had cost me dear. It will easily be seen that they may be summed up, or at least many of them, in one single injunction. My hope is that compliance with them will spare physicians practising analysis much unavailing effort and warn them of various possibilities which they might otherwise overlook. I must, however, expressly state that this technique has proved to be the only method suited to my individuality ; I do not venture to deny that a physician quite differently constituted might feel impelled to adopt a different attitude to his patients and to the task before him.

(a) To the analyst who is treating more than one patient in the day, the first necessity with which he is faced will seem the hardest. It is, of course, that of keeping in mind all the innumerable names, dates, detailed reminiscences, associations, and effects of the disease which each patient communicates during the treatment in the course of months or years, and not confounding them with similar material proceeding from other patients treated simultaneously or previously. When one is required to analyse six, eight, or even more patients daily, the effort of memory

---

[1] First published in *Zentralblatt*, Bd. II., 1912 ; reprinted in *Sammlung*. Vierte Folge. [Translated by Joan Riviere.]

necessary to achieve this evokes incredulity, astonishment, or even pity in the uninformed. Curiosity is inevitably aroused about the technique which makes it possible to deal with such abundance of material, and the expectation is that some special means are required for the purpose.

The technique, however, is a very simple one. It disclaims the use of any special aids, even of note-taking, as we shall see, and simply consists in making no effort to concentrate the attention on anything in particular, and in maintaining in regard to all that one hears the same measure of calm, quiet attentiveness —of ' evenly-hovering attention ', as I once before described it. In this way a strain which could not be kept up for several hours daily and a danger inseparable from deliberate attentiveness are avoided. For as soon as attention is deliberately concentrated in a certain degree, one begins to select from the material before one ; one point will be fixed in the mind with particular clearness and some other consequently disregarded, and in this selection one's expectations or one's inclinations will be followed. This is just what must not be done, however ; if one's expectations are followed in this selection there is the danger of never finding anything but what is already known, and if one follows one's inclinations anything which is to be perceived will most certainly be falsified. It must not be forgotten that the meaning of the things one hears is, at all events for the most part, only recognizable later on.

It will be seen, therefore, that the principle of evenly-distributed attention is the necessary corollary to the demand on the patient to communicate everything that occurs to him without criticism or selection. If the physician behaves otherwise he is throwing aside most of the advantage to be gained by the patient's obedience to the ' fundamental rule of psycho-analysis '. For the physician the rule may be expressed thus : All conscious exertion is to be withheld from the capacity for attention, and one's ' unconscious

memory ' is to be given full play ; or to express it in
terms of technique, pure and simple : One has simply
to listen and not to trouble to keep in mind anything
in particular.

What one achieves in this way will be sufficient
for all requirements during the treatment. Those
elements of the material which have a connection with
one another will be at the conscious disposal of the
physician ; the rest, as yet unconnected, chaotic and
indistinguishable, seems at first to disappear, but
rises readily into recollection as soon as the patient
brings something further to which it is related, and
by which it can be developed. The undeserved compliment of a ' remarkably good memory ' which the
patient pays when one reproduces some detail after a
year and a day is then accepted with a smile, whereas
a conscious effort to retain a recollection of the point
would probably have resulted in nothing.

Mistakes in recollection occur only at times and in
places where some personal consideration has intervened
(see below) ; that is, where there is a notable failure to
reach the ideal set up for the analyst. Confusion with
the communications of other patients arises very rarely.
In a disagreement with the patient whether he said
some particular thing, or how he said it, the physician
is usually right.[1]

(b) I do not recommend that during the sitting, in
the patient's presence, full notes should be made or a
shorthand record kept, and so on. Apart from the
unfavourable impression which this makes on many
patients, the same considerations as have been advanced
in regard to attention also apply here. A prejudicial
selection will of necessity be made in taking down

---

[1] The patient often asserts that he has previously mentioned some
particular thing, while one can assure him with calm authority that he
has now mentioned it for the first time. It then turns out that the
patient had previously had the intention to mention it, but had been
hindered in so doing by a resistance which had not yet been overcome.
The memory of his intention is indistinguishable in his mind from the
memory of the act itself.

notes or shorthand, and part of one's own mental activity is occupied in this way which would be better employed in interpreting what one hears. Exceptions may be made to this rule without reproach in the case of dates, the text of dreams, or single incidents of a noteworthy kind which can easily be detached from their context to serve an independent purpose as examples. I am not in the habit of doing this either, however. I write down examples from memory in the evening after work is over ; the text of a dream in which I find something useful I ask the patient to write down for me after he has related it.

(c) Note-taking during the sitting with the patient might be supported on the ground of an intention to publish a scientific study of the case. In theory this can hardly be denied. But in practice it must not be forgotten that exact reports of an analytic history of a case are less valuable than might be expected. Strictly speaking, they only convey that appearance of exactness which ' modern ' psychiatry presents in many conspicuous instances. They are wearisome to the reader as a rule, and yet they do not go far enough as a substitute for actual presence at the analysis. Altogether, experience shows that a reader who is willing to believe an analyst at all will give him credit for the touch of revision to which he has subjected his material ; but if the reader is unwilling to take analysis or the analyst seriously, the most faithful shorthand reports of the treatment of cases will not influence him. This does not seem to be the way to make up for the deficiency in evidence found in psycho-analytical descriptions of cases.

(d) It is indeed one of the distinctions of psycho-analysis that research and treatment proceed hand in hand, but still the technique required for the one begins at a certain point to diverge from that of the other. It is not a good thing to formulate a case scientific-ally while treatment is proceeding, to reconstruct its development, anticipate its progress, and take notes from time to time of the condition at the moment, as scientific interests would require. Cases which are thus destined at the start to scientific purposes and treated accordingly suffer in consequence ; while the most successful cases are those in which one proceeds, as it were, aimlessly, and allows oneself to be overtaken by any surprises, always presenting to them an open mind, free from any expectations. To swing over as required from one mental attitude to another, to avoid speculation or brooding over cases while the analysis proceeds, and to submit the material gained to the synthetic process only after the analysis is concluded, is the right course for the analyst. The distinction here drawn between the two different attitudes would have no significance if we already possessed all the knowledge (or even the essential knowledge) about the unconscious and the structure of the neuroses which is obtained by means of the analytic work. At the present time we are still far from this goal and must not cut ourselves off from the means by which we can test what we already know and learn more.

(e) I cannot recommend my colleagues emphatically enough to take as a model in psycho-analytic treatment the surgeon who puts aside all his own feelings, including that of human sympathy, and concentrates his mind on one single purpose, that of performing the operation as skilfully as possible. Under present conditions the affective impulse of greatest danger to the psycho-analyst will be the therapeutic ambition to achieve by this novel and disputed method something which will impress and convince others. This will not only cause a state of mind unfavourable for the work in him personally, but he will find himself in consequence helpless against certain of the patient's resistances, upon the struggle with which the cure primarily depends. The justification for this coldness in feeling in the analyst is that it is the condition which brings the greatest advantage to both persons involved, ensuring a needful protection for the physician's emotional life and the greatest measure of aid for the patient that is possible at the present time. An old surgeon once took for his motto the words : *Je le pansai, Dieu le guérit*. The analyst should content himself with a similar thought.

(*f*) All these rules which I have brought forward coincide at one point which is easily discernible. They all aim at creating for the physician a complement to the ' fundamental rule of psycho-analysis ' for the patient. Just as the patient must relate all that self-observation can detect, and must restrain all the logical and affective objections which would urge him to select, so the physician must put himself in a position to use all that is told him for the purposes of interpretation and recognition of what is hidden in the unconscious, without substituting a censorship of his own for the selection which the patient forgoes. Expressed in a formula, he must bend his own unconscious like a receptive organ towards the emerging unconscious of the patient, be as the receiver of the telephone to the disc. As the receiver transmutes the electric vibrations induced by the sound-waves back again into sound-waves, so is the physician's unconscious mind able to reconstruct the patient's unconscious, which has directed his associations, from the communications derived from it.

But if the physician is to be able to use his own unconscious in this way as an instrument in the analysis, he must himself fulfil one psychological condition in a high degree. He may tolerate no resistances in himself which withhold from his consciousness what is perceived by his unconscious, otherwise he would introduce into the analysis a new form of selection and distortion which would be far more injurious than that resulting from the concentration of conscious attention. It does not suffice for this that the physician should be of approximate normality himself ; it is a justifiable requisition that he should further submit himself to a psycho-analytic purification and become aware of those complexes in himself which would be apt to affect his comprehension of the patient's disclosures. There can be no reasonable doubt about the disqualifying effect of such personal defects ; every unresolved repression in the physician constitutes what W. Stekel has well named a ' blind spot ' in his capacity for analytic perception.

Years ago I replied to the question how one becomes an analyst with the answer : By the analysis of one's own dreams. This training certainly suffices for many people, but not for all those who wish to learn to analyse. Moreover, not everyone is able to interpret his own dreams without the help of another. I count it one of the valuable services of the Zürich school of analysis that they have emphasized this necessity and laid it down as a requisition that anyone who wishes to practise analysis of others should first submit to be analysed himself by a competent person. Anyone taking up the work seriously should choose this course, which offers more than one advantage ; the sacrifice involved in laying oneself bare to a stranger without the necessity incurred by illness is amply rewarded. Not only is the purpose of learning to know what is hidden in one's own mind far more quickly attained and with less expense of affect, but impressions and convictions are received in one's own person which may be sought in vain by studying books and attending lectures. In addition, the gain resulting from the lasting personal relationship which usually springs up between the learner and his guide is not to be estimated lightly.

Such analysis of a person who is for all practical purposes healthy will naturally remain uncompleted. Whoever knows how to appreciate the high value of the self-knowledge and increase in self-control so acquired will afterwards continue the analytic examination of his own personality by a self-analysis, and willingly recognize that, in himself as in others, he must always expect to find something new. That analyst, however, who has despised the provision of analysis for himself will be penalized, not merely by an incapacity to learn more than a certain amount from his patient, but by risking a more serious danger, one which may become a danger for others. He will easily yield to the temptation of projecting as a scientific theory of general applicability some of the peculiarities of his own personality which he has dimly perceived ; he will bring the psycho-analytic method into discredit, and lead the inexperienced astray.

(g) I will now add a few other rules which will make a transition from the attitude of the physician to the treatment of the patient.

The young and eager psycho-analyst will certainly be tempted to bring his own individuality freely into the discussion, in order to draw out the patient and help him over the confines of his narrow personality. One would expect it to be entirely permissible, and even desirable, for the overcoming of the patient's resistances, that the physician should afford him a glimpse into his own mental defects and conflicts and lead him to form comparisons by making intimate disclosures from his own life. One confidence repays another, and anyone demanding intimate revelations from another must be prepared to make them himself.

But the psycho-analytic relationship is a thing apart ; much of it takes a different course from that which the psychology of consciousness would lead us to expect. Experience does not bear witness to the excellence of an affective technique of this kind. Further, it is not difficult to see that it involves a departure from psycho-analytic principles and verges upon treatment by suggestion. It will induce the patient to bring forward sooner and with less difficulty what he already knows and would otherwise have kept back for a time on account of conventional objections. But this technique achieves nothing towards the discovery of the patient's unconscious ; it makes him less able than ever to overcome the deeper resistances, and in the more severe cases it invariably fails on account of the insatiability it rouses in the patient, who then tries to reverse the situation, finding the analysis of the physician more interesting than his own. The loosening of the transference, too—one of the main tasks of the cure—is made more difficult by too intimate an attitude on the part of the doctor, so that a doubtful gain in the beginning is more than cancelled in the end. Therefore I do not hesitate to condemn this kind of technique as incorrect. The physician should be impenetrable to the patient, and, like a mirror, reflect nothing but what is shown to him. In practice, it is true, one cannot object to a psychotherapeutist combining a certain amount of analysis with some suggestive treatment in order to achieve a perceptible result in a shorter time—as is necessary, for instance, in institutions ; but one may demand that he himself should be in no doubt about what he is doing and should know that his method is not that of true psycho-analysis.

(h) Another temptation arises out of the educative function which in a psycho-analytic treatment falls to the physician without any special intention on his part. As the inhibitions in development are undone it inevitably happens that the physician finds himself in a position to point out new aims for the impulses which have been set free. It is but a natural ambition for him then to endeavour to make something specially excellent out of the person whose neurosis has cost so much labour, and to set up high aims for these impulses. But here again the physician should restrain himself and take the patient's capacities rather than his own wishes as his standard. Talent for a high degree of sublimation is not found in all neurotics ; of many of them one can believe that they would never have fallen ill had they possessed the art of sublimating their impulses. In pressing them unduly towards sublimation, and cutting them off from the easier and simpler gratifications, life may often be made even harder for them than they feel it otherwise. A physician must always be tolerant of a patient's weakness, and must be content to win back a part of the capacity for work and enjoyment even for a person of but moderate worth. Ambitiousness in the educative direction is as undesirable as in the therapeutic. Moreover, it must not be forgotten that many people succumb to illness in the very effort towards sublimation beyond the limit of their capacity, and that in those who are capable of it the process usually takes place from within as soon as their inhibitions have been removed by the analysis. In my opinion, therefore, efforts to bring about sublimations of the impulses in the course of psycho-analytic treatment are no doubt always praiseworthy but most certainly not in all cases advisable.

(i) To what extent should the intellectual co-operation of the patient be called for in the treatment? It is difficult to say anything of general applicability on this point; the personality of the patient is here the principal deciding factor. In any case caution and self-restraint are to be observed in this matter. It is incorrect to set the patient tasks, such as collecting his memories, thinking over a certain period of his life, and so on. On the contrary, the patient has above all to learn, what never comes easily to anyone, that such mental activities as thinking over a matter, or concentrating the will and attention, avail nothing in solving the riddles of the neurosis; but that this can only be done by patiently adhering to the psycho-analytic rule demanding the exclusion of all criticism of the unconscious or of its derivatives. One must especially insist upon the following of the rule most rigidly with those patients whose habitual manœuvre it is to shirk analysis by sheering off into the intellectual, and who speculate much and often with great wisdom over their condition, thereby sparing themselves from taking steps to overcome it. For this reason I dislike resorting to analytical writings as an aid to patients; I require them to learn by personal experience, and I assure them that in this way they will acquire wider and more valuable knowledge than the whole literature of psycho-analysis could afford them. I recognize, however, that under the conditions of institution treatment it may be very advantageous to employ reading as a preparation for patients in analysis and as a means of creating an atmosphere favourable to influence.

The most urgent warning I have to express is against any attempt to engage the confidence or support of parents or relatives by giving them psycho-analytical books to read—either of an introductory or of an advanced kind. This well-meant step usually has the effect of evoking prematurely the natural and inevitable opposition of the relatives to the treatment, which in consequence is never even begun.

I will here express the hope that advances in the experience of psycho-analysts will soon lead to agreement upon the most expedient technique for the treatment of neurotic persons. As for treatment of the ' relatives ', I must confess myself utterly at a loss, and I have altogether little faith in any individual treatment of them.

FAUSSE RECONNAISSANCE ('DÉJÀ RACONTÉ') IN PSYCHO-ANALYTIC TREATMENT [1]

(1913)

IT not infrequently happens in the course of an analytic treatment that the patient, after reporting some fact that he has remembered, will go on to say : ' *But I've told you that already* '—while the analyst himself feels sure that this is the first time he has heard the story. If the patient is contradicted upon the point, he will often protest with energy that he is perfectly certain he is right, that he is ready to swear to it, and so on ; while the analyst's own conviction that what he has heard is new to him will become correspondingly stronger. To try to decide the dispute by shouting the patient down or by outvying him in protestations would be a most unpsychological proceeding. It is familiar ground that a sense of conviction of the accuracy of one's memory has no objective value ; and, since one of the two persons concerned must necessarily be in the wrong, it may just as well be the physician as the patient who has fallen a victim to a paramnesia. The analyst will admit as much to the patient, will break off the argument, and will postpone a settlement of the point until some later occasion.

In a minority of cases the analyst himself will then recollect that he has already heard the piece of information under dispute, and will at the same time discover the subjective, and often far-fetched, reason which led to this temporary forgetfulness. But in the great

[1] First published in *Zeitschrift*, Bd. I., 1913 ; reprinted in *Sammlung*, Vierte Folge. [Translated by James Strachey.]

majority of cases it is the patient who turns out to have been mistaken; and he can be brought to recognize the fact. The explanation of this frequent occurrence appears to be that the patient really did on some previous occasion have the intention of giving this information, that once or even several times he actually made some remark leading up to it, but that he was then prevented by resistance from carrying out his purpose, and afterwards confounded a recollection of his intention with a recollection of its performance.

Leaving on one side any cases in which there may still be some element of doubt, I will now bring forward a few others which are of special theoretical interest. With certain people it happens, and may even happen repeatedly, that they cling with particular obstinacy to the assertion that they have already told the analyst this or that, when the nature of the circumstances and of the information in question makes it quite impossible that they can be right. For what they claim to have told already once before and what they claim to recognize as something old, which must also be familiar to the physician, turn out to be memories of the greatest importance to the analysis — confirmatory facts for which the analyst has long been waiting, or solutions which wind up a whole section of the work and which he would certainly have made the basis of an exhaustive discussion. In the face of these considerations the patient himself soon admits that his recollection must have deceived him, though he is unable to account for its definite character.

The phenomenon presented by the patient in cases like this deserves to be called a ' *fausse reconnaissance* ', and is completely analogous to what occurs in certain other cases and has been described as a ' *déjà vu* '. In these other cases the subject has a spontaneous feeling such as ' I've been in this situation before ', or ' I've been through all this already ', without ever being in a position to confirm his conviction by discovering an actual recollection of the previous occasion.

This latter phenomenon, as is well known, has provoked a large number of attempts at explanation, which can be divided roughly into two groups.[1] One class of explanation looks upon the feeling which constitutes the phenomenon as deserving of credence, and assumes that something really has been remembered—the only question being what. The second and far larger class of explanation includes those which maintain, on the contrary, that what we have to deal with is an illusory memory, and that the problem is to discover how this paramnestic error can have arisen. This latter group comprises many widely different hypotheses. There is, for instance, the ancient view, ascribed to Pythagoras, that the phenomenon of the *déjà vu* is evidence of the individual having had a former life ; again, there is the hypothesis based upon anatomy (put forward by Wigan in 1860) to the effect that the phenomenon is based upon an absence of simultaneity in the functioning of the two cerebral hemispheres ; and finally there are the purely psychological theories, supported by the majority of more recent authorities, which regard the *déjà vu* as an indication of an apperceptive weakness, and assign the responsibility for its occurrence to such causes as fatigue, exhaustion and distraction.

In 1904 Grasset [2] put forward an explanation of the *déjà vu* which must be reckoned as one of the group which ' believes ' in the phenomenon. He was of opinion that the phenomenon indicates that at some earlier time there has been an *unconscious* perception, which only now makes its way into consciousness under the influence of a new and similar impression. Several other authorities have agreed with this view, and have maintained that the basis of the phenomenon is the recollection of something that has been dreamed and then forgotten. In both cases it would

[1] One of the most recent bibliographies of the subject is to be found in Havelock Ellis, *The World of Dreams*, 1911.
[2] *La sensation du déjà vu.*

be a question of the activation of an unconscious impression.

In 1907, in the second edition of my *Psycho-pathologie des Alltagslebens*, I proposed an exactly similar explanation for this form of apparent paramnesia without mentioning Grasset's paper or knowing of its existence. By way of excuse I may remark that I arrived at my conclusion as the result of a psycho-analytic investigation which I was able to make of an example of *déjà vu* in a female patient ; it was extremely clear, though it had occurred twenty-eight years earlier. I shall not reproduce the little analysis in this place. It showed that the situation in which the *déjà vu* occurred was really calculated to revive the memory of an earlier experience of the patient's. The patient, who was at that time a twelve-year-old child, was visiting a family in which there was a brother who was seriously ill and at the point of death ; while her own brother had been in a similarly dangerous condition a few months earlier. But with the earlier of these two similar events there had been associated a phantasy that was incapable of entering consciousness—namely, a wish that her brother should die. Consequently, the analogy between the two cases could not become conscious. And the perception of it was replaced by the phenomenon of ' having been through it all before ', the identity being displaced from the really common element on to the locality.

The name ' *déjà vu* ' is, as we know, applied to a whole class of analogous phenomena, such as the ' *déjà entendu* ', the ' *déjà éprouvé* ' and the ' *déjà senti* '. The case which I am now about to report, as a single instance out of many similar ones, consists of a ' *déjà raconté* ' ; and it could be traced back to an unconscious resolution which was never carried out.

A patient [1] said to me in the course of his associa-

---

[1] [A detailed analysis of this patient's case will be found in ' From the History of an Infantile Neurosis ', COLLECTED PAPERS, vol. iii. —Trans.]

tions : ' When I was playing in the garden with a knife (that was when I was five years old) and cut through my little finger—oh, I only *thought* it was cut through— but I've told you about that already '.

I assured him that I had no recollection of anything of the kind. He insisted with increasing conviction that it was impossible he could be mistaken. I finally put an end to the argument in the manner I have described above and asked him in any case to repeat the story. Then we should see where we were.

' When I was five years old, I was playing in the garden near my nurse, and was carving with my pocket-knife in the bark of one of the walnut-trees that also come into my dream.[1] Suddenly, to my unspeakable terror, I noticed that I had cut through the little finger of my (right or left ?) hand, so that it was only hanging on by its skin. I felt no pain, but great fear. I did not venture to say anything to my nurse, who was only a few paces distant, but I sank down on the nearest seat and sat there incapable of casting another glance at my finger. At last I grew calm, took a look at the finger, and saw that it was entirely uninjured.'

We soon agreed that, in spite of what he had thought, he could not have told me the story of this vision or hallucination before. He was very well aware that I could not have failed to exploit such evidence as this of his having had a *fear of castration* at the age of five. The episode broke down his resistance against assuming the existence of a castration complex ; but he raised the question : ' Why did I feel so certain of having told you this recollection before ? '

It then occurred to both of us that repeatedly and

---

[1] Cf. ' The Occurrence in Dreams of Material from Fairy Tales ' (1913), COLLECTED PAPERS, vol. iv. In telling the story again on a later occasion he made the following correction : ' I don't believe I was cutting the tree. That was a confusion with another recollection, which must also have been hallucinatorily falsified, of having made a cut upon a tree with my knife and of *blood* having come out of the tree.'

in various connections he had brought out the following
trivial recollection, and each time without our deriving
any profit from it :

'Once when my uncle went away on a journey he
asked me and my sister what we should like him to
bring us back. My sister asked for a book, and I
asked for a pocket-knife.' We now understood that
this association which had emerged months before had
in reality been a screen-memory for the repressed
recollection, and had been an attempt (rendered
abortive by the resistance) at telling the story of his
imagined loss of his little finger—an unmistakable
penis-equivalent. The knife which his uncle did in
fact bring him back was, as he clearly remembered, the
same one that made its appearance in the episode
which had been suppressed for so long.

It seems unnecessary to add anything in the way
of an interpretation of this little occurrence, so far
as it throws light upon the phenomenon of '*fausse
reconnaissance*'. As regards the subject-matter of the
patient's vision, I may remark that, particularly in
relation to the castration complex, similar hallucinatory
falsifications are of not infrequent occurrence, and that
they can just as easily serve the purpose of correcting
unwelcome perceptions.

The following notes upon their author's childhood
were put at my disposal in 1911. The writer, with
whom I am unacquainted and whose age is unknown
to me, is a man of university education residing in a
university town in Germany :

'In the course of reading your *Kindheitserinnerung
des Leonardo da Vinci*, I was moved to internal dissent
by the observations contained upon pages 29 to 31.
Your assertion that male children are dominated by an
interest in their own genitals provoked me to make a
counter-assertion to the effect that " if that is the
general rule, I at all events am an exception to it ".
I then went on to read the passage that follows (page 31
to the top of page 32) with the utmost amazement, such

amazement as one feels when one comes across a fact of an entirely novel character. In the midst of my amazement a recollection occurred to me which showed me, to my own surprise, that the fact could not be by any means so novel as it had seemed. For, at the time at which I was passing through the period of "infantile sexual inquiry", a lucky chance gave me the opportunity of inspecting the female genitals in a little girl of my own age, and in doing so *I quite clearly observed a penis of the same kind as my own*. Soon afterwards I was plunged into fresh confusion by the sight of some female statues and nudes; and in order to get over this "scientific" discrepancy I devised the following experiment. By pressing my thighs together I succeeded in making my genitals disappear between them; and I was glad to find that in that way all differences between my own appearance and that of a female nude could be got rid of. Evidently, I thought to myself, the genitals have been made to disappear in a similar way in female nudes.

' At this point another recollection occurred to me, which has always been of the greatest importance to me, in so far as it is *one* of the three recollections which constitute all that I can remember of my mother, who died when I was very young. My mother is standing in front of the wash-hand-stand and cleaning the glasses and washing-basin, while I am playing in the same room and committing some misdemeanour. As a punishment my hand is soundly slapped. Then to my very great terror I see that my little finger is falling off; and in fact it falls into the pail. Knowing that my mother is angry, I do not venture to say anything; but my terror grows still more intense when I see the pail carried off soon afterwards by the servant-maid. For a long time I was convinced that I had lost a finger— up to the time, I believe, at which I learnt to count.

' I have often tried to interpret this recollection, which, as I have already mentioned, has always been of the greatest importance to me on account of its

connection with my mother; but none of my interpretations has satisfied me. It is only now, after
reading your book, that I begin to have a suspicion
of a simple and satisfying answer to the conundrum.'

There is another kind of *fausse reconnaissance* which
not infrequently makes its appearance at the close of
a treatment, much to the physician's satisfaction.
After he has succeeded in forcing the repressed event
(whether it was of a real or of a psychical nature) upon
the patient's acceptance in the teeth of all resistances,
and has succeeded, as it were, in rehabilitating it—the
patient may say: '*Now I feel as though I had known
it all the time*'. With this the problem of the analysis
has been solved.

XXXI

FURTHER RECOMMENDATIONS IN THE TECHNIQUE OF PSYCHO-ANALYSIS[1]

ON BEGINNING THE TREATMENT. THE QUESTION OF THE FIRST COMMUNICATIONS. THE DYNAMICS OF THE CURE.

(1913)

H E who hopes to learn the fine art of the game of chess from books will soon discover that only the opening and closing moves of the game admit of exhaustive systematic description, and that the endless variety of the moves which develop from the opening defies description; the gap left in the instructions can only be filled in by the zealous study of games fought out by master-hands. The rules which can be laid down for the practical application of psycho-analysis in treatment are subject to similar limitations.

I intend now to try to collect together for the use of practising analysts some of the rules for the opening of the treatment. Among them there are some which may seem to be mere details, as indeed they are. Their justification is that they are simply rules of the game, acquiring their importance by their connection with the whole plan of the game. I do well, however, to bring them forward as 'recommendations' without claiming any unconditional acceptance for them. The exceptional diversity in the mental constellations concerned, the plasticity of all mental processes, and the great number of the determining factors involved prevent the formulation of a stereotyped technique, and also bring it about that a course of action, ordinarily

---

[1] First published in *Zeitschrift*, Bd. I., 1913; reprinted in *Sammlung*, Vierte Folge. [Translated by Joan Riviere.]

legitimate, may be at times ineffective, while one which is usually erroneous may occasionally lead to the desired end. These circumstances do not prevent us from establishing a procedure for the physician which will be found most generally efficient.

Some years ago I set forth the considerations of chief importance in the selection of patients, which I shall therefore not repeat here [1]; since that time other psycho-analysts have confirmed their validity. I will add, though, that since then, when I know little of a case, I have formed the practice of first undertaking it only provisionally for one or two weeks. If one breaks off within this period the patient is spared the distress of an unsuccessful attempt at cure; it was only ' taking a sounding ' in order to learn more about the case and to decide whether it was a suitable one for psycho-analysis. No other kind of preliminary examination is possible; the most lengthy discussions and questionings in ordinary consultation are no substitute. This experiment, however, is in itself the beginning of an analysis, and must conform to its rules; there may perhaps be this difference in that on the whole one lets the patient talk, and explains nothing more than is absolutely necessary to keep him talking.

For the purposes of diagnosis, also, it is an advantage to begin with a period of a few weeks designed as an experiment. Often enough, when one sees a case of neurosis with hysterical or obsessional symptoms, mild in character and of short duration (just the type of case, that is, which one would regard as suitable for the treatment), a doubt which must not be overlooked arises whether the case may not be one of incipient dementia præcox, so called (schizophrenia, according to Bleuler; paraphrenia, as I prefer to call it), and may not sooner or later develop well-marked signs of this disease. I do not agree that it is always possible to effect the distinction so easily. I know that there are psychiatrists who hesitate less often in their

[1] 'On Psychotherapy', COLLECTED PAPERS, vol. i.

differential diagnosis, but I have been convinced that they are just as often mistaken. For the psycho-analyst, however, the mistake is more serious than for so-called clinical psychiatrists. The latter has little of value to offer either to the one type of case or to the other ; he merely runs the risk of a theoretical mistake, and his diagnosis has but an academic interest. In an unsuitable case, however, the psycho-analyst has committed a practical error ; he has occasioned useless expense and discredited his method of treatment ; he cannot fulfil his promise of cure if the patient is suffering from paraphrenia instead of from hysteria or obsessional neurosis, and therefore he has particularly strong motives for avoiding mistakes in diagnosis. In an experimental course of a few weeks suspicious signs will often be observed which will decide him not to pursue the attempt further. Unfortunately I cannot assert that an attempt of this kind will invariably ensure certainty ; it is but one more useful precaution.[1]

Lengthy preliminary discussions before the beginning of the treatment, previous treatment by another method, and also previous acquaintance between physician and patient, have certain disadvantageous consequences for which one must be prepared. They result in the patient entering upon the analysis with a transference already effected, which must then be slowly uncovered by the physician ; whereas otherwise he is in a position to observe the growth and development of it from the outset. By this means the patient gains a start upon us which we do not willingly grant him in the treatment.

---

[1] There is much to be said on the subject of this uncertainty in diagnosis, on the prospects of analysis in the milder forms of para-phrenia, and on the explanation of the similarity between the two diseases, which I cannot bring forward in this connection. I should be willing to contrast hysteria and the obsessional neurosis, under the name of ' transference neuroses ', with the paraphrenic group, under the name of ' introversion neuroses ', in accordance with Jung's formula, if the term ' introversion ' (of the libido) were not alienated by such usage from its only legitimate meaning.

One must distrust all those who wish to put off beginning the treatment. Experience shows that at the appointed time they fail to return, even though their motive for the delay (that is, their rationalization of the intention) appears to the novice to be above suspicion.

Special difficulties arise when friendship or acquaintance already exists between the physician and the patient, or their families. The psycho-analyst who is asked to undertake treatment of the wife or child of a friend must be prepared for it to cost him the friendship, no matter what the outcome of the treatment ; nevertheless he must make the sacrifice unless he can propose a trustworthy substitute.

Both the general public and medical men—still fain to confound psycho-analytic with suggestive treatment —are inclined to attribute great importance to the expectations which the patient brings to the new treatment. They often believe that one patient will not give much trouble because he has a great belief in psycho-analysis and is fully convinced of its truth and curative power ; and that another patient will doubtless prove more difficult because he is of a sceptical nature and will not believe until he has experienced good results in his own person. Actually, however, this attitude on the part of the patient has very little importance ; his preliminary belief or disbelief is almost negligible compared with the inner resistances which hold the neurosis fast. A blissful trustfulness on the patient's part makes the relationship at first a very pleasant one ; one thanks him for it, but warns him that this favourable prepossession will be shattered by the first difficulty arising in the analysis. To the sceptic one says that the analysis requires no faith ; that he may be as critical and suspicious as he pleases ; that one does not regard his attitude as the effect of his judgement at all, for he is not in a position to form a reliable judgement on the matter ; his distrust is but a symptom like his other symptoms and will not interfere if he conscientiously carries out what the rule of the treatment requires of him.

Whoever is familiar with the nature of neurosis will not be astonished to hear that even a man who is very well able to carry out analysis upon others can behave like any other mortal and be capable of producing violent resistances as soon as he himself becomes the object of analytic investigation. When this happens it serves to remind us again of the dimensions which the mind has in regard to its depth, and it does not surprise us to find that a neurosis is rooted in mental strata that were never penetrated by an intellectual study of analysis.

Points of importance for the beginning of the treatment are the arrangements about time and money. In regard to time, I adhere rigidly to the principle of leasing a definite hour. A certain hour of my available working day is appointed to each patient ; it is his, and he is liable for it, even if he does not make use of it. This arrangement, which is regarded as a matter of course for teachers of music or languages among our upper classes, perhaps seems too rigorous for a medical man, or even unworthy of the profession. All the many accidents which may prevent the patient from attending every day at the same hour will be referred to, and some allowance will be expected for the numerous intercurrent ailments which may arise in the course of a lengthy analytic treatment. My only answer is : No other way is practicable. Under a less stringent régime the ' occasional ' non-attendances accumulate so greatly that the physician's material existence is threatened ; whereas strict adherence to the arrangement has the effect that accidental hindrances do not arise at all and intercurrent illnesses but seldom. One is hardly ever put in the position of enjoying a leisure hour which one is paid for and would be ashamed of ; the work continues without interruptions, and one is spared the disheartening and bewildering experience that an unexpected pause in the work always occurs just when it promises to be especially important and productive.

Nothing brings home to one with such overwhelming conviction the significance of the psychogenic factor in the daily life of mankind, the frequency of fictitious ' indispositions ', and the non-existence of chance as the practice of psycho-analysis for some years strictly on the principle of hire by the hour. In cases of indubitable organic illness, the occurrence of which cannot be excluded in spite of interest in the psychical work, I break off the treatment, regard myself as entitled to dispose otherwise of the hour which becomes free, and take the patient back again when he has recovered and I again have a free hour.

I work with my patients every day, except Sundays and public holidays, that is, usually six days a week. For slight cases, or the continuation of a treatment already well advanced, three days in the week will suffice. Otherwise, restriction of the time expended brings no advantage to physician or patient; it is not to be thought of at the beginning. Even short interruptions have a disconcerting effect on the work ; we used to speak jokingly of the ' Monday-crust ' when we began work again after the rest on Sunday ; with more frequent intervals the risk arises that one will not be able to keep pace with the patient's real life, that the analysis will lose contact with the present and be forced into by-paths. Occasionally one meets with patients to whom one must give more than the average time of one hour a day, because the best part of an hour is gone before they begin to open out and to communicate anything at all.

An unwelcome question which the patient asks the physician at the outset is : How long will the treatment last ? What length of time will you require to relieve me of my trouble ? If one has proposed an experimental course of a few weeks one can avoid a direct reply to this question by undertaking to give a more trustworthy answer later on. The answer is like that of Aesop in the fable of the Wanderer ; on being asked the length of the journey he answered ' Go ', and gave the explanation that he must know the pilgrim's pace before he could tell the time his journey would take him. This explanation helps one over the difficulty at the start, but the comparison is not a good one, for the neurotic can easily alter his pace and at times make but very slow progress. The question of the probable duration of the treatment is hardly to be answered at all, in fact.

As a result of the lack of insight on the part of patients combined with the lack of straightforwardness on the part of physicians, analysis is expected to realize the most boundless claims in the shortest time. As an example I will give some details from a letter which I received a few days ago from a lady in Russia. Her age is fifty-three; her illness began twenty-three years ago; for the last ten years she has been incapable of continued work; 'various cures in homes' have not succeeded in making an 'active life' possible for her. She hopes to be completely cured by psycho-analysis, of which she has read, but her illness has already cost her family so much that she cannot undertake a visit of more than six weeks or two months to Vienna. In addition to this there is another difficulty : she wishes to 'explain herself' from the beginning in writing, since any discussion of her complexes would excite an attack or render her 'temporarily dumb'. No one would expect a man to lift a heavy table with two fingers as if it were a little stool, or to build a large house in the time it would take to put up a wooden hut, but as soon as it becomes a question of the neuroses (which mankind seems not yet to have fitted into the general scheme of his ideas) even intelligent people forget the necessity for proportion between work, time and success—a comprehensible result, too, of the deep ignorance which prevails concerning the ætiology of neuroses. Thanks to this ignorance a neurosis is generally regarded as a sort of 'maiden from afar'; the world knows not whence it comes, and therefore expects it to vanish away some day.

Medical men support this happy belief ; even the experienced among them often fail to estimate properly the severity of nervous disorders. A friend and colleague of mine, to whose credit I account it that after several decades of scientific work on other principles he has betaken himself to the recognition of psycho-analysis, once wrote to me : What we need is a short, convenient form of treatment for out-patients suffering from obsessional neurosis. I could not supply him with it, and felt ashamed ; so I tried to excuse myself with the remark that probably physicians would also be very glad of a treatment for consumption or cancer which combined these advantages.

To speak more plainly, psycho-analysis is always a matter of long periods of time, of six months or a year, or more—a longer time than the patient expects. It is therefore a duty to explain this fact to the patient before he finally resolves upon the treatment. I hold it to be altogether more honourable, and also more expedient, to draw his attention, without alarming him unduly but from the very beginning, to the difficulties and sacrifices involved by analytic treatment ; thereby depriving him of the right to assert later on that he had been inveigled into a treatment the implications and extent of which he did not realize. The patient who lets himself be dissuaded by these considerations would later on have shown himself unsuitable ; it is a good thing to institute a selection in this way before the beginning of the treatment. With the progress of understanding among patients the number of those who stand this first test increases.

I do not bind patients to continue the treatment for a certain length of time ; I permit each one to break off whenever he likes, though I do not conceal from him that no success will result from a treatment broken off after only a small amount of work, and that it may easily, like an unfinished operation, leave him in an unsatisfactory condition. In the early years of my practice of psycho-analysis I had the greatest difficulty in prevailing upon patients to continue ; this difficulty has long since altered ; I must now anxiously exert myself to induce them to give it up.

The shortening of the analytic treatment remains a reasonable wish, the realization of which, as we shall hear, is being sought after in various ways. Unfortunately, it is opposed by a very important element in the situation—namely, the slowness with which profound changes in the mind bring themselves about, fundamentally the same thing as the ' inappreciation of time ' characteristic of our unconscious processes. When the patients are confronted with the great expenditure of time required for the analysis they often bethink themselves of suggesting a makeshift way out of the difficulty. They divide up their complaints and describe some as unendurable and others as secondary, saying, ' If only you will relieve me of this (for instance, a headache or a particular fear) I will manage by myself to endure life with the other troubles '. They exaggerate the selective capacity of the analysis in this. The analyst is certainly able to do a great deal, but he cannot determine beforehand exactly what results he will effect. He sets in operation a certain process, the ' loosening ' of the existing repressions : he can watch over it, further it, remove difficulties in the way of it, and certainly do much also to vitiate it ; but on the whole, once begun, the process goes its own way and does not admit of prescribed direction, either in the course it pursues or in the order in which the various stages to be gone through are taken. The power of the analyst over the symptoms of disease is comparable in a way to sexual potency ; the strongest man can beget a whole child, it is true, but he cannot effect the production of a head alone, or an arm, or a leg in the female organ, he cannot even prescribe the sex of the child. He, too, only sets in operation a highly complicated process, determined by foregone events, and ending with the severance of the child from the mother.

Again, a neurosis has the character of an organism ; its component manifestations are not independent of one another, they each condition and mutually support the others ; a man can only suffer from one neurosis, never from several accidentally combined in his person. Suppose one had freed the patient, according to his wish, from the one unendurable symptom, he might then have discovered that a symptom which was previously negligible had increased until it in turn had become intolerable. In general, the analyst who wishes the results to be as independent as possible of the influence of suggestion from himself (that is, of transference) will do best to refrain from using even the fraction of selective influence upon the results of the cure which is perhaps open to him. The patients who are most welcome to the psycho-analyst will be those who desire complete health so far as they are capable of it, and who will place as much time at his disposal for the cure as the process requires. Naturally, such favourable conditions are to be met with only in the minority of cases.

The next point to be decided on beginning the treatment is the money question, the physician's fee. The analyst does not dispute that money is to be regarded first and foremost as the means by which life is supported and power is obtained, but he maintains that, besides this, powerful sexual factors are involved in the value set upon it ; he may expect, therefore, that money questions will be treated by cultured people in the same manner as sexual matters, with the same inconsistency, prudishness and hypocrisy. He is therefore determined beforehand not to concur in this attitude, and in his dealings with patients to treat of money matters with the same matter-of-course frankness that he wishes to induce in them towards matters relating to sexual life. By voluntarily introducing the subject of fees and stating the price for which he gives his time, he shows the patient that he himself has cast aside false shame in these matters. Ordinary prudence then demands that the sums to be paid should not be allowed to accumulate until they are very large, but that payment should be made at fairly short regular intervals (every month or so). (It is well known that the value of the treatment is not enhanced in the patient's eyes if a very low fee is asked.) This is of course not the usual practice of neurologists or other physicians in our European cities. But the psycho-analyst may put himself in the position of surgeons, who are both honest and expensive because they deal in measures which can be of aid. In my opinion it is more dignified and ethically less open to objection to acknowledge one's actual claims and needs rather than, as the practice is now among medical men, to act the part of the disinterested philanthropist, while that enviable situation is denied to one and one grumbles in secret, or animadverts loudly, over the lack of con-sideration or the miserliness shown by patients. In estimating his fee the analyst must allow for the fact that, in spite of strenuous work, he can never earn as much as other medical specialists.

For the same reasons he may refrain from giving treatment gratuitously, making no exceptions to this in favour of his colleagues or their relatives. This last requisition seems to conflict with the claims of pro-fessional fellow-feeling ; one must consider, however, that gratuitous treatment means much more to a psycho-analyst than to other medical men—namely, the dedication of a considerable portion (an eighth or a seventh part, perhaps) of the time available for his livelihood over a period of several months. Another treatment conducted gratuitously at the same time would rob him of a quarter or a third of his earning capacity, which would be comparable to the effects of some serious accident.

Then the question arises whether the advantage to the patient would not outweigh the physician's sacrifice. I may rely on my own judgement in this matter, since I have given an hour daily, and sometimes two, for ten years to gratuitous treatment, because I wished, for the purpose of studying the neuroses, to work with the fewest possible hindrances. The advantages which I sought in this way were not forthcoming. Gratuitous treatment enormously increases many neurotic resistances, such as the temptations of the transference-relationship for young women, or the opposition to the obligatory gratitude in young men arising from the father-complex, which is one of the most troublesome obstacles to the treatment. The absence of the corrective influence in payment of the professional fee is felt as a serious handicap ; the whole relationship recedes into an unreal world ; and the patient is deprived of a useful incentive to exert himself to bring the cure to an end.

One may stand quite aloof from the ascetic view of money as a curse and yet regret that analytic therapy is almost unattainable for the poor, both for external and for internal reasons. Little can be done to remedy this. Perhaps there is some truth in the widespread belief that those who are forced by necessity to a life of heavy labour succumb less easily to neurosis. But at all events experience shows without a doubt that, in this class, a neurosis once acquired is only with very great difficulty eradicated. It renders the sufferer too good service in the struggle for existence ; the accompanying secondary 'epinosic gain' has here too much importance. The pity which the world has refused to his material distress the sufferer now claims by right of his neurosis and absolves himself from the obligation of combating his poverty by work. Any one who tries to deal by psychotherapeutic means with a neurosis in a poor person usually makes the discovery that what is really required of him in such a case is a very different, material kind of therapy—the sort of healing which, according to tradition, Emperor Joseph II. used to dispense. Naturally, one does occasionally meet with people of worth who are helpless from no fault of their own, in whom unpaid treatment leads to excellent results without exciting any of the difficulties mentioned.

For the middle classes the necessary expense of psycho-analysis is only apparently excessive. Quite apart from the fact that restored health and capacity for life on the one hand, and a moderate outlay in money on the other, cannot be measured in the same category ; if one contrasts a computation of the never-ceasing costs of nursing homes and medical treatment with the increase of capacity to live well and earn well after a successful analytic treatment, one may say that the patient has made a good bargain. Nothing in life is so expensive as illness—and foolishness.

Before I conclude these remarks on beginning the analytic treatment a word must be said about a certain ceremonial observance regarding the position in which the treatment is carried out. I adhere firmly to the plan of requiring the patient to recline upon a sofa, while one sits behind him out of his sight. This arrangement has an historic meaning ; it is the last vestige of the hypnotic method out of which psycho-analysis was evolved ; but for many reasons it deserves to be retained. The first is a personal motive, one that others may share with me, however. I cannot bear to be gazed at for eight hours a day (or more). Since, while I listen, I resign myself to the control of my unconscious thoughts I do not wish my expression to give the patient indications which he may interpret or which may influence him in his communications. The patient usually regards being required to take up this position as a hardship and objects to it, especially when scoptophilia plays an important part in the neurosis. I persist in the measure, however, for the intention and result of it are that all imperceptible influence on the patient's associations by the trans-ference may be avoided, so that the transference may be isolated and clearly outlined when it appears as a resistance. I know that many analysts work in a different way, though I do not know whether the main motive of their departure is the ambition to work in a different way or an advantage which they gain thereby.

The conditions of the treatment being now regulated in this manner, the question arises at what point and with what material it shall begin.

What subject-matter the treatment begins with is on the whole immaterial, whether with the patient's life-story, with a history of the illness or with recollections of childhood ; but in any case the patient must be left to talk, and the choice of subject left to him. One says to him, therefore, ' Before I can say anything to you, I must know a great deal about you ; please tell me what you know about yourself '.

The only exception to this concerns the fundamental rule of the psycho-analytic technique which the patient must observe. This must be imparted to him at the very beginning : ' One thing more, before you begin. Your talk with me must differ in one respect from an ordinary conversation. Whereas usually you rightly try to keep the threads of your story together and to exclude all intruding associations and side-issues, so as not to wander too far from the point, here you must proceed differently. You will notice that as you relate things various ideas will occur to you which you feel inclined to put aside with certain criticisms and objections. You will be tempted to say to yourself : " This or that has no connection here, or it is quite unimportant, or it is nonsensical, so it cannot be necessary to mention it ". Never give in to these objections, but mention it even if you feel a disinclination against it, or indeed just because of this. Later on you will perceive and learn to understand the reason for this injunction, which is really the only one that you have to follow. So say whatever goes through your mind. Act as if you were sitting at the window of a railway train and describing to some one behind you the changing views you see outside. Finally, never forget that you have promised absolute honesty, and never leave anything unsaid because for any reason it is unpleasant to say it.'[1]

Patients who date their illness from a particular time usually concentrate upon the events leading up to it; others who themselves recognize the connection of their neurosis with their childhood often begin with an account of their whole life-story. A consecutive narrative should never be expected and nothing should be done to encourage it. Every detail of the story will later have to be related afresh, and only with this repetition will additional matter appear enabling the significant connections which are unknown to the patient to be traced.

There are patients who from the first hour carefully

[1] Much might be said about our experience with the fundamental rule of psycho-analysis. One meets occasionally with people who behave as if they had instituted this rule for themselves; others offend against it from the beginning. It is indispensable, and also advantageous, to mention it at the first stage of the treatment; later, under the influence of resistances, obedience to it weakens and there comes a time in every analysis when the patient disregards it. One must remember how irresistible was the temptation in one's self-analysis to yield to those cavilling pretexts for rejecting certain thoughts. The feeble effect of the patient's agreement to the bargain made with him about the 'fundamental rule' is regularly demonstrated when something of an intimate nature about a third person rises to his mind for the first time; the patient knows that he must say everything, but he makes a new obstacle out of the discretion required on behalf of others. 'Must I really say everything? I thought that only applied to what concerns myself.' It is naturally impossible to carry out an analysis if the patient's relations with other people and his thoughts about them are excluded. *Pour faire une omelette il faut casser des œufs.* An honourable man readily forgets such of the private affairs of strangers as do not seem important for him to know. Names, too, cannot be excepted from communication; otherwise the patient's narratives become rather shadowy, like the scenes of Goethe's *Natural Daughter*, and do not remain in the physician's memory; moreover, the names withheld cover the approach to all kinds of important connections. One may perhaps leave names until the patient has become more familiar with the physician and the process of analysis. It is a most remarkable thing that the whole undertaking becomes lost labour if a single concession is made to secrecy. If at any one spot in a town the right of sanctuary existed, one can well imagine that it would not be long before all the riff-raff of the town would gather there. I once treated a high official who was bound by oath not to communicate certain State secrets, and the analysis came to grief as a consequence of this restriction. The psycho-analytic treatment must override everything which comes in its way, because the neurosis and the resistances are equally relentless.

prepare their communications, ostensibly so as to make better use of the time given to treatment. This appears to be eagerness on their part, but it is resistance. One must disallow this preparation ; it is employed to guard against the appearance of unwelcome thoughts ; [1] the patient may believe ever so honestly in his praise-worthy intention, but resistance will play its part in this kind of considered preparation and will see to it that in this way the most valuable part of the communication escapes. One will soon find that the patient invents yet other methods by which the required material may be withheld from analysis. He will perhaps talk over the treatment every day with some intimate friend, and in this discussion bring out all the thoughts which should occur to him in the presence of the physician. The treatment then suffers from a leak which lets through just what is most valuable. It will then soon be time to recommend the patient to treat the analysis as a matter between himself and his physician, and to exclude everyone else from sharing in it, no matter how closely bound to him or how inquisitive they may be. In later stages of the treatment the patient is not usually tempted in this way.

Certain patients wish their treatment kept secret, often because they have kept their neurosis secret, and I put no obstacle in the way of this. That in consequence the world hears nothing of some of the most brilliantly successful cures is of course a consideration not to be taken into account. Obviously the patient's decision in favour of secrecy at once reveals one feature of his inner history.

In advising at the beginning of treatment that as few persons as possible shall be informed of it, one protects patients to some extent from the many hostile influences seeking to detach them from the analysis. Such influences may be very mischievous at the outset of the cure ; later they are usually immaterial, or even

---

[1] Exceptions may be made only of such data as the family relationships, visits, operations, and so on.

useful in bringing into prominence resistances which are attempting concealment.

If during the course of the analysis the patient requires temporarily some other medical or special treatment, it is far wiser to call in some colleague outside analytic work than to administer this treatment oneself. Analysis combined with other treatment, for neurotic maladies with a strong organic connection, is nearly always impracticable ; the patients withdraw their interest from the analysis when there is more than one way leading them to health. Preferably one postpones the organic treatment until after the conclusion of the mental ; if the former were tried first, in most cases it would do no good.

To return to the beginning of the treatment. Patients are occasionally met with who begin the treatment with an absolute disclaimer of the existence of any thoughts in their minds which they could utter, although the whole field of their life-history and their neurosis lies before them untrodden. One must accede this first time as little as at any other to their request that one should propose something for them to speak of. One must bear in mind what it is that confronts one in these cases. A formidable resistance has come out into the open in order to defend the neurosis ; one takes up its challenge then and there, and grips it by the throat. Emphatic and repeated assurance that the absence of all ideas at the beginning is an impossibility, and that there is some resistance against the analysis, soon brings the expected confessions from the patient or else leads to the first discovery of some part of his complexes. It is ominous if he has to confess that while listening to the rule of the analysis he formed a determination in spite of it not to communicate this or that ; not quite so bad if he only has to declare the distrust he has of the treatment or the appalling things he has heard about it. If he denies these and similar possibilities when they are suggested to him, further pressure will constrain him to acknowledge that he has neglected certain thoughts which are occupying his mind. He was thinking of the treatment itself but not in a definite way, or else the appearance of the room he is in occupied him, or he found himself thinking of the objects round him in the consulting-room, or of the fact that he is lying on a sofa ; for all of which thoughts he has substituted ' nothing '. These indications are surely intelligible ; everything connected with the situation of the moment represents a transference to the physician which proves suitable for use as resistance. It is necessary then to begin by uncovering this transference ; thence the way leads rapidly to penetration of the pathogenic material in the case. Women who are prepared by events in their past lives for a sexual overture, or men with unusually strong, repressed homosexuality, are the most prone to exhibit this denial of all ideas at the outset of the analysis.

The first symptoms or chance actions of the patient, like the first resistance, have a special interest and will betray one of the governing complexes of the neurosis. A clever young philosopher, with leanings towards æsthetic exquisiteness, hastens to twitch the crease in his trousers into place before lying down for the first sitting ; he reveals himself as an erstwhile coprophiliac of the highest refinement, as was to be expected of the developed æsthete. A young girl on the same occasion hurriedly pulls the hem of her skirt over her exposed ankle ; she has betrayed the kernel of what analysis will discover later, her narcissistic pride in her bodily beauty and her tendencies to exhibitionism.

Very many patients object especially to the arrangement of reclining in a position where the physician sits out of sight behind them ; they beg to be allowed to undergo analysis in some other position, mostly because they do not wish to be deprived of a view of the physician. Permission is invariably refused ; one cannot prevent them, however, from contriving to say a few words before the beginning of the ' sitting itself ',

and after one has signified its termination and they
have risen from the sofa. In this way they make in
their own minds a division of the treatment into an
official part, in which they behave in a very inhibited
manner, and an informal 'friendly' part, in which
they really speak freely and say a good deal that they
do not themselves regard as belonging to the treatment.
The physician does not fall in for long with this division
of the time, he makes a note of what is said before or
after the sitting, and in bringing it up at the next
opportunity he tears down the partition which the
patient has tried to erect. It again is a structure
formed from the material of a transference-resistance.

*So long as the patient continues to utter without
obstruction the thoughts and ideas rising to his mind, the
theme of the transference should be left untouched.* One
must wait until the transference, which is the most
delicate matter of all to deal with, comes to be employed
as resistance.

The next question with which we are confronted is
a main one. It runs : When shall we begin our disclosures to the patient ? When is it time to unfold
to him the hidden meaning of his thoughts and associations, to initiate him into the postulates of analysis
and its technical devices ?

The answer to this can only be : Not until a depend-
able transference, a well-developed *rapport*, is established in the patient. The first aim of the treatment
consists in attaching him to the treatment and to the
person of the physician. To ensure this one need do
nothing but allow him time. If one devotes serious
interest to him, clears away carefully the first resistances that arise and avoids certain mistakes, such an
attachment develops in the patient of itself, and the
physician becomes linked up with one of the imagos
of those persons from whom he was used to receive
kindness. It is certainly possible to forfeit this primary
success if one takes up from the start any standpoint
other than that of understanding, such as a moralizing

attitude, perhaps, or if one behaves as the representative or advocate of some third person, maybe the husband or wife, and so on.

This answer of course involves a condemnation of that mode of procedure which consists in communicating to the patient the interpretation of the symptoms as soon as one perceives it oneself, or of that attitude which would account it a special triumph to hurl these ' solutions ' in his face at the first interview. It is not difficult for a skilled analyst to read the patient's hidden wishes plainly between the lines of his complaints and the story of his illness ; but what a measure of self-complacency and thoughtlessness must exist in one who can upon the shortest acquaintance inform a stranger, who is entirely ignorant of analytical doctrines, that he is bound by an incestuous love for his mother, that he harbours wishes for the death of the wife he appears to love, that he conceals within himself the intention to deceive his chief, and so forth ! I have heard that analysts exist who plume themselves upon these kinds of lightning-diagnoses and ' express '- treatments, but I warn everyone against following such examples. Such conduct brings both the man and the treatment into discredit and arouses the most violent opposition, whether the interpretations be correct or not ; yes, and the truer they are actually the more violent is the resistance they arouse. Usually the therapeutic effect at the moment is nothing ; the resulting horror of analysis, however, is ineradicable. Even in later stages of the analysis one must be careful not to communicate the meaning of a symptom or the interpretation of a wish until the patient is already close upon it, so that he has only a short step to take in order to grasp the explanation himself. In former years I often found that premature communication of interpretations brought the treatment to an untimely end, both on account of the resistances suddenly aroused thereby and also because of the relief resulting from the insight so obtained.

The following objection will be raised here : Is it then our task to lengthen the treatment, and not rather to bring it to an end as rapidly as possible ? Are not the patient's sufferings due to his lack of knowledge and understanding, and is it not a duty to enlighten him as soon as possible, that is, as soon as the physician himself knows the explanations ? The answer to this question requires a short digression concerning the significance of knowledge and the mechanism of the cure in psycho-analysis.

In the early days of analytic technique it is true that we regarded the matter intellectually and set a high value on the patient's knowledge of that which had been forgotten, so that we hardly made a distinction between our knowledge and his in these matters. We accounted it specially fortunate if it were possible to obtain information of the forgotten traumas of child-hood from external sources, from parents or nurses, for instance, or from the seducer himself, as occurred occasionally ; and we hastened to convey the information and proofs of its correctness to the patient, in the certain expectation of bringing the neurosis and the treatment to a rapid end by this means. It was a bitter disappointment when the expected success was not forthcoming. How could it happen that the patient, who now had the knowledge of his traumatic experience, still behaved in spite of it as if he knew no more than before ? Not even would the recollection of the repressed trauma come to mind after it had been told and described to him.

In one particular case the mother of an hysterical girl had confided to me the homosexual experience which had greatly influenced the fixation of the attacks. The mother herself had come suddenly upon the scene and had been a witness of it ; the girl, however, had totally forgotten it, although it had occurred not long before puberty. Thereupon I made a most instructive observation. Every time that I repeated the mother's story to the girl she reacted to it with an hysterical attack, after which the story was again forgotten. There was no doubt that the patient was expressing a violent resistance against the knowledge which was being forced upon her ; at last she simulated imbecility and total loss of memory in order to defend herself against what I told her. After this, there was no alternative but to abandon the previous attribution of importance to knowledge in itself, and to lay the stress upon the resistances which had originally induced the condition of ignorance and were still now prepared to defend it. Conscious knowledge, even if it were not again expelled, was powerless against these resistances.

This disconcerting ability in patients to combine conscious knowledge with ignorance remains unexplained by what is called normal psychology. By reason of the recognition of the unconscious, psychoanalysis finds no difficulty in it ; the phenomenon described is, however, one of the best confirmations of the conception by which mental processes are approached as being differentiated topographically. The patients are aware, in thought, of the repressed experience, but the connection between the thought and the point where the repressed recollection is in some way imprisoned is lacking. No change is possible until the conscious thought-process has penetrated to this point and has overcome the resistances of the repression there. It is just as if a decree were promulgated by the Ministry of Justice to the effect that juvenile misdemeanours should be dealt with by certain lenient methods. As long as this concession has not come to the knowledge of the individual magistrates, or in the event of their not choosing to make use of it but preferring to deal justice according to their own lights, nothing will be changed in the treatment accorded to youthful delinquents. For the sake of complete accuracy, though, it may be added that communicating to the patient's consciousness information about what is repressed does not entirely fail of any effect at all. It does not produce the hoped-for result of abolishing the symptoms, but it has other consequences. It first arouses resistances, but when these are overcome it sets a mental process in action, in the course of which the desired influence upon the unconscious memory is eventually effected.

At this point we should review the play of forces brought into action by the treatment. The primary motive-power used in therapy is the patient's suffering and the wish to be cured which arises from it. The volume of this motive-force is diminished in various ways, discoverable only in the course of the analysis, above all by what we call the 'epinosic gain'; the motive-power itself must be maintained until the end of the treatment; every improvement effects a diminution of it. Alone, however, the force of this motive is insufficient to overcome the illness; two things are lacking in it, the knowledge of the paths by which the desired end may be reached, and the amount of energy needed to oppose the resistances. The analytic treatment helps to supply both these deficiencies. The accumulation of energy necessary to overcome the resistances is supplied by analytic utilization of the energies which are always ready to be 'transferred'; and by timely communications to the patient at the right moment analysis points out the direction in which these energies should be employed. The transference alone frequently suffices to bring about a disappearance of the symptoms of the disease, but this is merely temporary and lasts only as long as the transference itself is maintained. The treatment is then nothing more than suggestion, not a psycho-analysis. It deserves the latter name only when the intensity of the transference has been utilized to overcome the resistances; only then does illness become impossible, even though the transference is again dissolved as its function in the treatment requires.

In the course of the treatment another helpful agency is roused — the patient's intellectual interest and understanding. But this alone is hardly worth

consideration by the side of the other forces engaged
in the struggle, for it is always in danger of succumbing
to the clouding of reasoning power under the influence
of resistances. Hence it follows that the new sources
of strength for which the sufferer is indebted to the
analyst resolve themselves into transference, and
instruction (by explanation). The patient only makes
use of the instruction, however, in so far as he is induced
to do so by the transference ; and therefore until a
powerful transference is established the first explanation should be withheld ; and likewise, we may add,
with each subsequent one, we must wait until each
disturbance of the transference by the transference-
resistances arising in succession has been removed.

XXXII

FURTHER RECOMMENDATIONS IN THE TECHNIQUE OF PSYCHO-ANALYSIS [1]

RECOLLECTION, REPETITION AND WORKING THROUGH

(1914)

IT seems to me not unnecessary constantly to remind students of the far-reaching changes which psycho-analytic technique has undergone since its first beginnings. Its first phase was that of Breuer's catharsis, direct concentration upon the events exciting symptom-formation and persistent efforts on this principle to obtain reproduction of the mental processes involved in that situation, in order to bring about a release of them through conscious operations. The aims pursued at that time, by the help of the hypnotic condition, were ' recollection ' and ' abreaction '. Next, after hypnosis had been abandoned, the main task became that of divining from the patient's free associations what he failed to remember. Resistances were to be circumvented by the work of interpretation and by making its results known to the patient ; concentration on the situations giving rise to symptom-formation and on those which lay behind the outbreak of illness was retained, while abreaction receded and seemed to be replaced by the work the patient had to do in overcoming his critical objections to his associations, in accordance with the fundamental psycho-analytic rule. Finally, the present-day technique evolved itself, whereby the analyst abandons concentration on any particular element or problem, contents himself with

¹ First published in *Zeitschrift*, Bd. II., 1914 ; reprinted in *Sammlung*, Vierte Folge. [Translated by Joan Riviere.]

studying whatever is occupying the patient's mind at the moment, and employs the art of interpretation mainly for the purpose of recognizing the resistances which come up in regard to this material and making the patient aware of them. A rearrangement of the division of labour results from this ; the physician discovers the resistances which are unknown to the patient ; when these are removed the patient often relates the forgotten situations and connections without any difficulty. The aim of these different procedures has of course remained the same throughout: descriptively, to recover the lost memories; dynamically, to conquer the resistances caused by repression.

One is bound to be grateful still to the old hypnotic technique for the way in which it unrolled before us certain of the mental processes of analysis in an isolated and schematic form. Only this could have given us the courage to create complicated situations ourselves in the analytic process and to keep them perspicuous.

Now in those days of hypnotic treatment ' recollection ' took a very simple form. The patient put himself back into an earlier situation, which he seemed never to confound with the present, gave an account of the mental processes belonging to it, in so far as they were normal, and appended to this whatever conclusions arose from making conscious what had before been unconscious.

I will here interpolate a few observations which every analyst has found confirmed in his experience. The forgetting of impressions, scenes, events, nearly always reduces itself to ' dissociation ' of them. When the patient talks about these ' forgotten ' matters he seldom fails to add : ' In a way I have always known that, only I never thought of it '. He often expresses himself as disappointed that not enough things come into his mind which he can hail as ' forgotten ', which he has never thought of since they happened. Even this desire on his part is fulfilled, however, particularly in cases of conversion-hysteria. The 'forgotten' material is still further circumscribed when we estimate at their true value the screen-memories which are so generally present. In many cases I have had the impression that the familiar childhood-amnesia, which is theoretically so important to us, is entirely outweighed by the screen-memories. Not merely is much that is essential in childhood preserved in them, but actually all that is essential. Only one must understand how to extract it from them by analysis. They represent the forgotten years of childhood just as adequately as the manifest content represents the dream-thoughts.

The other group of mental processes, the purely internal mental activities, such as phantasies, relations between ideas, impulses, feelings, connections, may be contrasted with impressions and events experienced, and must be considered apart from them in its relation to forgetting and remembering. With these processes it particularly often happens that something is 're-membered' which never could have been 'forgotten', because it was never at any time noticed, never was conscious ; as regards the fate of any such 'connection' in the mind, moreover, it seems to make no difference whatever whether it was conscious and then was forgotten or whether it never reached consciousness at all. The conviction which a patient obtains in the course of analysis is quite independent of remembering it in that way.

In the manifold forms of obsessional neurosis particularly, 'forgetting' consists mostly of a falling away of the links between various ideas, a failure to draw conclusions, an isolating of certain memories.

No memory of one special kind of highly important experience can usually be recovered : these are experiences which took place in very early childhood, before they could be comprehended, but which were *subsequently* interpreted and understood. One gains a knowledge of them from dreams, and is compelled to believe in them on irresistible evidence in the structure of the neurosis ; moreover, one can convince oneself that after his resistances have been overcome the patient no longer invokes the absence of any memory of them (sensation of familiarity) as a ground for refusing to accept them.   This matter, however, is one demanding so much critical caution and introducing so much that is novel and startling that I will reserve it for special discussion in connection with suitable material.[1]

To return to the comparison between the old and the new techniques ; in the latter there remains very little, often nothing, of this smooth and pleasing course of events belonging to the former.   There are cases which, under the new technique, conduct themselves up to a point like those under the hypnotic technique and only later abandon this behaviour ; but others behave differently from the beginning.   If we examine the latter class in order to define this difference, we may say that here the patient *remembers* nothing of what is forgotten and repressed, but that he expresses it in *action*.   He reproduces it not in his memory but in his behaviour ;   he *repeats* it, without of course knowing that he is repeating it.

For instance, the patient does not say that he remembers how defiant and critical he used to be in regard to the authority of his parents, but he behaves in that way towards the physician.   He does not remember how he came to a helpless and hopeless deadlock in his infantile searchings after the truth of sexual matters, but he produces a mass of confused dreams and associations, complains that he never succeeds at anything, and describes it as his fate never to be able to carry anything through.   He does not remember that he was intensely ashamed of certain sexual activities, but he makes it clear that he is ashamed of the treatment to which he has submitted himself, and does his utmost to keep it a secret ; and so on.

[1] [Cf. Freud, ' From the History of an Infantile Neurosis ', COLLECTED PAPERS, vol. iii.—Trans.]

Above all, the beginning of the treatment sets in with a repetition of this kind. When one announces the fundamental psycho-analytical rule to a patient with an eventful life-history and a long illness behind him, and then waits for him to pour forth a flood of information, the first thing that happens often is that he has nothing to say. He is silent and declares that nothing comes into his mind. That is of course nothing but the repetition of a homosexual attitude, which comes up as a resistance against remembering anything. As long as he is under treatment he never escapes from this compulsion to repeat ; at last one understands that it is his way of remembering.

The relation between this compulsion to repeat and the transference and resistance is naturally what will interest us most of all. We soon perceive that the transference is itself only a bit of repetition, and that the repetition is the transference of the forgotten past not only on to the physician, but also on to all the other aspects of the current situation. We must be prepared to find, therefore, that the patient abandons himself to the compulsion to repeat, which is now replacing the impulse to remember, not only in his relation with the analyst but also in all other matters occupying and interesting him at the time, for instance, when he falls in love or sets about any project during the treatment. Moreover, the part played by resistance is easily recognized. The greater the resistance the more extensively will expressing in action (repetition) be substituted for recollecting. The ideal kind of recollection of the past which belongs to hypnosis is indeed a condition in which resistance is completely abrogated. If the treatment begins under the auspices of a mild and unpronounced positive transference, it makes an unearthing of memories like that in hypnosis possible to begin with, while the symptoms themselves are for the time quiescent; if then, as the analysis proceeds, this transference becomes hostile or unduly intense, consequently necessitating repression, remembering immediately gives way to expression in action. From then onward the resistances determine the succession of the various repetitions. The past is the patient's armoury out of which he fetches his weapons for defending himself against the progress of the analysis, weapons which we must wrest from him one by one.

The patient reproduces instead of remembering, and he reproduces according to the conditions of the resistance ; we may now ask what it is exactly that he reproduces or expresses in action. The answer is that he reproduces everything in the reservoirs of repressed material that has already permeated his general character—his inhibitions and disadvantageous attitudes of mind, his pathological traits of character. He also repeats during the treatment all his symptoms. And now we can see that our special insistence upon the compulsion to repeat has not yielded any new fact, but is only a more comprehensive point of view. We are only making it clear to ourselves that the patient's condition of illness does not cease when his analysis begins, that we have to treat his illness as an actual force, active at the moment, and not as an event in his past life. This condition of present illness is shifted bit by bit within the range and field of operation of the treatment, and while the patient lives it through as something real and actual, we have to accomplish the therapeutic task, which consists chiefly in translating it back again into terms of the past.

Causing memories to be revived under hypnosis gives the impression of an experiment in the laboratory. Allowing ' repetition ' during analytic treatment, which is the latest form of technique, constitutes a conjuring into existence of a piece of real life, and can therefore not always be harmless and indifferent in its effects on all cases. The whole question of ' exacerbation of symptoms during treatment ', so often unavoidable, is linked up with this.

The very beginning of the treatment above all

brings about a change in the patient's conscious attitude towards his illness. He has contented himself usually with complaining of it, with regarding it as nonsense, and with underestimating its importance ; for the rest, he has extended the ostrich-like conduct of repression which he adopted towards the sources of his illness on to its manifestations. Thus it happens that he does not rightly know what are the conditions under which his phobia breaks out, has not properly heard the actual words of his obsessive idea or not really grasped exactly what it is his obsessive impulse is impelling him to do. The treatment of course cannot allow this. He must find the courage to pay attention to the details of his illness. His illness itself must no longer seem to him contemptible, but must become an enemy worthy of his mettle, a part of his personality, kept up by good motives, out of which things of value for his future life have to be derived. The way to reconciliation with the repressed part of himself which is coming to expression in his symptoms is thus prepared from the beginning ; yet a certain tolerance towards the illness itself is induced. Now if this new attitude towards the illness intensifies the conflicts and brings to the fore symptoms which till then had been indistinct, one can easily console the patient for this by pointing out that these are only necessary and temporary aggravations, and that one cannot overcome an enemy who is absent or not within range. The resistance, however, may try to exploit the situation to its own ends, and abuse the permission to be ill. It seems to say : ' See what happens when I really let myself go in these things ! Haven't I been right to relegate them all to repression ? ' Young and childish persons in particular are inclined to make the necessity for paying attention to their illness a welcome excuse for luxuriating in their symptoms.

There is another danger, that in the course of the analysis, other, deeper-lying instinctual trends which had not yet become part of the personality may come to be ' reproduced '. Finally, it is possible that the patient's behaviour outside the transference may involve him in temporary disasters in life, or even be so designed as permanently to rob the health he is seeking of all its value.

The tactics adopted by the physician are easily justified. For him recollection in the old style, reproduction in the mind, remains the goal of his endeavours, even when he knows that it is not to be obtained by the newer method. He sets about a perpetual struggle with the patient to keep all the impulses which he would like to carry into action within the boundaries of his mind, and when it is possible to divert into the work of recollection any impulse which the patient wants to discharge in action, he celebrates it as a special triumph for the analysis. When the transference has developed to a sufficiently strong attachment, the treatment is in a position to prevent all the more important of the patient's repetition-actions and to make use of his intentions alone, *in statu nascendi*, as material for the therapeutic work. One best protects the patient from disasters brought about by carrying his impulses into action by making him promise to form no important decisions affecting his life during the course of the treatment, for instance, choice of a profession or of a permanent love-object, but to postpone all such projects until after recovery.

At the same time one willingly accords the patient all the freedom that is compatible with these restrictions, nor does one hinder him from carrying out projects which, though foolish, are not of special significance ; one remembers that it is only by dire experience that mankind ever learns sense. There are no doubt persons whom one cannot prevent from plunging into some quite undesirable project during the treatment and who become amenable and willing to submit the impulse to analysis only afterwards.

Occasionally, too, it is bound to happen that the untamed instincts assert themselves before there is time for the curbing-rein of the transference to be placed on them, or that an act of reproduction causes the patient to break the bond that holds him to the treatment. As an extreme example of this, I might take the case of an elderly lady who had repeatedly fled from her house and her husband in a twilight state, and gone no one knew where, without having any idea of a motive for this ' elopement '. Her treatment with me began with a marked positive transference of affectionate feeling, which intensified itself with uncanny rapidity in the first few days, and by the end of a week she had ' eloped ' again from me, before I had time to say anything to her which might have prevented this repetition.

The main instrument, however, for curbing the patient's compulsion to repeat and for turning it into a motive for remembering consists in the handling of the transference. We render it harmless, and even make use of it, by according it the right to assert itself within certain limits. We admit it into the transference as to a playground, in which it is allowed to let itself go in almost complete freedom and is required to display before us all the pathogenic impulses hidden in the depths of the patient's mind. If the patient does but show compliance enough to respect the necessary conditions of the analysis we can regularly succeed in giving all the symptoms of the neurosis a new transference-colouring, and in replacing his whole ordinary neurosis by a ' transference-neurosis ' of which he can be cured by the therapeutic work. The transference thus forms a kind of intermediary realm between illness and real life, through which the journey from the one to the other must be made. The new state of mind has absorbed all the features of the illness ; it represents, however, an artificial illness which is at every point accessible to our interventions. It is at the same time a piece of real life, but adapted to our purposes by specially favourable conditions, and it is of a provisional character. From the repetition-reactions which are exhibited in the transference the familiar paths lead back to the awakening of the memories, which yield themselves without difficulty after the resistances have been overcome.

I might break off at this point but for the title of this paper, which requires me to discuss a further point in analytic technique. The first step in overcoming the resistance is made, as we know, by the analyst's discovering the resistance, which is never recognized by the patient, and acquainting him with it. Now it seems that beginners in analytic practice are inclined to look upon this as the end of the work. I have often been asked to advise upon cases in which the physician complained that he had pointed out his resistance to the patient and that all the same no change had set in; in fact, the resistance had only then become really pronounced and the whole situation had become more obscure than ever. The treatment seemed to make no progress. This gloomy foreboding always proved mistaken. The treatment was as a rule progressing quite satisfactorily ; only the analyst had forgotten that naming the resistance could not result in its immediate suspension. One must allow the patient time to get to know this resistance of which he is ignorant, to ' work through ' it, to overcome it, by continuing the work according to the analytic rule in defiance of it. Only when it has come to its height can one, with the patient's co-operation, discover the repressed instinctual trends which are feeding the resistance ; and only by living then through in this way will the patient be convinced of their existence and their power. The physician has nothing more to do than to wait and let things take their course, a course which cannot be avoided nor always be hastened. If he holds fast to this principle, he will often be spared the disappointment of failure in cases where all the time he has conducted the treatment quite correctly.

This ' working through ' of the resistances may in practice amount to an arduous task for the patient and a trial of patience for the analyst. Nevertheless, it is the part of the work that effects the greatest changes in the patient and that distinguishes analytic treatment from every kind of suggestive treatment. Theoretically one may correlate it with the ' abreaction ' of quantities of affect pent-up by repression, without which the hypnotic treatment remained ineffective.

XXXIII

FURTHER RECOMMENDATIONS IN THE TECHNIQUE OF PSYCHO-ANALYSIS [1]

Observations on Transference-Love

(1915)

EVERY beginner in psycho-analysis probably feels alarmed at first at the difficulties in store for him when he comes to interpret the patient's associations and deal with the reproduction of repressed material. When the time comes, however, he soon learns to look upon these difficulties as insignificant and instead becomes convinced that the only serious difficulties are encountered in handling the transference.

Among the situations to which the transference gives rise, one is very sharply outlined, and I will select this, partly because it occurs so often and is so important in reality and partly because of its theoretical interest. The case I mean is that in which a woman or girl patient shows by unmistakable allusions or openly avows that she has fallen in love, like any other mortal woman, with the physician who is analysing her. This situation has its distressing and its comical aspects as well as its serious ones; it is so complicated, and conditioned by so many factors, so unavoidable and so difficult to dissolve, that discussion of it has long been a pressing need of analytic technique. But since those who mock at the failings of others are not always themselves free from them, we have hardly been inclined to rush in to the fulfilment of this task. The obligation of professional discretion, which cannot be

---

[1] First published in *Zeitschrift*, Bd. III., 1915 ; reprinted in *Sammlung*, Vierte Folge. [Translated by Joan Riviere.]

disregarded in life but which is useless in our science, makes itself felt here again and again. In so far as psycho-analytical publications are a part of life, we have here an insoluble conflict. I have recently disregarded this matter of discretion for once [1] and shown how this same transference situation at first retarded the development of psycho-analytic therapy for ten years.

To a cultivated layman—and in their relation to psycho-analysis the attitude of such men is the best we encounter—matters concerned with love cannot be measured by the same standards as other things : it is as though they were written on a page by themselves which would not take any other script. If a patient falls in love with her doctor, then, such a man will think only two outcomes are possible—one comparatively rare, in which all the circumstances allow of a permanent legal union between them, and the other much commoner, in which physician and patient part, and abandon the work begun which should have led to her recovery, as though it had been prevented by some elemental phenomenon. There is certainly a third conceivable way out, which even appears compatible with continuing the treatment, and that is a love-relationship between them of an illicit character, not intended to last permanently ; but both conventional morality and professional dignity surely make this impossible. In any event our layman would beg the analyst to reassure him as unambiguously as possible that this third alternative is out of the question.

It is clear that the analyst's point of view must be different from this.

Let us take the case of the second possible alternative. After the patient has fallen in love with the physician, they part ; the treatment is given up. But very soon the patient's condition necessitates her making another attempt at cure with another physician;

[1] 'On the History of the Psycho-Analytic Movement', 1914, COLLECTED PAPERS, vol. i.

the next thing that happens is that she feels she has
fallen in love with the second physician, and just the
same again when she had broken off and begun again
with a third, and so on.   This phenomenon, which
occurs with such regularity and is one of the foundations
of psycho-analytical theory, may be regarded from two
points of view, that of the physician analysing and that
of the patient in need of analysis.

To the physician it represents an invaluable explanation and a useful warning against any tendency to
counter-transference which may be lurking in his own
mind.   He must recognize that the patient's falling in
love is induced by the analytic situation and is not to
be ascribed to the charms of his person, that he has
no reason whatever therefore to be proud of such a
' conquest ', as it would be called outside analysis.
And it is always well to be reminded of this.   For the
patient, however, there are two alternatives :   either
she must abandon her analytic treatment or she must
make up her mind to being in love with physicians as
to an inevitable destiny.[1]

I have no doubt that the patient's relatives and
friends would decide as emphatically in favour of the
first of the two alternatives as the analyst would for
the second.   In my opinion, however, this is a case
in which the decision cannot be left to the tender—or
rather, the jealous egoistic—mercies of the relatives
and friends.   The patient's welfare alone should decide.
The love of her relatives cannot cure her neurosis.
It is not necessary for the psycho-analyst to force
himself upon anyone, but he may take up the stand
that for certain purposes he is indispensable.   Anyone
who takes up Tolstoy's attitude to this problem can
remain in undisputed possession of his wife or daughter,
but must try to put up with her retaining her neurosis
and with the disturbance it involves in her capacity for

---

[1] We know that the transference can express itself by other less
tender feelings, but I do not propose to go into that side of the matter
here.

love. After all, it is the same situation as that of a gynecological treatment. Incidentally, the jealous father or husband makes a great mistake if he thinks the patient will escape falling in love with the physician if he hands her over to some other kind of treatment than that of analysis in order to get rid of her neurosis. The difference will be, on the contrary, that her falling in love in a way which is bound to remain unexpressed and unanalysed can never render that aid to her recovery which analysis would have extracted from it.

It has come to my knowledge that certain physicians who practise analysis frequently prepare their patients for the advent of a love-transference or even instruct them to ' go ahead and fall in love with the analyst so that the treatment may make progress '. I can hardly imagine a more nonsensical proceeding. It robs the phenomenon itself of the element of spontaneity which is so convincing and it lays up obstacles ahead which are extremely difficult to overcome.

At the first glance it certainly does not look as if any advantage to the treatment could result from the patient's falling in love in the transference. No matter how amenable she has been up till then, she now suddenly loses all understanding of and interest in the treatment, and will not hear or speak of anything but her love, the return of which she demands ; she has either given up her symptoms or else she ignores them ; she even declares herself well. A complete transformation ensues in the scene—it is as though some make-believe had been interrupted by a real emergency, just as when the cry of fire is raised in a theatre. Any physician experiencing this for the first time will not find it easy to keep a grasp of the analytic situation and not to succumb to the illusion that the treatment is really at an end.

On reflection one realizes the true state of things. One remembers above all the suspicion that everything impeding the progress of the treatment may be an

expression of resistance. It certainly plays a great
part in the outbreak of passionate demands for love.
One has long noticed in the patient the signs of an
affectionate transference on to the physician and could
with certainty ascribe to this attitude her docility, her
acceptance of the analytic explanations, her remarkable
comprehension and the high degree of intelligence
which she displayed during this period. This is now
all swept away ; she has become completely lacking in
understanding and seems to be swallowed up in her
love ; and this change always came over her just as
one had to bring her to the point of confessing or
remembering one of the particularly painful or heavily
repressed vicissitudes in her life-history. She had been
in love, that is to say, for a long time ; but now the
resistance is beginning to make use of it in order to
hinder the progress of the treatment, to distract her
interest from the work and to put the analyst into a
painful and embarrassing position.

If one looks into the situation more closely one can
recognize that more complicated motives are also at
work, of which some are connected with the falling in
love, and others are particular expressions of resistance.
To the first belong the patient's efforts to re-assure
herself of her irresistibility, to destroy the physician's
authority by bringing him down to the level of a
lover, and to gain all the other advantages which she
foresees as incidental to gratification of her love.
With regard to the resistance, one may presume that
at times it uses the declarations of love as a test for
the strait-laced analyst, so that compliance on his
part would call down on him a reprimand. But above
all one obtains the impression that the resistance acts
as an *agent provocateur*, intensifying the love of the
patient and exaggerating her readiness for the sexual
surrender, in order thereby to vindicate the action of
her repression more emphatically by pointing to the
dangers of such licentiousness. All this by-play, which
in less complicated cases may not be present at all, has

as we know been regarded by A. Adler as the essential element in the whole process.

But how is the analyst to behave in this situation if he is not to come to grief and yet believes that the treatment should be continued through this love-transference and in spite of it ?

It would be very simple for me now, on the score of conventional morality, emphatically to insist that the analyst must never in any circumstances accept or return the tender passion proffered him—that instead he must watch for his chance to urge the infatuated woman to take the moral path and see the necessity of renunciation, and induce her to overcome the animal side of her nature and subdue her passion, so as to continue the analytic work.

I shall not fulfil these expectations, however—neither the first nor the second. Not the first, because I am writing not for patients, but for physicians who have serious difficulties to contend with, and also because in this instance I can go behind moral prescriptions to the source of them, namely, to utility. I am on this occasion in the happy position of being able to put the requirements of analytic technique in the place of a moral decree without any alteration in the results.

Even more emphatically, however, do I decline to fulfil the second of the expectations suggested above. To urge the patient to suppress, to renounce and to sublimate the promptings of her instincts, as soon as she has confessed her love-transference, would be not an analytic way of dealing with them, but a senseless way. It would be the same thing as to conjure up a spirit from the underworld by means of a crafty spell and then to dispatch him back again without a question. One would have brought the repressed impulses out into consciousness only in terror to send them back into repression once more. Nor should one deceive oneself about the success of any such proceeding. When levelled at the passions, lofty language achieves very little, as we all know. The patient will only feel the humiliation, and will not fail to revenge herself for it.

Just as little can I advocate a middle course which would recommend itself to some as especially ingenious ; this would consist in averring one's response to the patient's feelings of affection, but in refraining from all the physical accompaniments of these tender feelings, until one could guide the situation along calmer channels and raise it on to a higher level. Against this expedient I have to object that the psycho-analytic treatment is founded on truthfulness. A great part of its educative effect and its ethical value lies in this very fact. It is dangerous to depart from this sure foundation. When a man's life has become bound up with the analytic technique, he finds himself at a loss altogether for the lies and the guile which are otherwise so indispensable to a physician, and if for once with the best intentions he attempts to use them he is likely to betray himself. Since we demand strict truthfulness from our patients, we jeopardize our whole authority if we let ourselves be caught by them in a departure from the truth. And besides, this experimental adoption of tender feeling for the patient is by no means without danger. One cannot keep such complete control of oneself as not one day suddenly to go further than was intended. In my opinion, therefore, it is not permissible to disavow the indifference one has developed by keeping the counter-transference in check.

I have already let it be seen that the analytic technique requires the physician to deny the patient who is longing for love the satisfaction she craves. The treatment must be carried through in a state of abstinence ; I do not mean merely corporal abstinence, nor yet deprivation of everything desired, for this could perhaps not be tolerated by any sick person. But I would state as a fundamental principle that the patient's desire and longing are to be allowed to remain, to serve as driving forces for the work and for the changes to be wrought, and that one must beware of granting this source of strength some discharge by surrogates. Indeed, one could not offer the patient anything but surrogates, for until the repressions are lifted her condition makes her incapable of true satisfaction.

Let us admit that this principle—of carrying through the analytic treatment in a state of renunciation—extends far beyond the case we are discussing, and that it needs close consideration in order to define the limits of its possible application. But we will refrain from going into this question now and will keep as closely as possible to the situation we started from. What would happen if the physician were to behave differently, and avail himself of a freedom perhaps available to them both to return the love of the patient and to appease her longing for tenderness from him ?

If he had been guided in his decision by the argument that compliance on his part would strengthen his power over the patient so that he could influence her to perform the tasks required by the treatment, that is, could achieve a permanent cure of her neurosis by this means, experience would teach him that he had miscalculated. The patient would achieve her aim, but he would never achieve his. There is an amusing story about a pastor and an insurance agent which describes what would happen. An ungodly insurance agent lay at the point of death and his relatives fetched the holy man to convert him before he died. The interview lasted so long that those outside began to have some hope. At last the door of the sick chamber opened. The free-thinker had not been converted—but the pastor went away insured.

If her advances were returned, it would be a great triumph for the patient, but a complete overthrow for the cure. She would have succeeded in what all patients struggle for, in expressing in action, in reproducing in real life, what she ought only to remember, to reproduce as the content of her mind and to retain within the mental sphere.[1] In the further course of the love-relationship all the inhibitions and pathological reactions of her love-development would come out yet there would be no possibility of correcting them, and the painful episode would end in remorse and a strengthening of her tendency to repression. The love-relationship actually destroys the influence of the analytic treatment on the patient ; a combination of the two would be an inconceivable thing.

It is therefore just as disastrous for the analysis if the patient's craving for love prevails as if it is suppressed. The way the analyst must take is neither of these ; it is one for which there is no prototype in real life. He must guard against ignoring the transference-love, scaring it away or making the patient disgusted with it ; and just as resolutely must he withhold any response to it. He must face the transference-love boldly but treat it like something unreal, as a condition which must be gone through during the treatment and traced back to its unconscious origins, so that it shall assist in bringing to light all that is most hidden in the development of the patient's erotic life, and help her to learn to control it. The more plainly the analyst lets it be seen that he is proof against every temptation, the sooner will the advantage from the situation accrue to the analysis. The patient, whose sexual repressions are of course not yet removed but merely pushed into the background, will then feel safe enough to allow all her conditions for loving, all the phantasies of her sexual desires, all the individual details of her way of being in love to come to light, and then will herself open up the way back from them to the infantile roots of her love.

With one type of woman, to be sure, this attempt to preserve the love-transference for the purposes of analytic work without gratifying it will not succeed. These are women of an elemental passionateness ;

[1] Cf. pp. 321 and 369 *et seq*.

they tolerate no surrogates ; they are children of
nature who refuse to accept the spiritual instead of
the material ; to use the poet's words, they are
amenable only to the ' logic of gruel and the argument
of dumplings '. With such people one has the choice :
either to return their love or else to bring down upon
oneself the full force of the mortified woman's fury.
In neither event can one safeguard the interests of
the treatment. One must acknowledge failure and
withdraw ; and may at leisure study the problem how
the capacity for neurosis can be combined with such
an intractable craving for love.

Many analysts must have discovered the way in
which other women, less violent in their love, can be
brought round gradually to the analytic point of view.
Above all, the unmistakable element of resistance in
their ' love ' must be insisted upon. Genuine love
would make the patient docile and intensify her
readiness to solve the problems of her case, simply
because the man she loved expected it. A woman who
was really in love would gladly choose the road to
completion of the cure, in order to give herself a value
in the physician's eyes and to prepare herself for real
life where her feelings of love could find their proper
outlet. Instead of this, she is showing a stubborn
and rebellious spirit, has thrown up all interest in her
treatment, and clearly too all respect for the physician's
well-founded judgement. She is bringing out a resistance, therefore, under the guise of being in love ; and
in addition to this, she has no compunction about
trying to lead him into a cleft stick. For if he refuses
her love, as duty and his understanding compel him
to do, she can take up the attitude that she has been
humiliated and, out of revenge and resentment, make
herself inaccessible to cure by him, just as she is now
doing ostensibly out of love.

As a second argument against the genuineness of
this love one advances the fact that it shows not a
single new feature connecting it with the present

situation, but is entirely composed of repetitions and 'rechauffés' of earlier reactions, including childish ones. One then sets about proving this by detailed analysis of the patient's behaviour in love.

When the necessary amount of patience is added to these arguments it is usually possible to overcome the difficult situation and to continue the work, the patient having either moderated her love or transformed it ; the aim of the work then becomes the discovery of the infantile object-choice and of the phantasies woven round it. I will now, however, examine these arguments critically and put the question whether they really represent the truth or whether by employing them we are not in our desperation resorting to prevarication and misrepresentation. In other words : can the love which is manifested in analytic treatment not truly be called real ?

I think that we have told the patient the truth, but not the whole truth without regard for consequences. Of our two arguments the first is the stronger. The part taken by resistance in the transference-love is unquestionable and very considerable. But this love was not created by the resistance ; the latter finds it ready to hand, exploits it and aggravates the manifestations of it. Nor is its genuineness impugned by the resistance. The second argument is far weaker ; it is true that the love consists of new editions of old traces and that it repeats infantile reactions. But this is the essential character of every love. There is no love that does not reproduce infantile prototypes. The infantile conditioning factor in it is just what gives it its compulsive character which verges on the pathological. The transference-love has perhaps a degree less of freedom than the love which appears in ordinary life and is called normal ; it displays its dependence on the infantile pattern more clearly, is less adaptable and capable of modification, but that is all and that is nothing essential.

By what other signs can the genuineness of a love

be recognized ? By its power to achieve results, its capacity to accomplish its aim ? In this respect the transference-love seems to give place to none ; one has the impression that one could achieve anything by its means.

Let us resume, therefore : One has no right to dispute the ' genuine ' nature of the love which makes its appearance in the course of analytic treatment. However lacking in normality it may seem to be, this quality is sufficiently explained when we remember that the condition of being in love in ordinary life outside analysis is also more like abnormal than normal mental phenomena. The transference-love is characterized, nevertheless, by certain features which ensure it a special position. In the first place, it is provoked by the analytic situation ; secondly, it is greatly intensified by the resistance which dominates this situation ; and thirdly, it is to a high degree lacking in regard for reality, is less sensible, less concerned about consequences, more blind in its estimation of the person loved, than we are willing to admit of normal love. We should not forget, however, that it is precisely these departures from the norm that make up the essential element in the condition of being in love.

The first of these three characteristics of the transference-love is what determines the physician's course of action. He has evoked this love by undertaking analytic treatment in order to cure the neurosis ; for him it is an unavoidable consequence of the medical situation, as inevitable as the exposure of a patient's body or being told some life-and-death secret. It is therefore plain to him that he is not to derive any personal advantage from it. The patient's willingness makes no difference whatever ; it merely throws the whole responsibility on him. Indeed, as he must know, the patient had from the beginning entertained hopes of this way of being cured. After all the difficulties are overcome she will often confess to a phantasy, an expectation that she had had as she began the treatment—'if she behaved well, she would be rewarded in the end by the doctor's love for her'.

For the physician there are ethical motives which combine with the technical reasons to hinder him from according the patient his love. The aim that he has to keep in view is that this woman, whose capacity for love is disabled by infantile fixations, should attain complete access over this function which is so inestimably important for her in life, not that she should fritter it away in the treatment, but preserve it for real life, if so be that after her cure life makes that demand on her. He must not let the scene of the race between the dogs be enacted, in which the prize was a chaplet of sausages and which a funny fellow spoilt by throwing one sausage on to the course ; the dogs fell upon it and forgot about the race and the chaplet in the distance luring them on to win. I do not mean to say that it is always easy for the physician to keep within the bounds prescribed by technique and ethics. Younger men especially, who are not yet bound by a permanent tie, may find it a hard task. The love between the sexes is undoubtedly one of the first things in life, and the combination of mental and bodily satisfaction attained in the enjoyment of love is literally one of life's culminations. Apart from a few perverse fanatics, all the world knows this and conducts life accordingly ; only science is too refined to confess it. Again, when a woman sues for love, to reject and refuse is a painful part for a man to play ; and in spite of neurosis and resistance there is an incomparable fascination about a noble woman who confesses her passion. It is not the grossly sensual desires of the patient that constitute the temptation. These are more likely to repel and to demand the exercise of toleration in order to regard them as a natural phenomenon. It is perhaps the finer impulses, those 'inhibited in their aim', which lead a man into the danger of forgetting the rules of technique and the physician's task for the sake of a wonderful experience.

And yet the analyst is absolutely debarred from giving way. However highly he may prize love, he must prize even more highly the opportunity to help his patient over a decisive moment in her life. She has to learn from him to overcome the pleasure-principle, to give up a gratification which lies to hand but is not sanctioned by the world she lives in, in favour of a distant and perhaps altogether doubtful one, which is, however, socially and psychologically unimpeachable. To achieve this mastery of herself she must be taken through the primordial era of her mental development and in this way reach that greater freedom within the mind which distinguishes conscious mental activity— in the systematic sense—from unconscious.

The analytic psychotherapist thus has a threefold battle to wage—in his own mind against the forces which would draw him down below the level of analysis; outside analysis against the opponents who dispute the importance he attaches to the sexual instinctual forces and hinder him from making use of them in his scientific method ; and in the analysis against his patients, who at first behave like his critics but later on disclose the over-estimation of sexual life which has them in thrall, and who try to take him captive in the net of their socially ungovernable passions.

The lay public, of whose attitude to psycho-analysis I spoke at the outset, will certainly seize the opportunity given it by this discussion of the transference-love to direct the attention of the world to the dangers of this therapeutic method. The psycho-analyst knows that the forces he works with are of the most explosive kind and that he needs as much caution and conscientious-ness as a chemist. But when has it ever been forbidden to a chemist, on account of its danger, to occupy himself with the explosives which, just because of their effective-ness, are so indispensable ? It is remarkable that psycho-analysis has to win for itself afresh all the liberties which have long been accorded to other medical work. I certainly do not advocate that the harmless methods of treatment should be abandoned. For many cases they suffice, and when all is said, the *furor sanandi* is no more use to human society than any other kind of fanaticism. But it is grossly to under-value both the origins and the practical significance of the psychoneuroses to suppose that these disorders are to be removed by pottering about with a few harmless remedies. No ; in medical practice there will always be room for the ' *ferrum* ' and the ' *ignis* ' as well as for the ' *medicina* ', and there a strictly regular, unmodified psycho-analysis, which is not afraid to handle the most dangerous forces in the mind and set them to work for the benefit of the patient, will be found indispensable.

Now this well-founded comparison of the psycho-analytic medical procedure with a chemical procedure might suggest a new direction for our therapy. We have *analysed* the patient, *i.e.* separated his mental processes into their constituent parts and demonstrated these instinctual elements in him singly and in isolation ; what could be more natural than a request that we should also help him to make a new and a better re-combination of them ? You know that this demand has actually been put forward. We have heard that after the analysis of the diseased mental organism a synthesis of it must follow! And, close upon this, concern was expressed that the patient might be given too much analysis and too little synthesis ; and then there followed a move to put all the weight on this synthesis as the main factor in the psychotherapeutic effect—seeing in it a kind of revivification of something destroyed by vivisection.

I cannot imagine, however, that any new task for us is to be found in this psycho-synthesis. If I were to permit myself to be honest and uncivil I should say it was nothing but a meaningless phrase. I will limit myself to remarking that it is only pushing a comparison so far that it ceases to have any foundation, or, if you prefer, that it is an unjustifiable exploitation of a name. A name, however, is only a label applied to it to distinguish a thing from other similar things, not a syllabus, a description of its content or a definition. And the two objects in a comparison need only touch at a single point and may be entirely different from each other in all else. The life of the mind is a thing so unique and peculiar to itself that no one comparison can reflect its nature. The work of psycho-analysis suggests analogies with chemical analysis, but just as much with the incursions of the surgeon or the manipulations of the orthopædist or the influence of the pedagogue. The comparison with chemical analysis has its limits, in this way : in mental life we have to deal with forces that are under a compulsion towards unification and combination. When we succeed in dissolving a symptom into its elements, in freeing an instinct from one concatenation, it does not remain in isolation, but immediately enters into combination again with something else.[1]

On the contrary, indeed! The neurotic human being brings us his mind racked and rent by resistances ; whilst we are working at analysis of it and at removing the resistances, this mind of his begins to grow together ; that great unity which we call his ego fuses into one all the instinctual trends which before had been split off and barred away from it. The psycho-synthesis is thus achieved during analytic treatment without our intervention, automatically and inevitably. We have created the conditions for it by dissolving the symptoms into their elements and by removing the resistances. There is no truth in the idea that when the patient's mind is dissolved into its elements it then quietly waits until somebody puts it together again.

Developments in our therapy will surely proceed in a different direction, therefore ; above all, in that which Ferenczi [2] has lately characterized as ' activity ' on the part of the analyst.

Let us hasten to agree upon what we mean by this activity. We defined our therapeutic task as consisting of two things : making conscious the repressed material and uncovering the resistances. In that we are active enough, to be sure. But are we to leave it to the patient to deal alone with the resistances we have pointed out to him ? Can we give him no other help in this besides the stimulus he gets from the transference ? Does it not seem natural that we should help him also in another way, by putting him into the mental situation most favourable to solution of the

---

[1] Even in chemical analysis something very similar occurs. Simultaneously with the isolation of the various elements, which the chemist forces upon them, syntheses which are no part of his intention come into existence, owing to the liberation of the elective affinities in their substances.

[2] Ferenczi, *Technische Schwierigkeiten einer Hysterieanalyse.*

conflict, which is our aim ?   After all, what he can
achieve depends partly on a number of external
circumstances which converge in their influence on
him.   Should we hesitate to alter this combination by
intervening in a suitable manner ?   I think activity
of such a kind on the part of the physician analysing
is unobjectionable and entirely justifiable.

You observe that this opens up a new vein in
analytic technique, which will require close application
in order to work it out and which will yield very definite
rules.   I shall not attempt to introduce you to-day
to this new technique which is still being evolved, but
will content myself with enunciating a fundamental
principle which will probably be the guiding force in
our work on this new problem.   It runs as follows :
*Analytic treatment should be carried through, as far as is
possible, under privation—in a state of abstinence.*

How far it is possible to determine this must be
left for more detailed discussion.   By abstinence, however, is not to be understood doing without any and
every satisfaction—that would of course not be
practicable ;   nor do we mean what it popularly
connotes, refraining from sexual intercourse ;   it means
something else which has far more to do with the
dynamics of illness and recovery.

You will remember that it was a *frustration* that
made the patient ill, and that his symptoms serve him
as substitutive gratifications.   It is possible to observe
during the treatment that every improvement in his
condition reduces the rate at which he recovers and
diminishes the instinctual energy impelling him towards
cure.   But this instinctual propelling force is indispensable for cure ;   reduction of it endangers our
aim, the patient's restoration to health.   What is the
conclusion that forces itself inevitably upon us ?
Harsh though it may sound, we must see to it that the
patient's sufferings, to a degree that is in some way or
other effective, do not prematurely come to an end.
When the symptoms have been dissected and the value

of them thus discounted, his sufferings become moderated, and then we must set up a sufficiently distressing privation again in some other sensitive spot, or else we run the risk of never achieving any further improvement except quite insignificant and transitory ones.

As far as I can see, danger threatens from two directions. On the one hand, when the illness has been broken down by the analysis the patient applies his most assiduous endeavours to creating for himself in place of his symptoms new substitutive gratifications, now lacking in the feature of suffering. He makes use of the colossal capacity for displacement in the libido that is now partly liberated, in order to invest with libido and promote to the position of substitutive gratifications the most diverse kinds of activities, pleasures, interests, habits, including those that he already possessed. He continually finds new distractions of this kind, into which the energy necessary to complete the cure escapes, and he knows how to keep them secret for a time. It is the analyst's task to detect these by-paths and to require him every time to abandon them, however harmless the performance which leads to satisfaction may be in itself. The half-cured person may also undertake escapades that are not so harmless, as when, for instance, if he is a man, he seeks prematurely to bind himself to a woman. It may be observed, incidentally, that unhappy marriage and bodily infirmity are the two things that most often dissolve a neurosis. They both gratify especially the sense of guilt (need for punishment) which binds many neurotics so fast to their neuroses. By a foolish choice in marriage they punish themselves ; a long organic illness they regard as a punishment by fate and then often cease to keep up their neurosis.

In all such situations activity on the part of the physician must take the form of energetic opposition to premature substitutive gratifications. It is easier for him, however, to prevent the second danger, one

not to be under-estimated, which jeopardizes the propelling forces of the analysis. The patient looks for
his substitutive gratification above all in the treatment
itself, in his transference-relationship with the physician,
and he may even strive to compensate himself through
this means for all the other privations laid upon him.
A certain amount must of course be permitted to him,
more or less according to the nature of the case and the
patient's individuality. But it is not good to let it
become too much. Any analyst who out of the fullness
of his heart and his readiness to help perhaps extends
to the patient all that one human being may hope to
receive from another, commits the same economic error
which our non-analytic institutions for nervous patients
are guilty of. They exert themselves only to make
everything as pleasant as possible for the patient, so
that he may feel well there and gladly take flight back
there again away from the trials of life. In so doing
they entirely forgo making him stronger for life and
more capable of carrying out the actual tasks of his
life. In analytic treatment all such cosseting must be
avoided. As far as his relations with the physician are
concerned, the patient must have unfulfilled wishes in
abundance. It is expedient to deny him precisely
those satisfactions which he desires most intensely and
expresses most importunately.

I do not think I have exhausted the range of useful
activity on the part of the physician with the statement
that a condition of privation is to be kept up during the
treatment. Activity in another direction during analytic
treatment has already, as you will remember, been a
point at issue between us and the Swiss school. We
rejected most emphatically the view that we should
convert into our own property the patient who puts
himself into our hands in seek of help, should carve his
destiny for him, force our own ideals upon him, and
with the arrogance of a Creator form him in our own
image and see that it was good. I still to-day maintain
this attitude of rejection, and I think that this is the

place for that medical discretion which we have had to ignore in other connections ; I have learnt, too, that such a far-reaching activity towards patients is not at all requisite for therapeutic aims. For I have been able, without affecting their individuality, to help people with whom I had nothing in common, neither nationality, education, social position nor outlook upon life in general. At the time of the controversy I spoke of, I had the impression, to be sure, that the objections of our spokesmen—I think it was Ernest Jones who took the chief part—were too harsh and uncompromising. We cannot avoid also taking for treatment patients who are so helpless and incapable of ordinary life that for them one has to combine analytic with educative influence ; and even with the majority now and then occasions arise in which the physician is bound to take up the position of teacher and mentor. But it must always be done with great caution, and the patient should be educated to liberate and fulfil his own nature, and not to resemble ourselves.

Our honoured friend, J. J. Putnam, in the land of America which is now so hostile to us, must forgive us if we cannot accept his proposal either, namely, that psycho-analysis should place itself in the service of a particular philosophical outlook on the world and should urge this upon the patient in order to ennoble him. I would say that after all this is only tyranny, even though disguised by the most honourable motives.

Lastly, another quite different kind of activity is necessitated by the gradually growing appreciation that the various forms of disease treated by us cannot all be dealt with by the same technique. It would be premature to discuss this in detail, but I can give two examples of the way in which a new kind of activity comes into question. Our technique grew up in the treatment of hysteria and is still directed principally to the cure of this affection. But the phobias have already made it necessary for us to go beyond our former limits. One can hardly ever master a phobia if one waits till the patient lets the analysis influence him to give it up. He will never in that case bring for the analysis the material indispensable for a convincing solution of the phobia. One must proceed differently. Take the example of agoraphobia ; there are two classes of it, one slight and the other severe. Patients belonging to the first indeed suffer from anxiety when they go about alone, but they have not yet given up going out alone on that account ; the others protect themselves from the anxiety by altogether giving up going about alone. With these last one succeeds only when one can induce them through the influence of the analysis to behave like the first class, that is, to go about alone and to struggle with their anxiety while they make the attempt. One first achieves, therefore, a considerable moderation of the phobia, and it is only when this has been attained by the physician's recommendation that the associations and memories come into the patient's mind enabling the phobia to be solved.

In severe cases of obsessive acts a passive waiting attitude seems even less well adapted ; indeed in general these cases incline to favour an asymptomatic process of cure, an interminable protraction of the treatment ; in their analysis there is always the danger of a great deal coming to light without its effecting any change in them. I think there is little doubt that here the correct technique can only be to wait until the treatment itself has become a compulsion, and then with this counter-compulsion forcibly to suppress the compulsion of the disease. You will understand, however, that these two instances I have given you are only samples of the new developments towards which our therapy is tending.

And now in conclusion I will cast a glance at a situation which belongs to the future—one that will seem fantastic to many of you, but which I think, nevertheless, deserves that we should be prepared for it in our minds. You know that the therapeutic effects we can achieve are very inconsiderable in number. We are but a handful of people, and even by working hard each one of us can deal in a year with only a small number of persons. Against the vast amount of neurotic misery which is in the world, and perhaps need not be, the quantity we can do away with is almost negligible. Besides this, the necessities of our own existence limit our work to the well-to-do classes, accustomed to choose their own physicians, whose choice is diverted away from psycho-analysis by all kinds of prejudices. At present we can do nothing in the crowded ranks of the people, who suffer exceedingly from neuroses.

Now let us assume that by some kind of organization we were able to increase our numbers to an extent sufficient for treating large masses of people. Then on the other hand, one may reasonably expect that at some time or other the conscience of the community will awake and admonish it that the poor man has just as much right to help for his mind as he now has to the surgeon's means of saving life ; and that the neuroses menace the health of a people no less than tuberculosis, and can be left as little as the latter to the feeble handling of individuals. Then clinics and consultation-departments will be built, to which analytically trained physicians will be appointed, so that the men who would otherwise give way to drink, the women who have nearly succumbed under their burden of privations, the children for whom there is no choice but running wild or neurosis, may be made by analysis able to resist and able to do something in the world. This treatment will be free. It may be a long time before the State regards this as an urgent duty. Present conditions may delay its arrival even longer ; probably these institutions will first be started by private beneficence; some time or other, however, it must come.

The task will then arise for us to adapt our technique to the new conditions. I have no doubt that the validity of our psychological assumptions will impress

the uneducated too, but we shall need to find the
simplest and most natural expression for our theoretical
doctrines. We shall probably discover that the poor
are even less ready to part with their neuroses than
the rich, because the hard life that awaits them when
they recover has no attraction, and illness in them
gives them more claim to the help of others. Possibly
we may often only be able to achieve something if we
combine aid for the mind with some material support,
in the manner of Emperor Joseph. It is very probable,
too, that the application of our therapy to numbers will
compel us to alloy the pure gold of analysis plentifully
with the copper of direct suggestion ; and even hypnotic
influence might find a place in it again, as it has in the
treatment of war-neuroses. But whatever form this
psychotherapy for the people may take, whatever the
elements out of which it is compounded, its most
effective and most important ingredients will assuredly
remain those borrowed from strict psycho-analysis
which serves no ulterior purpose.

LIST OF BOOKS AND PAPERS REFERRED
TO IN THE TEXT

Adler, ' Drei Psychoanalysen von Zahleneinfällen und obsedierenden Zahlen ', *Psychiatrisch-neurologische Wochenschrift*, Nr. 28, 1905.

Andreas-Salomé, Lou, ' " Anal " und " Sexual " ', *Imago*, Bd. IV., 1916.

Binswanger, *Die Pathologie und Therapie der Neurasthenie*, 1896.

Bleuler, ' Dementia Praecox oder Gruppe der Schizophrenien ', Aschaffenburg's *Handbuch der Psychiatrie*, 1911.

Breuer und Freud, *Studien über Hysterie*, 1895. Vienna. Fourth Edition, 1922.

Eckstein, Emma, *Die Sexualfrage in der Erziehung des Kindes*, 1904.

v. Ehrenfels, *Sexualethik*, Grenzfragen des Nerven- und Seelenlebens, LVI. Wiesbaden, 1907.

Ellis, Havelock, *Studies in the Psychology of Sex*, vol. i., ' The Evolution of Modesty ', 1904.

The World of Dreams, 1911.

Erb, W., *Über die wachsende Nervosität unserer Zeit*, 1893.

Ferenczi, ' Introjection and Transference ' (1909), *Contributions to Psycho-Analysis*, translated by Ernest Jones, Boston, 1916. First published in German, *Jahrbuch*, Bd. I., 1909.

' Stages in the Development of the Sense of Reality ' (1913), *Contributions to Psycho-Analysis*, translated by Ernest Jones, Boston, 1916. First published in German, *Zeitschrift*, Bd. I., 1913.

' Technische Schwierigkeiten einer Hysterieanalyse ', *Zeitschrift*, Bd. V., 1919.

'Zur Symbolik des Medusenhauptes', *Zeitschrift*, Bd. IX., 1923.

Freud, *Beyond the Pleasure Principle*, London, 1922. Translated by C. M. Hubback from *Jenseits des Lustprinzips*, Vienna, 1920.

Das Ich und das Es, Vienna, 1923.

Die Traumdeutung, Vienna, 1900. Seventh Edition, 1922.

Drei Abhandlungen zur Sexualtheorie, 1905. Fifth Edition, 1922.

Group Psychology and the Analysis of the Ego, London, 1922. Translated by James Strachey from *Massenpsychologie und Ichanalyse*, Vienna, 1921.

Totem und Tabu, Vienna, 1913.

Zur Psychopathologie des Alltagslebens, first published in the *Monatsschrift für Psychiatrie und Neurologie*, Bd. X., 1901. Also published in book form by the Internationaler Psychoanalytischer Verlag, Vienna, 1904. Tenth Edition, 1924.

Grasset, 'La sensation du "déjà vu"', *Journal de psychologie normale et pathologique*, T. 1, 1904.

Janet, Pierre, *Névroses et idées fixes*, 1898.

Jeremias, *Babylonisches im neuen Testament*, 1906.
  Das alte Testament im Lichte des alten Orients, Zweite Auflage, 1906.

Jones, Ernest, 'Hate and Anal Erotism in the Obsessional Neurosis' (1913), *Papers on Psycho-Analysis*, Third Edition, 1923. First published in German, *Zeitschrift*, Bd. I., 1913.

Jung, 'Die Bedeutung des Vaters für den Schicksal des Einzelnen', *Jahrbuch*, Bd. I., 1909.
  'Die psychologische Diagnose des Tatbestandes', *Juristischpsychiatrische Grenzfragen*, Bd. IV., 2, 1906.
  'Symbole und Wandlungen der Libido', *Jahrbuch*, Bd. III., 1911.

v. Krafft-Ebing, 'Nervosität und neurasthenische Zustände', Nothnagel's *Handbuch der speziellen Pathologie und Therapie*.

Lipschütz, A., *Die Pubertätsdrüse und ihre Wirkungen*, Berne, 1919.

Löwenfeld, *Die psychische Zwangserscheinungen*, 1904.

Marcinowski, 'Die erotischen Quellen der Minderwertigkeitsgefühle', *Zeitschrift für Sexualwissenschaft*, Bd. IV., 1918.

Multatuli, *Briefe*, 1906.

Pick, A., 'Über pathologische Träumerei und ihre Beziehungen zur Hysterie', *Jahrbuch für Psychiatrie und Neurologie*, Bd. XIV., 1896.

Sadger, J., 'Die Bedeutung der psychoanalytischen Methode nach Freud', *Centralblatt für Nervenheilkunde und Psychiatrie*, Nr. 229, 1907.
  'Jahresbericht über sexuelle Perversionen', *Jahrbuch*, Bd. VI., 1914.

Stekel, W., *Die Sprache des Traumes*, Wiesbaden, 1911.